THE DHARMA FLOWER SUTRA

THE WONDERFUL DHARMA

LOTUS FLOWER

SUTRA.

TRANSLATED INTO CHINESE BY TRIPITAKA MASTER KUMARAJIVA
OF YAO CH IN

Vol 2: Chapter 1. Introduction

with the commentary of

Tripitaka Master Hua

Translated into English by
THE BUDDHIST TEXT TRANSLATION SOCIETY
SAN FRANCISCO
1977

Translated by the Buddhist Text Translation Society

Primary translation: Bhikshuni Heng Yin
Reviewed by: Bhikshuni Heng Ch'ih
Edited by: Upasika Kuo-lin Lethcoe
Certified by: The Venerable Master Hua

Printed in the United States of America

First Printing--1978

For information address:

Sino American Buddhist Association
Gold Mountain Monastery
1731 15th Street
San Francisco, California 94103
U.S.A.
(415) 621-5202
(415) 861-9672

ISBN 0-917512-22-7

TABLE OF CONTENTS

The Venerable Tripitaka Master Hua,
Certifier

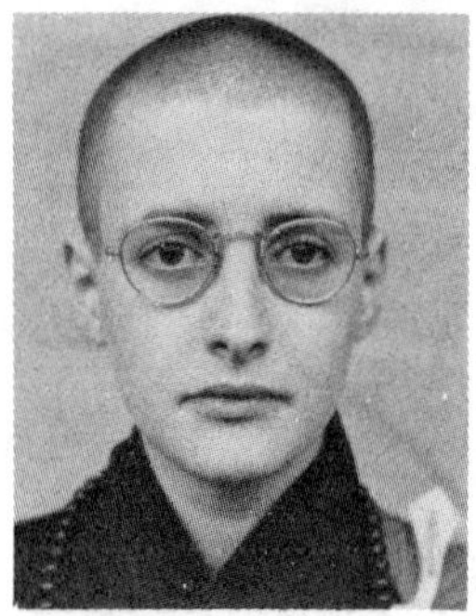

Bhikshuni Heng-yin,
Primary Translation

Bhikshuni Heng-ch'ih,
Revisions

Upasika Kuo-lin
Lethcoe, Ph.D., Editor

Bhikshuni Heng-hsien, Ph.D.
Translating-assistant to
the Certifier

INTRODUCTION

In this, the second volume of *The Wonderful Dharma Lotus Flower Sutra,* we present the First Chapter proper with the commentary of the Venerable Tripitaka Master Hua. The ancients said:

> To develop your wisdom,
> study the *Shurangama.*
> To become a Buddha,
> study the *Dharma Flower.*

In the *Dharma Flower Sutra,* the Buddha sets forth the One Buddha Vehicle; all beings possess the Buddha nature and are destined for Buddhahood. Although we are all potential Buddhas, it is only through cultivation and practice of the principles of the Buddhadharma that we can actualize that potential. Therefore, the commentary of the Venerable Master is filled with analogies, examples, expedients, and exhortations, all for the purpose of leading us to Buddhahood. He truly brings the teachings of Shakyamuni Buddha to *life* so that their application to us, today, is immediately obvious.

In Chapter One the stage is set for the Buddha's speaking of the Sutra. On Vulture Peak, near the City of the House of Kings, Shakyamuni Buddha has gathered with a great assembly of Bhikshus, Arhats, Bodhisattvas, and the gods and dragons and the eightfold division. He manifests six portents and the Bodhisattva Maitreya asks the Bodhisattva Manjushri to explain the reason for them. Manjushri explains in detail, comparing the present portents to those he saw in the distant past, in the Dharma assembly of Sun-Moon-Lamp Buddha. After manifesting the portents, that Buddha spoke *The Wonderful Dharma Lotus Flower Sutra.* Thus, the Bodhisattva Manjushri concludes that Shakyamuni Buddha is about to speak *The Dharma Flower* as well.

The Venerable Master's commentary provides a

wealth of information on the lives of the Buddha's disciples, as well as detailed explanations of terms and concepts basic to an understanding of the Buddhadharma. Included in this volume, also, is the outline of Ming Dynasty Master Ngou-i.

The combination of Shakymuni Buddha's most perfect Lotus teaching, "purely perfect and solitarily wonderful," with the compassionate commentary of the Master makes this work a particularly priceless Dharma jewel. The Master teaches the Dharma of the heart, the Dharma which is aimed only at showing us how to break our attachments and gain liberation. The Buddha's teaching now blooms, lotus-like, in the West. It is up to us to study and practice it, and quickly bear the Bodhi-fruit!

Bhikshuni Heng-yin

Co-chairperson, Primary Trans. Comm.
Buddhist Text Translation Society
International Institute for the
Translation of Buddhist Texts

San Francisco
December 1977

Chapter One: Introduction

CHAPTER ONE: OUTLINE

- A1. general intro. to root and branches divisions (75-
  - B1. time and place Dharma was heard (75
  - B2. audience (75-
    - C1. members of (75-
      - D1. sound hearers (75-
        - E1. bhikshus (75-
          - F1. well known (75-
            - G1. category and number (75-
            - G2. position and virtues (75-
            - G3. partial listing of names (91-
          - F2. lesser known (126
        - E2. bhikshunis (126
      - D2. Bodhisattvas (128
        - E1. category and number (128-
        - E2. position and virtues (128-
        - E3. partial listing of names (144-
      - D3. other members of assembly (158-
        - E1. desire realm heaven gods (158-
        - E2. gods of forms realm heavens (162-
        - E3. dragons (165-
        - E4. kinnaras (170-
        - E5. gandharvas (171-
        - E6. asuras (172-
        - E7. garudas(176-
        - E8. humans (178-
    - C2. summation (178

CHAPTER ONE: OUTLINE

Sutra:

CHAPTER ONE: INTRODUCTION

THUS HAVE I HEARD...

Commentary:

The Wonderful Dharma Lotus Flower Sutra contains twenty-eight chapters. The first chapter narrates the causes and conditions leading up to the speaking of the Sutra. Although the first passage of text of all Sutras is an introduction, this is the only Sutra that devotes an entire chapter to an introduction.

THUS HAVE I HEARD...Every Dharma assembly must fulfill six requirements: faith, hearing, time, host, place, and audience. THUS fills the requirement of faith. I HAVE HEARD fills the requirement of hearing. Dharma which is "Thus" can be believed; dharma which is not "Thus" cannot be believed.

Who is the "I" referred to here? There are four types of "I" or "self." First of all there is the attached self of the common person. Then there is the divine self of non-Buddhist religions. Thirdly, there is the false self which Bodhisattvas assume in order to accord with worldly convention, and, fourthly, there is the true self of the Buddha's Dharma-body.

Here, Ananda uses the false self. Having certified to the fruit, Ananda basically has no "self," but he complies with worldly convention and says, "Thus have I heard," in order to be intelligible to common people who all have a self.

You may ask, "Why does the text say, "I" heard? Basically isn't it the ear which hears? Why doesn't it say "the ear heard?"

The ear is just one part of the body. The "I" refers to the entire body. Therefore, Ananda said, "I have heard."

Four Reasons for "Thus have I heard"

Ananda spoke the words "Thus have I heard" for four reasons:

1. To resolve the assembly's doubts.
2. To honor the Buddha's instructions.
3. To end the assembly's debates.
4. To distinguish Buddhist Sutras from the writings of other religions.

What doubts did the assembly hold? When Ananda compiled the Sutras and took the Dharma seat, he manifested the characteristics of the Buddha and thus caused the assembly suddenly to give rise to three doubts:

First of all, the Bodhisattvas, Arhats, and Bhikshus thought perhaps Shakyamuni Buddha hadn't entered Nirvana after all, but had returned again to lecture on the Sutras.

Others thought, "This must be a Buddha from another place who has come to teach us."

Still others thought, "Ananda has become a Buddha! Otherwise, how could he manifest the thirty-two marks and eighty minor characteristics of a Buddha? How could he, surrounded by this dazzling purple-golden light, appear so splendid?"

But when Ananda took the Dharma seat and said, "Thus I have heard," the three doubts were all resolved. The Bodhisattvas, Arhats, and Bhikshus then knew Ananda was saying, "This is the Dharma. It is thus. Thus it was that I personally heard this Dharma from the Buddha. It is not my own invention."

The second reason the words "Thus have I heard" were used was in order to honor the Buddha's instructions. When the Buddha was about to enter Nirvana, he told Ananda, "All the Sutras should begin with the words 'Thus have I heard.'"

The third reason was to end the assembly's debates. Ananda was one of the youngest of the Buddha's disciples. If he hadn't made it clear that the Sutras he was speaking were the Buddha's and not his own, there would certainly have been objections. "You say you can speak Sutras? Well so can we!" people would have said. But when Ananda said that the Sutras were not his own but were the Buddha's, all the assembly, including his elders, his peers, and his juniors, had nothing to say. They were the Buddha's Sutras. This silenced their objections and ended all debates.

The fourth reason was to distinguish the Buddha's Sutras from the writings of other religions. The texts of other religions begin their works with the words "A" or "O" meaning "non-existence" or "existence," respectively. They say that all the ten thousand dharmas either exist or do not exist. The Buddhist Sutras are "Thus." They fall neither into the extreme of emptiness nor into the extreme of existence. They expound the Middle Way.

Ananda's Four Questions

One day, Shakyamuni Buddha announced, "Tonight, at midnight, I am going to enter Nirvana." When Ananda heard this, he was so upset that he cried like a baby. "Buddha! Buddha!" he called out. "Please don't enter Nirvana! Don't cast us all aside!" He cried until his brains got addled.

Just then a blind man named Aniruddha came by. Although his eyes were sightless, his Heavenly Eye was open. Because he was blind, he didn't gaze around to the north, east, south or west. He wasn't burdened with a lot of extraneous thoughts, and his mind was very clear. "Venerable One," he said to Ananda, "why are you crying?"

"The Buddha is about to enter Nirvana," Ananda replied. "How can I possibly *not* cry?"

"But how can you do your work if you cry?" said Aniruddha. "After the Buddha goes to Nirvana, we will have much to do. There is work to be done. There are questions to be asked."

"What questions?" asked Ananda. "The Buddha is leaving. He's going to Nirvana. What could be more important than that?"

Aniruddha said, "There are four extremely important matters which must be settled."

"What are they?" asked Ananda.

"Compiling the Sutras is one," said Aniruddha. "With what words should we begin each Sutra?"

"Right," said Ananda. "I never would have thought of it myself."

"Secondly," Aniruddha continued, "we have taken the Buddha as our teacher, but after the Buddha enters Nirvana, who will be our teacher?"

"What is the third?" said Ananda.

"Now, we live with the Buddha. After the Buddha enters Nirvana, where are we going to live?"

"That is very important," said Ananda. "Without a place to live, how can we cultivate the Way? What is the fourth question?"

"The Buddha can discipline evil-natured Bhikshus," said Aniruddha. "But after he goes to Nirvana, how are we going to control them?"

"These are very important questions," said Ananda. "I'll go ask right away." He wiped his eyes, blew his nose, and ran to the Buddha. "Buddha?" he said, "excuse me, but may I ask you some questions? I have four questions which I would like to ask before you enter Nirvana. Is that all right?"

"Of course," said the Buddha.

"World Honored One, you have spoken many Sutras. In the future when we compile and edit them, with what words shall we begin them?" asked Ananda.

"All the Sutras spoken by the Buddhas of the past, present, and future begin with the words 'Thus have I heard,'" said the Buddha. "These words mean: 'The Dharma which is thus can be believed; I personally heard it from the Buddha.'"

Ananda continued, "You are our Master, but when you enter Nirvana, who will be our teacher?"

The Buddha said, "Take the Pratimoksha, the precepts, as your teacher. To accord with the Buddha's regulations, Bhikshus and Bhikshunis must receive the complete precepts. If one does not rely upon the precepts in cultivation, the Dharma will become extinct. If the precepts are relied upon, the Buddhadharma will remain in the world. For every person who cultivates according to the precepts, Buddhism has just that much more light. If ten people cultivate according to the precepts, then Buddhism will give off ten parts of light. If a hundred, a thousand, ten thousand people cultivate according to the precepts and do not violate them, then boundless, limitless light will destroy all the darkness of evil in the world. Therefore, in cultivation, holding the precepts is essential."

Then Ananda said, "We have always lived with you, Buddha. After you enter Nirvana, where shall we live?"

The Buddha replied, "You should dwell in the Four Applications of Mindfulness: mindfulness with regard to the body, feelings, thoughts, and dharmas."

"Lastly, Buddha," said Ananda, "how should we treat evil-natured Bhikshus? What should our policy towards them be?"

The Buddha said, "Simply be silent and they will go away. Fight evil people with concentration. If they are evil, don't be evil in return. Evil-natured Bhikshus show no consideration for anyone. They insist on being number one. There is no way to reason with them. All you can do is refuse to talk to them. They will become ashamed of themselves and may even come around to following the rules. The best method is not to argue with them. If you simply ignore them, they will quickly lose interest. Do not talk to them. Pay no attention to them and they will soon pack up and leave." This was the way the Buddha answered Ananda's four questions.

The word *thus* expresses the credibility of the Dharma which is about to be heard. The Dharma which you may believe is "thus." Dharma which you may not believe is not "thus."

"Thus" means "it is thus." "Thus" represents the unchanging noumenal principle. "It is thus" represents the phenomena which change according to conditions. Because it accords with conditions and is yet unchanging and because it is unchanging and yet accords with conditions, the Dharma is said to be "thus."

It accords with conditions, yet does not change.
It does not change and yet accords with conditions.
It is thus, thus unmoving;
The Dharma, clear and constantly bright--
Thus it is.

"Thus" also means it is "sealed with approval." If you do things correctly, if you do things in accord with the Buddha's heart, then it is "thus." If you are at variance with the Buddha's heart, then it is not "thus."

"I have heard" is Ananda saying, "The Dharma which is thus is that which I personally heard the Buddha speak. It is not my own invention or my own creation. I heard it from the Buddha."

Ananda was quite a bit younger than the Buddha. In fact, the Buddha left home when he was nineteen and accomplished the way when he was thirty. Ananda was born on the day the Buddha accomplished the Way and, at twenty, he left home and served the Buddha. Therefore, he did not hear the Dharma taught by the Buddha during the first twenty years of teaching. How, then, was Ananda able to compile the Sutras if he hadn't even heard those first twenty years of the Buddha's teaching?

That's a good question. Ananda was the Buddha's cousin; he left home when he was twenty and made the vow to remember and record all the Buddha's words. But, since he hadn't heard the first years of the Buddha's teaching, he requested the Buddha to repeat it all for him. So the Buddha, in secret, respoke all the Sutras to Ananda who, by means of his excellent memory, remembered them all perfectly. Thus, from beginning to end, all the Dharma the Buddha spoke went past his ears directly into his heart and was never forgotten. Therefore, it is said,

> "The great sea of the Buddhadharma
> flowed right into Ananda's heart."

Ananda was actually a great Bodhisattva who manifested provisionally as an Arhat. All the Sutras of the past Buddhas were compiled by Ananda. That is why, after his enlightenment, he was able to remember all the Dharma spoken by the Buddhas of the past. The Dharma spoken by all the Buddhas is essentially the same.

More On the Four Applications of Mindfulness

The first Application of Mindfulness is to contemplate the body as impure. Our bodies constantly perspire, no matter how often we wash them. If you don't wash, they soon begin to stink. Impurities always ooze from the nine openings on the body. Tears and matter flow from the eyes. Wax accumulates in the ears. Mucus comes from the nose. Phlegm and saliva come from the mouth. Add excrement and urine from the eliminatory orifices and that makes nine. Therefore, you should contemplate the body as impure.

Living beings burdened with heavy greed should cultivate the contemplation of impurity and view the uncleanness of the body. Those afflicted with sexual desire should apply this contemplation to counteract lust. No matter how beautiful the woman or how attractive the man, they are still basically unclean. Since they are impure, how can you cling to them? Understanding their basic impurity, you won't keep longing for them, and your sexual desire will diminish.

The second is to contemplate feelings as suffering. Everything you experience, be it pleasant or unpleasant, moves your mind. When your mind moves, that is suffering. There are many kinds of suffering. There are the Three Sufferings, the Eight Sufferings and all the limitless sufferings. The Three Sufferings are:

1. The suffering within suffering: This is the poverty and misery to which all living beings are subject.

2. The suffering of decay: You may presently enjoy wealth and honor, but eventually they decay. Perhaps you have a sizeable fortune but then lose it in a stock market crash, or perhaps your real estate gets appropriated for a freeway project...

3. The suffering of process: All of us undergo the suffering of the life-process itself. From birth we pass into the prime of life; from the prime of life, we pass into old age. The shifting and changing in every thought is called the suffering of process.

The Eight Sufferings are:

1. The suffering of birth,
2. old age,
3. sickness, and
4. death.
5. The suffering of being separated from what one loves.
6. The suffering of being around what one hates.
7. The suffering of not getting what one wants.
8. The suffering of the raging blaze of the five skandhas. Form, feeling, thought, activity, and consciousness are like a raging fire. They are our constant shadow which we can never escape. Whether pleasant or unpleasant, feelings are all a kind of suffering, for pleasant feelings are the cause of unpleasant feelings. Feelings may be pleasant, unpleasant, or neutral. From the point of view of the three sufferings, unpleasant feelings are the suffering within suffering; pleasant feelings are the suffering of decay, and neutral feelings are the suffering of process.

The Three Sufferings are present within the Three Realms: the Desire Realm, the Form Realm, and the Formless Realm. No matter what you feel, it is bound up with suffering. If you can understand this, you won't crave pleasure, and you'll be able to avoid suffering.

The third application of mindfulness is to contemplate thoughts as impermanent. In our minds, when one thought is produced, the former thought is extinguished. When yet another thought arises, the preceding one perishes. Thoughts succeed one another like the waves on the sea. Thought after thought arises without cease, but they are all impermanent. Every thought is vain and unreal. Therefore, you should contemplate thoughts as impermanent.

The fourth Application of Mindfulness is to contemplate dharmas as without self. What are dharmas? Generally, they are divided into five categories. They are explained in detail in the *Shastra to the Door of Understanding the Hundred Dharmas*, by Bodhisattva Vasubandhu.

There are eleven form dharmas.

There are eight mind dharmas.

There are fifty-one dharmas belonging to the mind.

There are twenty-four dharmas non-interactive with the mind.

There are six unconditioned dharmas.

Altogether there are a hundred dharmas. Although there are so many dharmas, among them all there is no self. Therefore, you should not be attached to dharmas. The *Vajra Sutra* says, "Even dharmas should be cast aside. How much the more so that which is non-dharma?" When you have cultivated to the extreme limit where both people and dharmas are empty, you must give up attachment to dharmas. If you become attached to the existence of dharmas, you contract the Dharma Attachment. There are two kinds of attachments, the Self Attachment and the Dharma Attachment. Before people have understood the Buddhadharma, they are attached to the self. Everything revolves around themselves. With attachment they become obstructed, perverted, and filled with dream-thoughts.

Once you understand the Buddhadharma, you may give rise to Dharma Attachments. So the Buddha spoke the Four Applications of Mindfulness and taught us to contemplate dharmas as devoid of self. Contemplate all dharmas as having no self. Since there is no self, how could there be dharmas? Therefore you must contemplate dharmas as without a self.

Although there are Four Applications, you can divide them up and apply each of the four characteristic qualities--impurity, suffering, impermanence, and non-self--to the body, feelings, thought, and dharmas, making a total of sixteen contemplations in all.

Contemplate the body as impure; feelings, thoughts, and dharmas are also impure. Contemplate feelings as suffering: the body, thoughts, and dharmas are also suffering. Contemplate thoughts as impermanent and also the body, feelings, and dharmas. Contemplate dharmas as without self, and also the body, feelings and thoughts. The Buddha told his disciples that after his Nirvana they should always dwell in these Four Applications.

The outline has been taken from Master Chih Che's commentary to the Sutra by Master Ngou-i of the Ming Dynasty. It has three major headings:

A1. general introduction to the root and branches divisions of the Sutra.

A2. specific explanation of root and branches divisions of the Sutra.

A3. propagational section of root and branches division of the Sutra.

We will now begin with section A1:

Sutra:

(Thus have I heard...) A1

AT ONE TIME THE BUDDHA DWELT ON MOUNT GRDHRAKUTA, NEAR THE CITY OF THE HOUSE OF THE KINGS,[B1] TOGETHER WITH A GATHERING OF GREAT BHIKSHUS, TWELVE THOUSAND IN ALL.[B2C1D1E1F1G1] ALL WERE ARHATS WHO HAD EXHAUSTED ALL OUTFLOWS AND HAD NO FURTHER AFFLICTIONS. HAVING ATTAINED SELF-BENEFIT, THEY HAD EXHAUSTED THE BONDS OF ALL EXISTENCE AND THEIR HEARTS HAD ATTAINED SELF-MASTERY.[G2]

Outline:

- A1. general intro. to root and branches divisions
  - B1. time and place Dharma was heard.
  - B2. audience
    - C1. members of
      - D1. sound-hearers
        - E1. bhikshus
          - F1. well known
            - G1. their category and number
            - G2. statement of their position and praise of their virtues

Commentary:

AT ONE TIME fills the time requirement, not giving the exact date, for that would lead to endless speculation among historians. It was the "time" when the Sutra was spoken. The BUDDHA fills the host requirement. The Buddha is the enlightened one. There are three kinds of enlightenment. 1. Basic enlightenment. This is the inherent Buddha nature in all beings, our enlightenment potential which does not depend on cultivation.

2. Initial enlightenment is the resolve to study the Buddhadharma and actualize that enlightenment potential.

Eventually, you will come to understand it completely. When you understand it completely, you realize Buddhahood and that is the third:

3. Ultimate enlightenment.

There are also the following three types of enlightenment:

1. Self-enlightenment. Those who are self-enlightened are different from common people who are unenlightened. This refers to the Shravakas and Pratyeka Buddhas.

2. The enlightenment of others. These are the Bodhisattvas who are different from the Shravakas and Pratyeka Buddhas. These Bodhisattvas teach everyone the doctrines which they themselves have understood so that they can become enlightened too. This is the spirit of the Bodhisattva who benefits himself and benefits others. Those of the Two Vehicles only benefit themselves; they do not benefit others. They gain their own understanding, but do not seek to lead others to that same understanding. The Buddha called the people of the Two Vehicles "self-understanding Arhats." He scolded them and said they were "withered sprouts and sterile seeds," because they did not concern themselves with propagating the Buddhadharma.

3. The perfection of enlightenment and practice. This is the enlightenment of the Buddha. Although Bodhisattvas enlighten others, they have not perfected their enlightenment and practice. Only the Buddha has perfected both self-enlightenment and the practice of enlightening others.

> Having perfected the three types of
> enlightenment and
> Complete with the ten thousand virtues,
> He is therefore called, "The Buddha."

Shakyamuni Buddha was born in India, the son of King Shuddhodana of the Kshatriya caste who was the ruler of Kapilavastu. His personal name was Siddhartha. He left the home-life when he was nineteen, realized Buddhahood at age thirty, and taught the Dharma for forty-nine years in over three hundred Dharma assemblies. His disciple Ananda was thirty years younger than the Buddha and left home when he was twenty. He heard the Buddha's teachings for only twenty-nine years. But the Buddha used his spiritual penetrations to respeak the first twenty years of his teaching to Ananda, who remembered them exactly and recorded and compiled them.

THE BUDDHA DWELT ON MOUNT GRDHRAKUTA, NEAR THE CITY OF THE HOUSE OF THE KINGS. This fills the requirement of place. The City of the House of Kings (Rajagrha) was the capital city of Magadha in central India. The city was surrounded by five mountains--one of which was Mount Grdhrakuta, "Vulture Peak," so named because it was shaped like a vulture.

TOGETHER WITH A GATHERING OF GREAT BHIKSHUS, TWELVE THOUSAND IN ALL. Most of the Sutras list a gathering of one thousand twelve hundred and fifty Bhikshus, but there was an especially large gathering at the *Dharma Flower Sutra* assembly.

GREAT Bhikshus are those about to certify to the fruit of Arhatship.

BHIKSHU: Because the word contains many meanings, it is not translated but is left in Sanskrit. The three meanings of the word Bhikshu are:

1. Mendicant. Bhikshus do not prepare their own food. In the Buddha's time, some of them practiced the ascetic practice of eating only once a day before noon; others practiced the ascetic practice of not eating after noon. When it was time to eat, they took their bowls into the city and begged from door to door, and lay people would give them offerings of food.

2. Frightener of Mara. When one who has left home is about to receive the complete precepts, the Precept Masters, consisting of Three Masters and Seven Certifiers, ask him, "Are you a great hero?"

"I am a great hero,"he answers.

"Have you brought forth the Bodhi heart?" they ask.

"I have brought forth the Bodhi heart," he answers.

The moment he answers the second question, an earth travelling yaksha ghost tells a space travelling yaksha ghost, who informs a heaven travelling yaksha,who in turn informs the sixth desire heaven, where Mara dwells, saying,"Among people, such a person has left home. The Buddha's retinue has increased by one and the retinue of Mara has decreased by one. Hearing this, the demon king is jealous and frightened. Therefore, Bhikshus are called Frighteners of Mara.

3. Destroyers of evil. Bhikshus destroy the evils of affliction and ignorance as well as the poisons of greed, hatred, and stupidity. The assembly of Bhikshus who were Shravakas , fill the requirement of audience. How many were there? Twelve thousand.

Every Sutra begins with these six requirements because unless all six requirements are filled, the Buddha will not speak the Dharma. For example there must be an *audience* to listen and a *place* in which to speak the Dharma. Thirdly, a *host* speaker is needed, a Dharma Master who genuinely understands the Buddhadharma.

If you merely have an audience and a place, but no one speaks the Dharma, you can't convene a Dharma assembly. Next, you need a *time,* for example, seven to nine in the evening. There must be a *hearing,* that is you need to come and listen. If you listen, but you do not believe it, then the requirement of *faith* is lacking. You may think, "The Dharma Master speaks extremely well. He's most articulate. The more I hear, the more I want to listen," in which case the requirement of *faith* is met.

This completes the discussion of the six requirements.

The phrase TOGETHER WITH A GATHERING OF GREAT BHIKSHUS, TWELVE THOUSAND IN ALL denotes the number present. ALL WERE ARHATS denotes their position. The following phrases, ALL WERE ARHATS WHO HAD EXHAUSTED ALL OUTFLOWS AND HAD NO FURTHER AFFLICTIONS; HAVING GAINED PEACE AND PERSONAL BENEFIT THEY HAD EXHAUSTED THE BOND OF ALL EXISTENCE AND THEIR HEARTS HAD ATTAINED SELF MASTERY, praise their virtues.

ALL WERE ARHATS: The Sanskrit word Arhat has three meanings which correspond to the three meanings of the word Bhikshu. Cultivation in the causal ground as a Bhikshu leads to the result of Arhatship.

1. One Worthy of Offerings. In the causal ground a Bhikshu is a mendicant. As a result, an Arhat is Worthy of Offerings, worthy of receiving offerings from men and gods, and both should make offerings to him. "Arhat" also means "One Who Should Make Offerings"--that is one who should make offerings to the other Bhikshus. For example, when the Buddha was in the world, the Bhikshus and common people made offerings to the Buddha; but one time the Buddha transformed himself into a cultivator of the Way and made offerings to all the Bhikshus in turn.

2. Slayer of Thieves. In the causal ground, a Bhikshu destroys evil; in the result ground, the Arhat is a Slayer of Thieves. He slays the thieves of ignorance and affliction, and the six thieves of the eyes, ears, nose, tongue, body, and mind.

You may ask, "They have slain the thieves. But have they slain the non-thieves?"

Yes, as a matter of fact they have. Not only have they slain the thieves, they have slain the non-thieves as well.

Someone may wonder, "What are the non-thieves?"

In the Small Vehicle, the Shravakas and Pratyeka Buddhas look upon certain things as not being thieves which at the Bodhisattva level are seen as thieves. These they have also slain.

3. One Without Birth. In the causal ground a Bhikshu frightens Mara, and as a result becomes an Arhat, One Without Birth. He is neither produced nor destroyed. At the Fourth Stage of Arhatship, one awakens to the Patience of the Non-Production of Dharmas; within the great trichiliocosm, one sees not the slightest dharma produced nor the slightest dharma destroyed. As it is an unspeakable, ineffable state, it can only be endured in the heart. Therefore, it is called the Patience of the Non-Production of Dharmas.

There are four levels of Arhatship: First, Second, Third, and Fourth.

The First Stage Arhat is called a Shrotaapana. At the First Stage of Arhatship, birth and death have not yet been ended. It is called the "position of seeing the Way." Shrotaapana means "stream enterer." They have entered the stream of the Dharma Nature of the Sages, and go against the stream of the six sense objects of the common person. The six sense objects are: forms, sounds, smells, tastes, tangible objects, and dharmas. Those who have certified to the First Fruit of Arhatship do not "enter into" forms, sounds, smells, tastes, tangible objects, or dharmas.

Forms: Because they have the power of concentration, forms do not move their minds. Whether or not a form is beautiful--no matter how nice-looking it is--when they encounter it, their minds are not affected, and they do not "enter into" forms.

Sounds: Most people like to hear songs and music. First Stage Arhats are simply not affected by sounds, be they good sounds, bad sounds, pleasant sounds, irritating sounds, right sounds, or wrong sounds. They are not "turned by" sounds; they are able to "turn" the sounds. That is, they are in control.

Smells: Because they are turned by smells, people are fond of pleasant smells and displeased by bad ones. If you are "fond" of or "displeased" by smells, you have thoughts of love and hate and are therefore affected by smells.

Tastes: Because we are turned by tastes, we like to eat a little more of the tasty foods and tend to avoid the bad ones. At the First Stage of Arhatship one is not affected by tastes.

Tangible objects: Ordinary people are all greedy for objects of touch. Emotional love between men and women arises when one has not seen through and set aside the desire for objects of touch. People desire that their bodies come in contact with other bodies because they are not able to "turn" the objects of touch. Arhats at the First Stage are not affected by objects of touch. They are not greedy for beautiful things to touch or lovely things to hold onto.

Dharmas: If you have attachment, then there are many different kinds of dharmas. First Stage Arhats are not attached to any dharmas whatever.

If someone claims that he has certified to the fruit, obtained the Way, and become enlightened, you can test him out. Invite him to lunch and present him with two dishes, one delectable and the other nauseating. Then let him take his pick. But don't tell him you are testing him or of course he will take the bad food. But, in deliberately wanting to eat the bad food, he also betrays a susceptibility to objects of taste. Why? Because he really likes the good food, but he knows you are testing him and so deliberately he eats the bad food. He is still being turned and is merely putting on an act. If he is truly not turned by smells and tastes he won't do *any* picking, he'll just eat the good along with the bad because he makes no distinctions. This proves the cultivator has a bit of skill but it's still not for sure that he has certified to the First Fruit. You cannot casually claim to have certified to the fruit; you must be able to prove it.

Second Stage Arhats are called Sakrdagamin, which means "once returner." First Stage Arhats must undergo seven more rebirths, but Second Stage Arhats are called once returners because they need only be born once in the heavens and once among men.

Third Stage Arhats are called Anagamin, which means "never returner". They do not again undergo birth and death.

The First Stage of Arhatship is called the Position of Seeing the Way. The Second and Third Stage called the Positions of Cultivating the Way, because they still have to cultivate. The Fourth Stage is called the Position Beyond Study. They need study no more. At the Position Beyond Study, birth and death, that is Share-Section, has been ended, but they still haven't ended Change Birth and Death. There are two kinds of birth and death: Share Section Birth and Death and Change Birth and Death.

"Share" refers to our bodies. Everyone has a body, which is a certain size and weight, and that is called our share. Everyone has their own particular life-span. Change Birth and Death refers to the uninterrupted birth and death of the succession of thoughts which flow through the mind. Arhats have not ended Change Birth and Death. It is only at the Bodhisattva level that Change Birth and Death is ended. This has been a general discussion of the word Arhat.

The realm of the spiritual penetrations and miraculous functions of Fourth Stage Arhats is an inconceivable experience, subtle and difficult to describe. Their spiritual powers are completely different from those of non-Buddhist religions. They have the five eyes and the six spiritual penetrations. They can jump up into empty space and stand suspended right in the air. They can walk in the air too, and stand on their heads while suspended in space. They can emit flames from the top of their bodies and water from their feet, or they emit water from the top of their bodies and fire from their feet. They can fly and perform all kinds of miraculous transformations. In general, they can manifest eighteen different kinds of transformations. Because they have spiritual powers, they belong to the Four Sagely Realms: the Buddhas, Bodhisattvas, Pratyeka Buddhas and Shravakas.

Once there was an Arhat who accepted a young disciple. As the two of them went out travelling one day, the disciple carried their belongings on his back. He thought, "There's really nothing finer than the Bodhisattva Way. I am definitely going to study it and help all living beings." Just as the disciple had that thought, the Arhat knew.

"Ah!" the Arhat thought, "He has decided to become a Bodhisattva. I am only an Arhat, so I should carry the baggage," and he took the pack from the disciple.

As they continued down the road, the disciple began thinking about Shariputra. When Shariputra had tried to cultivate the Bodhisattva Way, he met a person who asked for his eye. Accordingly, he plucked out his left eye and gave it to him. However, the man stomped it into the dust, saying that he had no use for his left eye, he wanted Shariputra's *right* eye. At that point, Shariputra's Bodhisattva came to an abrupt end. "The Bodhisattva Way is obviously too difficult for me," the disciple thought. "I'll cultivate the Arhat-dharmas and take care of myself."

When his teacher saw that his disciple, who had previously turned from the Small towards the Great, had now returned from the Great to the Small, and had, so speak, shifted into reverse, he handed the pack back to him and said, "Here, I can't carry this any more."

Pretty soon, the disciple's Bodhisattva heart popped up again; he again turned from the Small to the Great, and the Arhat shouldered the pack again. The disciple's curiosity got the best of him. "Why are you passing this thing back and forth like that?" he asked.

"When you bring forth the Bodhisattva heart," said the Arhat, "I, as a mere Arhat, should rightfully carry the pack. When you retreat, I'm in no position to carry it and must return it to you."

Hearing this, the disciple knew that his teacher was indeed extraordinary. He brought forth the Bodhisattva heart and diligently practiced the Bodhisattva Way. The Arhat had spiritual penetrations which permitted him to feel free wherever he went.

When the Venerable Ananda was about to compile the Sutras, he had not yet obtained the Fourth Stage of Arhatship, the extinction of outflows. The Arhats, who gathered to organize the convocation for compiling the Sutras, decided that in order to take part one had to be a Fourth Stage Arhat. Consequently, Ananda, who was only a Third Stage Arhat, was left standing outside the door. They wouldn't let him in and he was extremely upset. "I remember all the Sutras the Buddha spoke, but now I can't even attend the meeting. What am I to do?" He was so nervous--not angry, mind you, but nervous, that he certified to the Fourth Fruit of Arhatship. "I've certified to the Fourth Fruit," he cried. "Open the door and let me in!"

But the Arhats inside just said, "Really? If you've certified to the Fourth Fruit, you don't need to have the door opened. Climb in through the keyhole." Ananda did just that. So you see, Arhats don't need to open the door to go into a room. If someone claims to be an Arhat, but still has to use the door, you can be sure that he is lying.

HAVING EXHAUSTED ALL OUTFLOWS: At the Fourth Stage of Arhatship one has exhausted all outflows.

There is not just one kind of outflow. How many kinds are there? Broadly speaking, there are 84,000 outflows and 84,000 afflictions. Afflictions themselves are outflows. Do you enjoy being afflicted? That's an outflow. Where do outflows go? They flow out into the Three Realms, the desire realm, the form realm, and the formless realm.

All faults are called outflows. All thoughts of desire are outflows. If you like to eat good food, that is an outflow. If you like to listen to good sounds, that is an outflow. Liking to live in a nice house or to run a prosperous business is an outflow. In general, whatever you like, whatever you are greedy for and can't set aside, is an outflow. So how many are there? How many things can't you set aside?

Outflows are like water pouring through a leaky bottle. No matter how much water you pour, it flows right through. With outflows, when you do acts of merit and virtue, the merit and virtue flow right out; you can't keep it. Human bodies are riddled with outflows. The eyes, ears, nose, tongue, and eliminatory orifices all flow with matter. The false thoughts in the mind are also outflows. There are simply *too* many of them. An inexhaustible number, even more than 84,000.

ALL OUTFLOWS refers to major shortcomings and minor faults. All of your peculiar, undesirable habits are outflows. To get even more basic, smoking, drinking, gambling and chasing after women are all outflows. Chasing after men is an outflow too. Don't think it applies only to men. It works both ways. Women, in fact, have more outflows than men. Women have a monthly outflow. To be more explicit about it, when you cannot keep your semen, energy, and spirit in check, you have outflows. The biggest outflow occurs through the male and female reproductive organs as a function of sexual desire. There are many, many outflows.

However, these Arhats had exhausted all their outflows. Exhausted means that they had put them to an end. It does *not* mean that their outflows had flowed out until they were all gone. When you read the Sutras you have to be careful to interpret these things correctly. They had no outflows, they did not flow out. It was not the case that all their outflows had flowed out. Fourth Stage Arhats have obtained the Penetration of the Extinction of Outflows, which is one of the Six Spiritual Penetrations. These twelve thousand Arhats had exhausted all outflows and had not the slightest fault. They were sages.

HAVING NO FURTHER AFFLICTIONS: All of the great Arhats had obtained the Penetration of the Extinction of Outflows, and therefore had no further afflictions. If they had not obtained that Penetration, they would still have afflictions. "Further" means that they will never become afflicted again.

They have done what they had to do,
And will undergo no further becoming.

Because they have ended birth and death, they have no affliction.

How many kinds of affliction are there? In general, there are 84,000 kinds of affliction. But that's really too many to discuss and so we will concentrate them into the term "ignorance." Afflictions all arise from ignorance. There are three kinds of affliction which are also known as the three poisons. The three poisons envenom our Buddha natures. The reason from beginningless time until the present we have not realized Buddhahood is because of the three poisons. They poison us to the point that

Drunk we live and
Dreaming, we die.

And we simply cannot return to the root, go back to the source, and return to our original face.

What are the three poisons? Number one: greed. Number two: hatred. Number three: stupidity.

Greed is insatiable. No matter what it is, you always want more and you want to appropriate everything to yourself. Everyone has his own greedy tendencies and nations all have their own greedy inclinations. National leaders are greedy to annex neighboring nations and individuals are greedy for wealth. They think one house is not enough and so they buy two. Then two houses are not enough so they buy a third. Three houses still don't satify them, and so they build a multi-storied mansion--all to keep up with the Jones'es. "I am the richest," they think. However, when the time comes, they can't buy off their own lives. No matter how rich they are, they can't bribe King Yama into letting them live forever. So greed is a deadly poison. It makes intelligent people muddled and sends good people down evil paths.

Hatred is also difficult to change. One spark of anger burns down a forest of virtue. The firewood gathered in a thousand days is burned up by a single spark. You may foster great merit and virtue, but as soon as you lose your temper, it all goes up in a blaze.

What is meant by "Offerings to the Triple Jewel?" If there is no hatred on your face, that is an offering to the Triple Jewel. To be pleasant and agreeable is just an offering to the Buddha. If you make offerings to the Triple Jewel, but do so in anger, with your face all twisted up with rage, no matter how fine your offerings, they will not please the Buddha.

With no words of anger, the mouth puts forth a wonderful fragrance. If you don't scold people, your mouth is very fragrant.

The absence of hatred in the heart is a true jewel, but thoughts of anger are difficult to subdue. In the *Vajra Sutra,* Subhuti asks how a Bodhisattva should subdue his heart. This refers to subduing afflictions and false thinking.

Although it is easy to be greedy or hateful, it is also easy to spot these afflictions as they arise. Stupidity, on the other hand, is deeply rooted and difficult to expose. Stupidity refers to being unclear about principle, taking what is right as wrong and what is wrong as right, saying what is white is black and what is black is white. Stupid people continually have false thoughts such as, "Wouldn't it be nice if the flowers were always blooming?"

Now, flowers bloom and flowers fade, and that is the way of nature. But stupid people want them to be fresh every day.

"Why isn't the bright moon full all month long?" they wonder and they get quite upset when they see it wane. Stupid people want the moon to be always full. Thieves find the full moon's light inconvenient for their nightly robberies and would much prefer to see no moon at all.

Those who like to drink wine think, "I have to have money in order to buy wine, but if all the rivers, streams, lakes, and oceans were filled with wine, wouldn't that be great? All I'd have to do is walk down to the riverbank and take a drink." These are examples of stupid false thoughts.

People who are greedy for money go to work to earn it and feel that they are toiling bitterly. "If all the trees had leaves of cash," they think, "all I'd have to do is pick my money off the trees!" All these things could simply never come to pass, but stupid people keep wishing, wishing for the impossible.

Other examples of stupidity are: those who have never been to school, but want to get a Doctorate; those who have not planted the fields but want to reap a harvest. Also, if you don't cultivate but want to become a Buddha, that is the *height* of stupidity. If you haven't even taken refuge with the Triple Jewel, and still expect to become a Buddha, that's absurd.

Everyone is poisoned by these three poisons. They turn us upside-down, make us confused, and prevent our wisdom from manifesting.

"Well, then," you ask, "what is to be done?"

Do *not* give rise to thoughts of greed. Do *not* give rise to thoughts of anger. Do *not* give rise to thoughts of stupidity. Extinguish greed, hatred, and stupidity and diligently cultivate precepts, samadhi, and wisdom.

Speaking of morality, samadhi, and wisdom, what, exactly, are they?

Morality

Morality means to stop evil and avoid error. This means to put an end to thoughts of greed. Thoughts of greed give rise to evil thoughts which are covetous of others' goods. How do thoughts of greed arise? They arise because one does not understand how to practice morality. Morality teaches you to be content, to be satisfied with what you have and not to long for others' valuables. One who upholds the moral precepts can bring thoughts of greed under control.

Samadhi

Samadhi is a Sanskrit word which means "right concentration," or "right reception." One who lacks the power of concentration will give rise to thoughts of hatred and will see everyone else as being in the wrong and everything as just not working right. When not doing that, one will see oneself as in the wrong and get angry at oneself to the point that one may even slap one's own cheek! Then, fearing the other cheek might get jealous, one will slap it, too.

The Chinese term for "jealous" literally means "drinking vinegar."

During the Ch'in dynasty, there was an Emperor who had an official who was scared to death of his own wife. If he was late coming home his wife made him kneel beside the bed. Kneeling to have audience with the Emperor was one thing, but kneeling before his own wife was really too much and he had to remain kneeling until she gave him permission to rise. Since he was on very good terms with the emperor, he finally confided in him.

The Emperor said, "Don't worry. I have a method which will cause your wife never to push you around again." Then he sent out an order calling the official's wife to the palace. The "old lady tiger" presented herself before the Emperor.

"Why do you make your husband kneel beside the bed when he comes home late?" said the Emperor. "That's not a proper thing to do. Besides, he hasn't been involved in any indiscreet affairs with other women, and even if he had, it is still not your place to oversee his business. If you reform your conduct and stop managing your husband, we'll forget the whole thing. If you continue to restrict his freedom, I will force you to drink this cup of poison; I will have you put to death. If it suits you to quit watching over your husband, you won't have to drink the poison. If you insist on watching over him, you will have to drink it and you will certainly die."

The woman was amazingly bold. "Fine," she said, "I'll die right here and now." She took the cup and drank the contents. Of course, it wasn't really poison; it was only vinegar. The Emperor had only said it was poison to see whether she would dare to drink it. The woman was braver than he thought. She would rather have died than quit watching over her husband. So in China they say, "drink vinegar," when they wish to refer to a woman who keeps too close track of her husband. Luckily, it was only vinegar. It may have soured her stomach, but it didn't kill her.

People with quick tempers will vent their anger on themselves if there is no one else around. They will even hit themselves! Why? Because they have no samadhi power. People who have samadhi will not become angry. Angry tempers will only blaze if one has no samadhi.

Wisdom

Why are you stupid? Because you lack wisdom. All day your heart is pre-occupied with false thoughts and gets no rest. You recognize nothing clearly.

For people with wisdom:

> When something happens, they respond;
> When it's over, they are still.

They take care of matters as they arise; when they are done, they set their hearts at rest. Their hearts are not the slaves of their bodies. If you lack wisdom, you are unable to contol your body because your mind is under its control and does its bidding. If you have genuine wisdom, then all matters are taken care of with razor-sharp intelligence. Students of the Buddhadharma should be clear about all matters. Those who understand the Buddhadharma have wisdom. Those who do not understand the Buddhadharma are stupid. Wise people will not act stupidly, and stupid people are incapable of acting wisely.

I'll now be perfectly frank and tell you the absolute truth: stupidity is *just* wisdom.

You may object, "You're confusing me! If that's the case, why bother to strive for wisdom and get rid of stupidity?"

Don't take my statement on face value alone. I am saying that the basic substance of stupidity transforms into wisdom. It is not the case that wisdom is to be found apart from stupidity. Wisdom is found right within stupidity: it's simply a matter of your not being able to use it. When you are able to use it, it's wisdom; when unable to use it, it is stupidity.

The same applies to samadhi. Samadhi is just anger and anger is samadhi. If you truly wish to gain samadhi, you should know that it is to be transformed right out of your anger. Morality, too, is transformed from greed. Don't look for them outside, for they are all contained within your self-nature. If you are able to use them, they are morality, samadhi, and wisdom. If you are unable to use them, they remain greed, hatred, and stupidity. The wonderful is found right at this point, and this is also the point where you may not understand.

HAVING ATTAINED SELF-BENEFIT: means that they have already arrived at the level of self-benefit. How have they arrived at this level? Previously, the text said, "who had exhausted all outflows and had no further afflictions." Why are we unable to obtain self-benefit? Because we are continually "flowing out." Free from outflows and devoid of afflictions, these Arhats have themselves attained genuine benefit. What is the genuine benefit? It is true understanding, the attainment of genuine wisdom. People without wisdom have not obtained the genuine benefit. To obtain wisdom, to certify to the fruit of Arhatship, is called attaining self-benefit.

Self-benefit also is just enlightening oneself, that is, self-enlightenment. Enlightened oneself, one benefits oneself. If you are then able to take the doctrines which you yourself have become enlightened to and teach them to all living beings, that is called benefitting others, enlightening others.

All the great Arhats in the *Lotus Sutra* assembly were self-enlightened. However, they did not enlighten others. They only knew self-benefit; they did not benefit others, and so the text says, "...having attained self-benefit."

...THEY HAD EXHAUSTED THE BONDS OF ALL EXISTENCE AND THEIR HEARTS HAD ATTAINED SELF-MASTERY. "Exhausted" means "non-existent." What is non-existent? There are three realms of existence which further divide into twenty-five planes of existence. The three realms of existence are:

1. existence in the desire realm (which contains fourteen planes);
2. existence in the form realm (which contains seven planes);
3. existence in the formless realm (which contains four planes).

To further break down the twenty-five planes of existence, the fourteen planes in the desire realm are: the four evil destinies, the four continents, and the six desire heavens as follows:

4 continents: Purva-videha in the East;
Jambudvipa in the South;
Apara-godaniya in the West;
Uttarakuru in the North.

4 evil destinies: the hells;
the path of hungry ghosts;
the path of animals;
the path of asuras.

These evil destinies come into existence through the creation of evil karma.

6 desire heavens: the Heaven of the Four Great Kings (chaturmaharajika);
the Heaven of the Thirty-three (trayastrimsha);
the Suyama heaven;
the Tushita Heaven;
the Nirmanarati Heaven;
the Paranirmitavashavartin Heaven.

The seven planes in the form realm are:

4 the Four Dhyana Heavens;
1 the Great Brahma Heaven (which is within the first Dhyana);
2 the Pure Dwelling Heavens (the five heavens from which there is no return) and
the Heaven of No-Thought (both of which are found in the Fourth Dhyana).

The four planes in the formless realm are:

4 the Four Stations of Emptiness:
the station of boundless space;
the station of boundless consciousness;
the station of nothing whatever;
the station of neither perception nor non-perception.

That makes a total of twenty-five planes of existence in the three realms.

Some people who don't understand the Buddhadharma think arriving at the level of the Fourth Dhyana is an extraordinary accomplishment. Actually, it is still within the twenty-five planes of the three realms and is nothing special. The ultimate goal of cultivation is still far off. But a confused teacher may tell everyone that it is the highest level of attainment. For example, there was an unlearned Bhikshu who mistook the Fourth Dhyana for the Fourth Fruit of Arhatship. When he had exhausted the merit that had enabled him to dwell there and began to fall, he slandered the Dharma. "The Buddha said that those who reach the Fourth Fruit do not undergo birth and death. How come I'm falling?" Having slandered the Buddha, he fell eternally into the four evil destinies.

The unlearned Bhikshu did not fall alone. Several tens of thousands of his disciples also fell with him. So, as I have said repeatedly:

> One with confused understanding transmits
> confused understanding;
> In one transmission, two don't understand.
> When the teacher plummets into the hells,
> The disciples reverently follow right along.

And neither the teacher nor the disciples know how they got there. The disciples are so fond of their teacher that they even follow him to hell. How pathetic! The teacher thinks, "How did I manage to bring my disciples to hell?" He himself doesn't know how it happened.

The Arhats present in the *Lotus Sutra* assembly had extinguished the bonds of all becoming and transcended the Three Realms, the realm of desire, the realm of form, and the formless realm. So it says, "They had transcended the Three Realms and were not within the five elements." They had gained genuine liberation from birth and death; they exhausted the bonds of all becoming...

AND THEIR HEARTS HAD ATTAINED SELF-MASTERY. The hearts of the Great Arhats then knew a boundless joy. Self-mastery is true happiness. There is nothing more comfortable, more joyful. So Avalokiteshvara is called "The Bodhisattva Who Contemplates with Self-Mastery," which means that the Bodhisattva sits in meditation and is always very happy, extremely comfortable, and knowing not even the slightest trace of vexation. Self-mastery refers to having no further afflictions, having attained self-benefit, and having exhausted all the bonds of existence.

In this state, the heart has obtained true freedom and genuine wisdom. One is, therefore, extremely happy.

This kind of happiness is a true inner-happiness. It is not an artificial emotional display of giggling and laughter. It's an inner-happiness, not an outside one. Don't think that your laughing and joking is happiness; it's really just upside-down affliction. Why is it upside-down? It shows that because you had no samadhi power you were influenced by some situation that pleased you and responded with laughter. There's no real happiness in that; that's just being upside-down.

Sutra:

THEIR NAMES WERE: AJNATAKAUNDINYA, MAHAKASHYAPA, URUVILVAKASHYAPA, GAYAKASHYAPA, NADIKASHYAPA, SHARIPUTRA, GREAT MAUDGALYAYANA, MAHAKATYAYANA, ANIRUDDHA, KAPPHINA, GAVAMPATI, REVATA, PILINDAVATSA, VAKKULA, MAHAKAUSHTHILA, NANDA, SUNDARANANDA, PURNAMAITRAYANIPUTRA, SUBHUTI, ANANDA, AND RAHULA -- AND OTHER GREAT ARHATS SUCH AS THESE, WHOM THE ASSEMBLY KNEW AND RECOGNIZED. G3

Outline:

G3. partial listing of names

Commentary:

Above have been listed the names of twenty-one of the Sound Hearer Disciples who were among the twelve thousand Bhikshus present on Vulture Peak when Shakyamuni Buddha spoke the *Lotus Sutra*.

THEIR NAMES WERE:

1. AJNATAKAUNDINYA

Ajnatakaundinya was the first person whom the Buddha took across. He was one of the five Bhikshus to whom the Buddha preached in the Deer Park in Benares shortly after his enlightenment.

Shakyamuni Buddha sat beneath the Bodhi Tree and one night he saw a bright star and awoke to the Way. Having become enlightened, he contemplated to see who he should cross over first. "There are so many people in the world," he thought. "Who should I save first?"

When the Buddha first accomplished the Way, he sighed three times and said, "Strange indeed! Strange indeed! All living beings have the Buddha nature. All can become Buddhas. It is merely because of false thinking and attachment that they are unable to certify to that attainment."

The Buddha merely said that all beings can become Buddhas. He did *not* say that they actually *were* Buddhas. But Buddhist disciples, or rather, pseudo-Buddhist disciples, say, "Everyone *is* Buddha!" They see no difference between ordinary people and the Buddha. This is a case of "the blind leading the blind" and "blinding the eyes of men and gods."

After Shakyamuni Buddha sighed three times, he used the Wonderful Observing Wisdom to determine who he should save first. "Ah!" he concluded, "Ajnatakaundinya is among the five Bhikshus now at the Deer Park. I should cross them over first." In past lives, these five people had exclusively concentrated on trying to ruin Shakyamuni Buddha. Limitless kalpas ago when they all decided to cultivate the Way, the five Bhikshus had slandered and bullied Shakyamuni Buddha. Sometimes they beat him, other times they berated him. Sometimes they ate his flesh, other times they drank his blood. Violent, weren't they? But while he was cultivating the causal ground, when the five beat him, he made the following vow, "You are all truly aiding me in my cultivation. In the future, when I realize Buddhahood, I will certainly save you first. That is my vow. Because you are treating me badly now, I shall be expecially good to you.

When they scolded Shakyamuni Buddha, he said, "You scold me now, but I do not hate you. Not only do I not hate you, but I vow that when I become a Buddha, I will save you first." If it had been us, we would surely have hit them or kicked them right back. But not only did Shakyamuni Buddha not defend himself, he resolved to be good to them. Once, the five of them got together in a small mob and approached him saying, "We have no meat to eat. You're such a cultivator,do you think you could give us a little piece of your flesh?" Sure enough, Shakyamuni Buddha cut off a clean, lean piece of flesh for them. As they ate it, they muttered, "This meat is no good at all. Dog meat tastes better than this, to say nothing of pork, beef, or mutton. It's tasteless. Your offering is not being relished." Still, they ate it. So they even scolded him while eating his flesh! Shakyamuni Buddha had thought that by offering them his flesh, they might be moved to shame and reform their conduct. Who would have thought that they would, on the one hand eat his flesh, and on the other hand, scold him? This would have been the last straw for most people. "I didn't buy this in the meat market," they would have said. "I cut it off my *own* body. And you have the nerve to scold me?" But Shakyamuni Buddha just said, "Okay. You can eat my flesh and in the future when I succeed in my cultivation and become a Buddha, I will take you across first, because this flesh I have given you to eat is a Buddha-seed which I am planting in each of you."

The same thing happened when they drank Shakyamuni Buddha's blood. They said it was spoiled, bad blood. Shakyamuni Buddha was able to endure all of this, even to the point that, when the King of Kalinga cut off his arms and legs, he still harbored not the slightest trace of hatred in his heart.

The King of Kalinga who was a former incarnation of Ajnatakaundinya, and went to the mountains on a big-game hunting expedition, took along his concubines. They had been confined to the palace, as if in jail, for many years. Now, "seeing the sky," they frolicked in the mountains, enjoying the beautiful surroundings. Suddenly they spotted a person sitting in a cave. His body was covered with dust and his hair was matted into a big lump. The concubines didn't dare approach him. At first they thought he was a monster, but then they saw that he was just a strange person.

As a cultivator in the causal ground, Shakyamuni Buddha was practicing as this "Patient Immortal" and rarely saw anyone. When he saw the concubines, he decided to take them across. "Don't be afraid," he said. "I won't eat you. I don't eat people. I'm a person myself, in fact."

The concubines said, "What are you doing here? What do you eat and why are your clothes so tattered? Can you walk? Why do you just sit there?"

The causal cultivator Shakyamuni Buddha said, "I am cultivating the Way. I exclusively cultivate patience."

The concubines said, "What is patience?" They had no idea what it was.

The Patient Immortal said, "Patience means that no matter how impolite people are to you, you do not get angry or upset. Everything continues just as if nothing had happened. And then he explained the methods of cultivating patience. As he spoke, his enthusiasm grew, and the concubines, who had never heard such wonderful Dharma, were enthralled. Soon the speaker and his listeners all had entered samadhi, and were oblivious to what was going on around them. If one listens to the Dharma with a true heart, one will not notice anything else that is going on. If one does not listen with a true heart, one will be distracted by every noise on the street. The Patient Immortal and his audience were completely absorbed in the practice of patience when along came the King of Kalinga. Sneaking up on the scene, he saw his concubines listening intently to the old cultivator, and he was immediately overcome with jealousy. "Just what do you think you are doing, seducing my women?" he screamed at the cultivator.

The Patient Immortal looked to see who was speaking and recognized that an emperor had come on the scene and said, "I'm teaching them the Dharma-door of patience."

"Oh, really?" said the King. "Patience,eh? What, exactly do you mean by that, anyway? Are you patient?"

"Yes,I am," said the Immortal.

"Very well," said the King. "I'll just give your patience a little test. If you are patient, that means you can endure any kind of pain, doesn't it?"

"Yes," said Shakyamuni Buddha.

"Well, I'm going to slice off your hand with my sword and see how patient you are," said the King.

"Go ahead," said Shakyamuni Buddha. The King drew his royal sword and with one neat swing sliced off Shakyamuni Buddha's hand.

"Does it hurt?" asked the King.

"No," said Shakyamuni Buddha.

"Are you angry?" asked the King.

"I am not angry," said the Buddha.

"All right, I'll cut off the other hand and see what you do," and he cut off the other hand. "Now, does that hurt?" he asked.

Shakyamuni Buddha said, "It does not hurt."

"Do you hate me?" the King asked.

"I do not hate you," said Shakyamuni Buddha.

"I don't believe you! I think you are lying," said the King. "How could you possibly not hate someone who had cut off both of your hands? It's impossible! I'll cut off your leg and see if *that* makes you hate me. I'll get the truth out of you yet," he said and cut off Shakyamuni Buddha's leg. Ordinary people would certainly have been crying bitter tears by this time, but Shakyamuni Buddha remained as if nothing had happened.

The King asked, "Does that hurt?"

"No," said Shakyamuni Buddha, "it's really nothing."

"Ah, it's nothing, huh? Do you hate me?"

"No, I don't hate you."

"All right then, you're missing two hands and one leg. The other leg isn't much use to you, O patient one who knows no pain, so we'll just cut that one off too," and he sliced off Shakyamuni Buddha's other leg. "Hurts, doesn't it?" said the King. "You've lost both your hands and both your legs. What are you going to do now? Tell the truth! Does it hurt? If you tell the truth, we'll forget it. If you don't tell the truth, I've got yet another test in store."

Shakyamuni Buddha said, "It still doesn't hurt."

"Do you hate me?"

"No."

The King said, "That's just what you *say*. You don't dare admit that you hate me because I am a King. No matter how much it hurts, you continue to lie, because you don't dare tell the truth. Right?"

"Wrong," said Shakyamuni Buddha. "And if I truly don't hate you, my hands and feet will grow back on my body. If I do hate you, my hands and legs won't grow back." As soon as he said that, immediately his hands and legs grew back as if they had never been severed. Then, all the Dharma Protectors and good spirits flew into a rage and sent down a great hailstorm which pounded the King of Kalinga unmercifully. Shakyamuni Buddha interceded on the King's behalf saying, "Don't blame him. He just came to test me and aid me in the accomplishment of my Way-karma. In the future when I become a Buddha, he is the first person I am going to take across to Buddhahood. He shall be the first to be enlightened."

In fact, the King of Kalinga in a later life became the Bhikshu Ajnatakaundinya, the first person Shakyamuni Buddha liberated.

Therefore, Ajnatakaundinya's name means, "liberated to the original limit."[1] It also means, "the first to be liberated,"[2] for he was the first to become enlightened.

2. MAHAKASHYAPA

"Maha" means great. Kashyapa, his family name, means "drinking light,"[3] or "waves of light."[4] It also means "great turtle clan,"[5] for it is said that his

---

1 解本際 -*chieh pen chi.*

2 最初解 -*tsui ch'u chieh*

3 飲光 -*yin kuang.*

4 光波 -*kuang po.*

5 大龜氏 -*ta kuei shih.*

ancestors saw a big turtle with a chart on its back which they used to cultivate the Way and from this took their family name. The Chinese would consider the name "turtle" to be an insult, but Kashyapa's name nonetheless means "big turtle."

Kashyapa's personal name was Pippala, which is the name of the tree to which his parents prayed in order to have their son. "Drinking light" doesn't mean that he actually drank light, of course. It refers to the fact that Kashyapa's body emitted a light which outshone and seemed to "drink up" all other light.

Where did the light come from? Kashyapa's wife also left the home-life and became the Bhikshuni Purple-Golden Light. Long ago after the Nirvana of Vipashyin Buddha, she was a poor woman. One day, she came across the ruins of a temple and stupa. Inside, she saw a Buddha image. Someone had put a straw hat on it to protect it from the wind and rain which blew in through holes in the roof but still it was badly weathered, cracked and peeling. She compassionately resolved to repair the temple and regild the image. "How can I allow the Buddha to be battered by the wind and rain?"

Since she was poor, she went out begging to raise the funds for her project. Every day she took the money she had collected and exchanged it for gold. After about ten years of begging, she had accumulated quite a bit of gold and made arrangements to have the temple rebuilt. She also went to visit a goldsmith to see about having her gold refined to regild the image. The goldsmith asked her where she got so much gold. "I saw a Buddha image which was cracked and peeling," she said, "and I begged for ten years to get enough money to buy this gold in order to repair it."

The goldsmith said, "We should share this merit and virtue." Actually, he was so struck by her goodness in wanting to repair the image that he fell in love with her and wanted her to think well of him. "You can furnish the gold," he said, "and I will contribute the labor, free." When the image and the temple had been restored, the goldsmith asked the woman for her hand im marriage. "You are truly a good-hearted woman. You are the finest woman I have ever met. I had intended to remain unmarried, but now I have changed my mind. Won't you marry me?"

The woman thought it over: "He isn't a bad sort, himself. After all, he did help me regild the image..." and she consented. Once they were married, they vowed to be husband and wife in every life. How powerful was their love! For ninety-one kalpas, in every life, they were husband and wife. Because they had regilt the Buddha image, their bodies shone with a golden light. Thus, Kashyapa's name means "drinking light" because his light swallowed up all other light.

Kashyapa was born in India, in Magadha. When he grew up, his parents wanted him to marry, but he said, "The woman I marry must shine with golden light just like I do. Otherwise, I will not marry." Sure enough, in a neighboring country such a woman was found and they were married. They both left home and cultivated the Way. When they certified to the Fruit of Arhatship, they discovered that they had been married to each other throughout many lifetimes. You shouldn't make a mistake however, and think to imitate them by making a vow to be married to someone for life after life. Kashyapa and his wife vowed to be married and then to cultivate the Way, to take refuge with the Triple Jewel, to leave the home-life and master the Way. Don't just make a vow to be married to someone in every life. If you do, you'll just get farther and farther off the track until you finally end up in the hells. You must cultivate the Way.

So Kashyapa and his wife took refuge with the Buddha and certified to the fruit, and Kashyapa became the first Patriarch in Buddhism.

If you would like to meet Mahakashyapa, he is still in this world. He is in Southwestern China, sitting in samadhi on Chicken Foot Mountain in Yünnan Province. Although it has been over three thousand years since the Buddha's Nirvana, Mahakashyapa is still sitting in meditation waiting for Maitreya Buddha to appear in the world. He will then give Maitreya the bowl which the Four Heavenly Kings gave Shakyamuni Buddha and which Shakyamuni Buddha gave him. Then, his job will be completed.

Those with sincere hearts who travel to Chicken Foot Mountain may see Mahakashyapa. On the mountain there are always three kinds of light: Buddha-light gold light, and silver light. If you are sincere, you may hear a bell ringing inside the mountain. It rings by itself and can be heard for several hundred miles.

Mahakashyapa was the oldest of the disciples and the foremost of the Buddha's disciples in ascetic practices. He was the oldest of the disciples, but the older he got, the more vigorous he became, the stronger he grew, and the harder he worked. He was the son of a rich Brahman of Magadha and the King of Magadha had even bowed to him as his Master. When he left the home-life, he thought, "Cultivators are called 'Poor Ones of the Way.' They have no business being rich," and gave away all of his wealth.

He also thought, "Cultivators must endure bitterness, bear weariness, and fear no suffering whatever," and he concentrated on cultivating ascetic practices. Ascetic practices refers to undergoing suffering, that is, not eating well, not wearing fine clothes, and not living in a comfortable dwelling. The harder something is to bear, the more the ascetic must bear it. In all the ways ordinary people wish to find enjoyment, through eating, dwelling, and clothing, the ascetic wishes to undergo suffering.

One day, when the Buddha was speaking the Dharma, he moved over and asked Kashyapa to sit beside him. At that time, Kashyapa was very old, perhaps a hundred and forty or a hundred and fifty. The Buddha said, "You're getting old, Kashyapa. Your energy is failing. You should give up ascetic practices. Eat better, wear better clothes, and move to a more suitable dwelling. I don't know if you can bear up under such ascetic practices at your age." But, Kashyapa chose not to obey the Buddha, and continued his ascetic practices as before.

Seeing this, the Buddha praised him highly saying, "The Buddhadharma will dwell long in the world largely because of Kashyapa's cultivation of ascetic practices. His ability to practice them means that the Buddhadharma will certainly long endure." Thus Patriarch Kashyapa was foremost in ascetic practices.

Once, when the Buddha was about to speak the Dharma, a god from the Great Brahma Heaven made an offering to him of a golden flower and then lay down on the ground and asked the Buddha to use his body for a chair and speak the Dharma for living beings. The Buddha sat down on the brahma god, took the flower in his fingers and in the midst of hundreds of tens of thousands of men and gods, gave a subtle smile. Kashyapa also smiled slightly, and with that, the Mind Seal Dharma was transmitted. So it is called the transmission of "twirling the flower and giving a subtle smile." Then the Buddha said, "I have the Right Dharma-Eye Treasury, the wonderful Mind of Nirvana, the Actual Mark which is unmarked, transmitted outside the teaching, the sealing of the Mind by means of the Mind. I have just transmitted it to Mahakashyapa. In this way Kashyapa became the First Indian Patriarch.

Since the time of the Buddha, the Dharma has been transmitted to only one Patriarch in each generation. Shakyamuni Buddha transmitted his entire Dharma to his disciple Mahakashyapa and Arya Mahakashyapa transmitted it to Arya Ananda who became the Second Patriarch. From Arya Ananda, the Dharma went to Arya Shankavasa from Arya Shankavasa it went to Arya Upagupta, and so on to the Twenty-Eighth Indian Patriarch, Great Master Bodhidharma, who took the Dharma to China where it was transmitted to the Second Chinese Patriarch, Great Master Hui K'o, to the Third Patriarch, Great Master Seng Ts'an. From Great Master Seng Ts'an, the Dharma went to the Fifth Patriarch, Great Master Hung Jen, who passed the Dharma to the Sixth Patriarch, Great Master Hui Neng. Then the flower of the Dharma bloomed with five petals: the five Lineages of Lin-chi, Fa-yen, Ts'ao Tung, Wei-yang, and Yün-men and so forth until the present. And now the Buddhadharma has come to the West.

The Twelve Ascetic Practices

Ascetic practices are called "dhutangas," a Pali word from the root √dhu, which means "to shake out." They are also called duskara-charya, "bitter practices." "To shake out," means to strike up your spirits and raise up your energy, to shake yourself free of affliction and ignorance as you would shake the dust out of a robe. When we have a Ch'an meditation session, we are also encouraged to strike up our spirits, to be vigorous, and to fear no suffering or difficulty. The harder it is, the more you should resolve to do it! As old as Patriarch Kashyapa was, he still kept up his ascetic practices.

There are twelve ascetic practices. The first two deal with clothing, five deal with food and five with dwelling.

1. *Wearing rag robes.* One finds old, unwanted clothing on refuse heaps, washes it, and stitches it into a robe.

"What are the advantages of wearing such a robe?" you may ask.

If you wish to know the advantages, there are many. If you want to talk about the disadvantages, there are also many. Wearing rag robes, you yourself do not become greedy for fine clothes or become vain as often happens when one puts on a new garment. It helps do away with one's own greed and it also helps to lessen the greed of others. When people see you, they think,

"That old cultivator is dressed in rags, not fine clothes. He's a true adept and I should imitate him." By means of your example, other Bhikshus also resolve to cultivate the Way. So, there are many advantages to the practice.

And what are the disadvantages? When you wear rags, thieves leave you alone. For example, when I was living at Nan Hua Monastery in the late 1940's, I wore the same rag robe that I had worn in Manchuria when I sat in mourning for three years beside my mother's grave. When I had finished the term of mourning, I continued to wear it in memory of her. In Manchuria, when my disciples took refuge, each of them gave me an inch-sized patch for my robe; it was really ragged but I had alot of patches.

At Nan Hua Monastery, one night a gang of thieves started pounding on the monastery gate trying to get in. "Open up!" they screamed, but no one let them in. When I finally opened the door, they surrounded me.

"Why didn't you open the door?" they demanded.

"You are thieves and bandits, " I said. "Think about it. If you had been in my place, would you have opened the door for me?"

Then I said, "There are valuables in my room. Go get them." But when they took a good look at me, dressed in rags, they decided I probably had nothing worth taking and so they didn't go. Actually, there were two living treasures in my room at the time--two frightened young novices who were hiding under the bed.

"Where is the money?" they demanded.

"Look at my robe," I said. "Do I look like a rich man?"

"No," they agreed, "but your students must have money."

"Sirs," I replied, "if the teacher is penniless, surely the students will be even poorer." As the bandits ran through the temple, I followed them, ordering them to leave and warning them not to take anything.

The following day, at a general assembly, the Venerable Abbot Hsü Yün announced, "In the monastery, only one person was not afraid of the thieves," and then he mentioned my name.

"No," I replied, "the Sixth Patriarch was unmoved and Master Han Shan was also unruffled. Master Tan T'ien was quite calm, although he had less samadhi-power and stuck out his head to take a look. These three great teachers all did far better than I. I had no samadhi at all. I just hounded them around the temple grounds." (The bodies of the three masters have not decayed. They have been gilded and are kept at the monastery so that the faithful can pay reverance to them. The body of Master Tan T'ien seems to lean forward a bit.)

Thus, when you wear rag robes, thieves keep their distance. The rich also stay away, and this saves a lot of trouble. Another important factor: women leave you alone. After you've worn your rag-robe for a while it takes on a rare fragrance which women find offensive. One could never finish speaking of the advantages of wearing rag robes.

2. *Possessing only three robes*. Cultivating this bitter practice, one owns nothing except one's three robes. It is said,

> Owning nothing beyond the limits of
> one's person,
> Vexation and annoyance do not arise.

Bhikshus who undertake this practice have only three robes, a begging bowl, and a sitting cloth. The first is the samghati, the great, or host, robe. It is worn when entering the king's palace, when taking the seat to speak the Dharma, and when begging for food. It is commonly made of twenty-five strips of cloth sewn into 108 patches. Each strip has four long and one short piece. The patches represent fields in which, through making offerings, the faithful can plant causes for future blessings.

The second is the uttarasangha; the robe worn when entering the assembly. Made of seven pieces, it is interpreted as meaning "the upper robe" and is worn when attending ceremonies of worship, such as cultivating repentances, reciting Sutras, sitting in meditation, reciting the precepts, and attending the Pravarana.

The third is the antarvasaka, the all-purpose work robe, made of five pieces which is worn in the monastery when doing manual labor and standing in attendance, and on the road when coming and going.

A bhikshu who cultivates ascetic practices should only have three robes, his bowl and his bowing cloth.

The first two ascetic practices deal with clothing. The next five deal with that most important human activity: eating.

3. *Begging for food*. In the morning, Bhikshus take their begging bowls and go into the city to collect alms for their midday meal. They do not cook their own food. In Thailand, Burma, and Ceylon, the donor will prepare an extra bowl of food as an offering to the

Triple Jewel. They offer it to the first Bhikshu who passes by their house on his begging rounds. They kneel respectfully, hold the bowl over their heads, pour the contents into the Bhikshu's bowl and then bow three times.

4. *Consecutive begging*. One begs from house to house, paying no attention to whether families are rich or poor. In the *Shurangama Sutra* we read:

"At that time, Ananda, holding his begging-bowl, went into the city to beg consecutively. From the beginning of his begging-tour to the last donor, he did not question the purity or filth of the vegetarian hosts or concern himself with whether they were of noble kshatriya families or chandalas. He practiced equal compassion and did not seek out only the lowly, for he had resolved to perfect the limitless merit and virtue of all living beings."

The practice of consecutive begging helps rid one of discrimination and allows one to give all living beings an equal opportunity to plant blessings. It is an act of great unselfishness.

5. *Eating only one meal at midday*. In the morning and evening one does not eat; one eats only one meal per day, and that is taken before noon. This is an excellent practice, but, unfortunately it is not an easy one. Why? Because it is said, "The people take food as their foundation." Everybody likes to eat. Human beings are born with the desire for food and, whenever they get the slightest bit hungry, want to eat something. This usually happens in the morning and evening as well as at lunchtime.

Eating once a day takes care of a lot of problems. Eating two less meals a day, one spends less time cooking and eating as well as less time on the toilet.

It would be impossible to enumerate in full all the virtues derived from the practice of eating only once a day. In general, if you eat a little less you'll have a little less trouble. If you eat too much you'll have more trouble.

Whenever Bhikshus eat, they must observe Four Recollections and Five Contemplations. With every bite of food, one in turn ruminates on them.

The Four Recollections are:

1. I vow to cut off all evil.
2. I vow to cultivate all good.
3. I vow to save all living beings.
4. I vow to cause the world to quickly be at peace.

The Five Contemplations are:

1. Consider the amount of work involved in bringing the food to the table

How much human labor was involved in getting the food to the table? Take, for example, the rice. It had to be planted, tended, and harvested. Although today we use machines, formerly people had to grind it and remove the husks. Then, it has to be cooked and served. A lot of effort went into every single grain. The ancients had a verse:

Hoeing the grain in the midday sun,
The farmer's sweat falls into the earth;
Who would have guessed how much toil
Went into every single grain in the pan?

So the people of all nations should take care not to waste material goods or casually throw things away. One should consider the difficulty involved in making and distributing goods. The reason that some countries are now stricken with famine is because in the past they were wasteful. Those who believe in Buddhism should be particularly careful in matters of cause and effect and always be thrifty. Use what you can and give what is left over to others. Don't throw things away. It is said,

If there's wasted rice in the house
There will be hungry people on the streets.

If you waste food, it is as if you were taking it from the mouths of others. If you have more than you can eat, give it away. Don't waste it. So the first of the Four Recollections is to consider the amount of work involved in getting the food to the table.

2. Reflect on whether or not one's virtuous conduct is sufficient to entitle one to receive this offering.

Think it over: what virtuous practice have you done to entitle you to receive offerings from the ten directions. Is your merit sufficient or is it lacking? If it is lacking, you should hurry and cultivate the Way!

3. Guard the mind from transgressions, principally that of greed. Avoid the offenses created primarily through greed, but also those comitted through hatred and stupidity. Don't greedily gobble down the good food and leave the bad food sitting there. Look on all the food as the same and do not discriminate among the good and bad flavors.

4. Regard the food as medicine to prevent the body from collapsing. While he eats, the Bhikshu should

think of his food as medicine. "Why am I eating? I am actually taking medicine because if I don't eat, I'll wither and die."

5. Take this food only in order to accomplish the karma of the Way. "I eat only because I want to work hard and cultivate the Way. If I don't eat, I won't be able to stand up or sit properly. I could still sleep, but that can't be considered cultivation. Since I want to cultivate, I can't avoid eating. But I do so only because I want to cultivate.

Bhikshus must always observe these Four Recollections and Five Contemplations when they eat. There are a great many advantages to be gained by eating one meal a day.

6. *Eating a fixed and moderate amount of food.* This is the fourth of the five ascetic practices dealing with food. A moderate amount means that, just because the food is good, you don't gorge yourself with it. Eating a fixed amount means that you eat the same amount every day. For example, every day you eat exactly two bowls of food, whether the food is tasty or not. You wouldn't eat only one bowl of bad food one day and the next day, when the menu has improved, eat three. Those who cultivate ascetic practices should reduce the amount of food they consume. If they can eat two bowls, then they should eat one and a half.

7. *Not drinking juices after noon.* After midday, one does not drink milk, juice, broth, coffee, tea, or honey. Only water is permitted. It's a very difficult practice because even tea is prohibited!

Those are the five which deal with food. Next are the five which deal with dwelling:

8. *Dwelling in an Aranya.* Aranya is a Sanskrit word whcih means "a still and quiet place." The noise of the bustling city does not reach one who dwells deep in the mountain groves in an Aranya. It is therefore an excellent place in which to cultivate.

9. *Dwelling beneath a tree.* Dwelling in an aranya, one still has a fixed "place" in which one dwells. Why would one want to live at the base of a tree?

Cultivators take the earth and sky as their cottage and the four seas as their home. They dwell wherever they happen to be. Dwelling at the base of a tree, one avoids the rain and is very refreshed as well. However, one may only dwell for two nights beneath any one tree. On the third day, one has to find another tree. Bhikshus who genuinely cultivate, and who are lofty and pure in their practices, wish to avoid recognition and offerings. After two days, they leave. No one can find them, and no affinities are established.

10. *Dwelling in the open.* Dwelling beneath a tree, one is still protected from the wind and rain by the leaves and branches. Dwelling in the open, one truly takes the earth and sky as one's house. Living in this way one is very natural and free. One bathes in the light of the moon and stars. It is said,

> When the moon arrives at the heart of heaven,
> And the wind blows across the face of
> the waters,
> There's a kind of clear mental flavor--
> Guess how few have tasted it?

Very few people have any idea how wonderful such a life-style is.

11. *Dwelling in a graveyard.* You sleep with the dead, sit in the graveyard and enjoy a camaraderie with the ghosts. What for? In order to contemplate impermanence and understand the ephemeral nature of human life. Sooner or later, we're *all* going to die. After we die, we decompose into a heap of bleached out bones in the grave. Cultivating at the graveyard you awaken to the doctrine that all is impermanence and you will be able to relinquish your attachments and will not become involved in the workings of greed, hatred, and stupidity.

12. *Always sitting and never lying down.* When you cultivate this practice, your ribs never touch the mat. In India there was a Venerable Master Hsieh who throughout his whole life never once lay down. One who sleeps in a prone position may develop a need for more and more sleep and never think to get up and cultivate. If you always sit, when you wake up you're all ready to begin cultivating, to sit in Dhyana meditation. This practice is a great aid in cultivation.

Some people may practice only one or perhaps a few of the twelve ascetic practices. There is nothing fixed about it. It depends upon how strong one is. Although a very old man, Mahakashyapa practiced all twelve ascetic practices in accord with the Dharma. Thus, he was foremost of those who cultivate asceticism.

3. URUVILVA KASHYAPA
4. GAYA KASHYAPA
5. NADI KASHYAPA

These three brothers had all been fire worshippers before they took refuge with the Buddha. Believing that fire was the most powerful of spiritual forces and the and the mother of all creation, they worshipped it with slavish devotion, bowing and making offerings to it. Would you say this was stupid or not? As meaningless as it was, they continued to do it until they met Shakyamuni Buddha.

Uruvilva's name means "papaya grove,"[1] as it is said that he liked to cultivate in a papaya grove. He and his five hundred disciples lived on the river Neranjara. Further down the river lived his brothers Nadi, which means "river,"[2] and Gaya, which means "city,"[3] or "elephant-head mountain."[4] They had three hundred and two hundred disciples respectively. Thus, between the three of them, the Kashyapa brothers had one thousand disciples.

After the Buddha attained enlightenment, he went to the Deer Park and converted the five Bhikshus. Then he considered who to cross over next. Seeing that conditions were favorable to save the three Kashyapa Brothers, he went to visit Uruvilva Kashyapa. He knew that if he converted him he would cross over his large following as well, but he could not come right out and tell Uruvilva as much; so he spoke expediently and said, "It has grown dark and I cannot travel any farther, may I please spend the night in your cave?"

"A fierce dragon lives in there," said Uruvilva. "He will surely scorch you to death."

"That's no problem," said the Buddha. "The dragon cannot harm me."

"Do as you please," said Uruvilva.

In the middle of the night, the dragon belched fire and tried to burn the Buddha, but the Buddha had entered the fire-light samadhi and couldn't be harmed. The Buddha used his spiritual powers to put the dragon in his begging bowl. He then preached the Dharma to it, and the dragon took refuge.

Uruvilva Kashyapa was amazed. Although he considered himself a cultivator of some skill, he realized he couldn't fathom the Buddha's realm or match the Buddha's powers. He and his five hundred disciples took refuge with the Buddha. When his brothers heard

---

1 木瓜林 -*mu kua lin.*

2 河 -*ho*, or 江 -*chiang.*

3 城 -*ch'eng.*

4 象頭山 -*Hsiang t'ou shan.*

that he had become a Bhikshu, they also resolved to leave the home life and, along with their five hundred followers, joined the Sangha. Soon after leaving home, they gave proof to the sagely fruit.

6. SHARIPUTRA

There's a special story about Shariputra which makes him hard to forget: Shariputra's mother often used to debate with her younger brother Mahakaushtila, and she lost every time. Strangely enough, when she became pregnant with Shariputra, she began winning all the debates. Mahakaushthila figured that the child in his older sister's womb was surely a wise one and was helping his mother, augmenting her eloquence and intelligence. "I had better get some rhetorical skills," he thought, "otherwise, I'll be defeated by my own little nephew which would be truly disgraceful;" he went to southern India to study. He was so industrious that he studied night and day and didn't take time to cut his hair, shave his beard, or even cut his fingernails. They grew to several inches in length and everyone called him, "The Long-Nailed Brahman." He didn't deliberately let them grow, as do the long-haired, bearded ones of today, who have dropped out of school. He was simply too busy to attend to his grooming. A model student, he labored day and night to the exclusion of all other activities. When he had mastered the Indian books of medicine, divination, physiognomy, and astrology as well as literature and debating skills, he returned and asked his sister, "Where is my nephew?"

"He has left home under the Buddha," she replied.

Kaushthila was outraged. "My nephew began preaching when he was eight years old and has astounded the entire country by out-debating several hundred philosophers. How could such an intelligent child leave the home life under a mere Shramana. It's pathetic." Arrogant and upset, he went to see the Buddha. "I'll have to see what special tricks that Shramana has that he managed to fool my brilliant nephew into becoming his disciple."

When he met the Buddha, no matter how he tried to counter him, he failed. He had studied for so many years, not even bothering to cut his nails, in preparation for his debate with his nephew. Who would have guessed it would all have come to nothing? His nephew had left home under the Buddha and he himself had no idea what branch of his learning to use against the Buddha. He finally decided to set up his established doctrine.

"What is your doctrine?" the Buddha asked him.

"I take non-accepting as my doctrine," Kaushthila replied. "No matter what you say, I won't accept it because I take non-accepting as my principle. Let's see what you can do with that. Speak up!"

"Fine," said the Buddha, "you take non-accepting as your doctrine, but let me ask you, do you or do you not accept your view of non-accepting?"

What a question! If he answered that he accepted his view, in accepting it he would be contradicting his own view of non-accepting. On the other hand, if he said that he did not accept his own view, he wouldn't have any doctrine at all and how could he take non-accepting as his doctrine. If he accepted it, he would contradict himself and if he refused it, he wouldn't have a doctrine at all. He didn't have a leg to stand on; he was like a rootless tree. To make matters worse, before he began, he had made a bet with the Buddha saying, "If I win the debate, then my nephew comes home with me. If I lose, I'll cut off my head and give it to you." Now, scared to lose his head, he had no recourse but to run. When he'd run about five miles, he stopped and thought, "I am a human being after all. How can I go back on my word? I agreed to cut off my head if I lost. How can I run like a coward?" He decided to return, cut off his head, and consider the matter closed.

When he arrived, he asked the Buddha for a knife and the Buddha said, "What do you want it for?"

"I agreed to cut off my head if I lost the debate," said Kaushthila, "and so now I owe you my head. Isn't that correct?"

"There is no such dharma within my Buddhadharma," said the Buddha. "You lost, so let's just forget it. What's the use of cutting off your head?"

The Buddha then spoke the Dharma to him and he obtained the purification of the Dharma-eye. When his Dharma-eye opened, he realized the marvelous, unfathomable profundity of the Buddhadharma. "I spent all that time learning non-Buddhist teachings. They are not even a ten-thousandth part as good as the Buddhadharma," he said, and he left home under the Buddha. So, not only did he not regain his nephew, he joined the Buddha's Sangha himself.

Shariputra's name is Sanskrit. It means "egret-son."[1] Shari means "egret" because his mother's eyes

---

1 鶖鷺子 *-ch'ou lu tzu.*

were as keen and beautiful as an egret's. Putra means "son." Another explanation of Shariputra's name is "body-son,"[1] after the Sanskrit word for body, sharira, because his mother was physically very beautiful. Shariputra also means "pearl-son"[2] because his eyes were like pearls and sharira is also the term for the pearl-like relics left after the cremation of a sage.

Shariputra was the foremost of the Shravaka Disciples in wisdom. He wasn't exactly number two when it came to spiritual powers, either. His spiritual powers were also great. One time, Mahamaudgalyayana decided to compare his spiritual powers with Shariputra's. Shakyamuni Buddha had gone elsewhere to speak the Dharma. When he did this, his disciples always went along to hear the Dharma too because they didn't have any tape recorders in those days and if they missed a lecture, they couldn't make it up. This time, Shariputra had entered samadhi. Mahamaudgalyayana called to him, but he wouldn't come out of samadhi. "All right," said Mahamaudgalayana, "I'll use my spiritual powers to snap you out of it," and he applied every ounce of spiritual power he had to get Shariputra to come out of samadhi, but he couldn't budge even so much as the corner of Shariputra's robe. How great would you say Shariputra's spiritual powers were? Mahamaudgalyayana was generally recognized as foremost in spiritual powers but he lost to Shariputra, and this proves that Shariputra's spiritual powers were even greater than his.

Thus, Shariputra was foremost in wisdom and had great spiritual powers. When he was eight years old he began studying with the Buddha and in seven days he had penetrated the actual mark of all Dharmas, mastered all the Buddha's teachings, and could defeat all the philosophers in India.

7. GREAT MAUDGALYAYANA

Mahamaudgalyayana's name is Sanskrit and means "descended from people connected with means."[3] It is also interpreted as meaning "turnip root."[4] This is because his ancestors cultivated an Indian ascetic

---

1 身子 -*shen tzu*

2 珠子 -*chu tzu.*

3 采菽氏 -*ts'ai shu shih.*

4 萊菔根 -*lai fu ken.*

practice of eating only foods that grew wild in the forests and never eating foods that had been planted or harvested. His personal name was Kolita, or "jujube tree," because his parents prayed to a local tree spirit in seeking to have a son, just as Mahakashyapa's parents had done. In this case, Maudgalyayana's parents consulted the spirit of a koli tree and named their son Kolita in honor of the spirit.

Maudgalyayana's mother may have consulted spirits, but she didn't believe in the Buddha, the Dharma, or the Sangha. She slandered the Triple Jewel and spoke ill of it. Because of these heavy offenses, at death she fell into the hells. When Maudgalyayana attained the fruit of Arhatship and gained the five eyes and the six spiritual penetrations, he took a look at the entire world and finally located his mother in the hells. Seeing her suffering and starving, he took her a bowl of food. Her greedy nature had accompanied her from the human realm to the realm of hungry ghosts, and so she immediately covered the bowl with one hand, hid it behind her sleeve, and ran off to eat it in secret, fearing the other ghosts might grab it away from her. But because her karmic obstacles were so heavy, the delicious food turned to fire in her mouth. Although he was foremost in spiritual powers, he had no mantra or method to free his mother. Completely at a loss, he went to ask his teacher's advice. The talents this disciple had developed were useless in this situation. He returned to the Jeta Grove and asked Shakyamuni to be compassionate and save his mother.

Shakyamuni Buddha said, "Your mother's karmic obstacles were created through slandering the Triple Jewel. You alone do not have the power to save her. We shall set up the Ullambana Festival, the day of the Buddha's rejoicing, to be held on the 15th day of the seventh month, which is the last day of the Sangha's annual rain's retreat. On that day offerings will be made to the Sangha of the ten directions. Before they accept the offerings and eat the food the Sangha will recite mantras and Sutras to liberate deceased relatives and friends who may have fallen into evil destinies, those who were hanging upside-down. Those making the offerings must take care that the food is not tasted until it has been offered to the Buddha, Dharma and Sangha. Maudgalyayana's mother was freed from the hells by the united power of the Sangha and was reborn in the heavens; she left suffering and attained bliss. After that, every year on that day, the ceremony is observed in all monasteries and temples to save relatives and friends from this life and from seven lives past.

You may say, "But my parents haven't died."

You can save your parents from seven lives past, and your present parents will also gain an increase in blessings and long-life.

Mahamaudgalyayana's spiritual powers were extraordinarily great. Once, when Shakyamuni Buddha was on his way to the Heaven of the Thirty-Three to speak the Dharma, he passed by Mount Sumeru. On the way he met two poisonous dragons which were jealous of the Buddha. "Does a Shramana like you really think you can speak the Dharma in the heavens?" they said. "We won't permit it!" And they spit out clouds of poisonous black fog to kill the Buddha. Several Bhikshus asked the Buddha for permission to fight the dragons, but the Buddha would not allow them to because he knew their powers would be insufficient. He did, however, grant Maudgalyayana permission to do battle with them. The dragons manifested in huge bodies which wound around Mount Sumeru seven times with their tails in the ocean and their heads on the mountain peak. Now, Mount Sumeru is very large. Our four continents, in fact, are on its four sides. Maudgalyayana manifested a body twice as large which coiled itself around Mount Sumeru fourteen times! The dragons sent down a rain of vajra sand, but Maudgalyayana transformed it into precious lotus petals; This only increased the dragons' fury. Maudgalyayana then shrunk himself into a small body, the size of a bug. He flew into the dragons' ears and buzzed into their eyes. Then he drilled into their noses and into their stomachs and bit their inner organs until they were in so much pain that they finally submitted. Maudgalyayana once again manifested in the body of a Shramana and took the two dragons back to the Buddha. The dragons then took refuge and joined the assembly.

Mahamaudgalyayana is Earth-Store (Kshitigarbha) Bodhisattva. He couldn't bear to see his mother suffering in the hells. He also couldn't bear to see anyone else's mother or any one at all suffering. Accordingly, he vowed to be Earth Store Bodhisattva and to manage the business of getting people out of the hells, saying,

If the hells are not empty,
I vow not to realize Buddhahood
When all beings are crossed over,
I will then accomplish bodhi.

8. MAHAKATYAYANA

Maha means "great." Katyayana means "literary elegance,"[1] because this Venerable One was foremost of the Buddha's disciples in debate and spoke with great elegance and refinement. His name is also interpreted as "fan-cord"[2] because his father died shortly after he was born, and his mother wanted to remarry, but the child Katyayana was a tie, like a fan-cord, which prevented her from doing so.

Katyayana's name is also interpreted as "good shoulders,"[3] because his shoulders were well-formed and good-looking, and as "victorious thinker,"[4] because he could out-think everyone else.

Katyayana, an eloquent exponent of the Dharma, was quick to utilize his reasoning to bring home his points. Once, he met a non-Buddhist who held to the view of annihilationism; that is, he did not believe in rebirth but believed that after death there was nothing at all. He confronted Katyayana with his position saying, "Buddhists believe that after death there is rebirth. I do not hold that doctrine, and I can prove that it is false. If there is rebirth, and beings are destined to suffer in future incarnations, then why has not even one of them ever returned to tell of his torment? This proves that there is no rebirth. When people die, it's all over, like a lamp that's been blown out."

Katyayana said, "Suppose a criminal were arrested, tried, given a jail sentence. Would he be free to return home?"

"No," came the reply.

"The beings in the hells are even less free to come and go," said Katyayana.

"That may be the case," said the annihilationist, "but what about those born in the heavens? Not one has ever returned to talk about it. Beings in the hells may have no freedom, but certainly heavenly beings should be free to come back and give a brief report."

---

[1]文飾 -*wen shih.*
[2]扇繩 -*shan sheng.*
[3]好肩 -*hao chien.*
[4]思勝 -*ssu sheng.*

Katyayana said, "That's a very reasonable question. However, people born in the heavens are like beings who have climbed out of the toilet and been washed clean. They wouldn't be likely to want to jump back into the toilet, would they?

The annihilationist had nothing to say.

"Besides," Katyayana continued, "one day and one night in, for example, the Heaven of the Thirty-three, is equal to one hundred years in the world of men. Born there, it would take several days to get settled. By the time they thought to return, several hundred years would have passed in the world of men. You would have long been dead and your bones turned to dust. How would you know they had returned?

The annihilationist was speechless. Each of the Buddha's ten great disciples possessed a quality whereby he excelled others. Mahakatyayana, the foremost in debate, was articulate, eloquent, and unbeatable.

9. ANIRUDDHA

The Venerable Aniruddha's name means "never poor,"[1] because in limitless kalpas past he made an offering to a Pratyeka Buddha. At the time he made the offering, he did not know the mendicant was a Pratyeka Buddha. The Pratyeka Buddha, who lived in the mountains, had vowed to come down and beg only once every seven days at only seven houses. If he obtained no food, he would simply return and go hungry for another week. On this particular round, having obtained no food, he was returning carrying his empty bowl anticipating another week of hunger. Aniruddha knew this and was pained at heart. Times were hard, and famine was rampant. Families had trouble supporting themselves, and had nothing left over to give those who had left home. Aniruddha, a poor farmer who scraped his living out of the soil, ate the very coarsest, cheapest kind of unhusked rice, which he carried to the fields with him each day. When he saw the Bhikshu, he said: "That a cultivator such as yourself should have to undergo starvation is too pitiful. Won't you accept my offering of coarse rice? If it is not unacceptable, you may have it."

"If you wish to give it, I'll accept it," said the Pratyeka Buddha, "but what will *you* eat?"

---

[1] 無貧 -*wu p'in.*

"I can skip lunch today," said Aniruddha. "It doesn't matter."

When the Pratyeka Buddha had finished eating, he revealed his spiritual powers by manifesting the Eighteen Miraculous Changes which include things like emitting water from the upper part of one's body and fire from the lower part, and emitting water from the lower part of one's body and fire from the upper part, and suspending oneself in space--things which Arhats and Pratyeka Buddhas can do but which ordinary people find most unusual. After that, he said, "I accepted your offering and from now on, in every life, you will never again be poor," then he left.

Aniruddha continued to work in the fields when along hopped a rabbit. Strangely enought, it jumped and frisked around and around Aniruddha as tamely as a horse, dog or cat. "Don't bother me," Aniruddha finally said, "I'm working and I don't have time to play with you."

Then the rabbit jumped up onto Aniruddha's back. No matter how Aniruddha tried to brush it off, it wouldn't budge. It was as if it had grown roots right into Aniruddha's shoulders. Aniruddha continued working, but he was getting worried. "What's going to become of this rabbit on my back?" he wondered. As poor as he was, he still had a wife; when he returned home that evening, he asked her to knock the rabbit off his back. As she did so, the rabbit died and turned into gold! Aniruddha broke off its front leg and exchanged it for a large sum of cash. To his surprise, the front leg grew back again! The same thing happened whenever he broke off one of the back legs. He had struck it rich! No one knew how much he was worth because he could always break off part of the golden rabbit. Not only was he a rich man in that life, but throughout ninety-one kalpas he was wealthy, honored and never poor again.

When he made the offering, he did not know the Bhikshu was a Pratyeka Buddha. After the Pratyeka Buddha accepted it, he transferred merit to him, so that Aniruddha received the retribution of never being poor.

Aniruddha, the Buddha's first cousin, liked best to sleep. In fact, every time the Buddha lectured on the Dharma Aniruddha would doze off with his head resting on the table and snoring like thunder. Once the Buddha scolded him saying:

Hey! Hey! How can you sleep,
Like an oyster or a clam?
Sleep, sleep for a thousand years,
But you'll never hear the Buddha's name.

After the reprimand, in a burst of vigor Aniruddha decided never to sleep again but to truly dedicate himself to studying the Buddhadharma. He went for seven days and nights without sleeping and as a result he went blind. Shakyamuni Buddha, knowing that he had gone blind because of his great vigor in studying the Buddhadharma, took pity on his little cousin and taught him the Vajra Bright-illumination Samadhi. Thereafter, Aniruddha cultivated according to Dharma and obtained the Penetration of the Heavenly Eye. In fact, his Heavenly Eye covered half of his head, enabling him to view the world system of three thousand great thousand worlds just as we would regard an amala fruit or an apple in our hands. Thus Aniruddha was foremost in possessing the Heavenly Eye.

10. KAPPHINA

Kapphina's name means "house-constellation"[1] because when Kapphina's parents had reached the age of forty or fifty, they still had no son. Going to a temple, they prayed to one of the 28 constellations. They received a response and had a son. He was the foremost of the Buddha's disciples in the knowledge of astrology.

11. GAVAMPATI

The Venerable Gavampati's name means "cow cud"[2] or "cow king"[3] because when he was finished eating he continued to smack his lips like a cow chewing its cud. When cows are done eating, they go to sleep, but they continue to munch on their cud.

Because of this habit, Shakyamuni Buddha was afraid that people would ridicule him and consequently fall; so he sent Gavampati to the heavens to receive offerings of the gods.

Why did he have this habit? It was retribution for having created evil karma with his mouth by one sentence of slander. Long ago, in limitless ages past,

---

1 房宿 -*fang su*.

2 牛呞 -*niu tz-u*.

3 牛王 -*niu wang*.

he met an elderly Pratyeka Buddha who had lost his teeth and chewed his food very slowly. "Old Master," said Gavampati, "you sound just like a cow chewing its cud!"

The Pratyeka Buddha said, "The retribution you will incur for having slandered me will be extremely grave. Hurry and repent!"

Gavampati, who was a Shramenera at the time, ridiculed the Master saying, "Repent of what? Why should I beg your forgiveness?" As a result of his slander, for five-hundred lifetimes he was reborn as a cow. When he finally became a person, his cow-like habits remained, and when he was done eating, he still worked his jaws like a cow. Such was the retribution for slandering a Pratyeka Buddha. From this we should take special care in every movement and word not to casually slander or berate others. Watch yourself.

12. REVATA

Revata's name means "constellation"[1] because his parents also prayed to a constellation[2] for their son's birth. It also means "false unity."[3] Because he was poor and had no place to live, one night he stayed in an old abandoned shack. That night two ghosts came--a big one and a little one. The big one was twenty feet tall and the small one was two feet tall.

They came in, dragging a corpse and asked him, "Shall we eat this corpse or not?" What they meant was, "If you tell us to eat the corpse, we will eat you. If you tell us not to eat the corpse, we won't have anything to eat, and so we'll have to eat you. They were obviously going to eat him no matter what he said, so he didn't say anything.

The big ghost bit off the corpse's legs and the little ghost ripped off Revata's legs and stuck them on the corpse. Then the ghost ate the corpse's arms and the little ghost ripped off Revata's arms and stuck them on the corpse. The big ghost ate the entire corpse and the little ghost replaced its parts, one by one, with parts of Revata's body.

Revata panicked. "My body has been used to repair the corpse and so now I don't have a body!" The next day he ran frantically through town asking everyone he

---

[1]星宿 *-hsing su.*

[2]That of 室星, (a) Markab, (b) Scheat, Pegasus.

[3]假和合 *-chia ho ho.*

met, "Do I have a body? Please tell me!"

"What?" they said. They had no idea what he meant and supposed that he was insane. Then he met some High Masters. "Shramanas," he asked, "Do I have a body?" Among the High Masters were certified Arhats who knew that he had the potential to leave the home-life.

"Your body is fundamentally false," they said. "If you cultivate and certify to the fruit and obtain the bright light of the self-nature, *that* is true. What difference, then, would it make whether or not you have a body? The body is basically a combination of causes and conditions. When the causes and conditions disperse, the body is destroyed. There is nothing that is you and nothing that is *not* you."

Just as they said that, Revata was enlightened. Although he had been eaten by ghosts, the whole affair had been basically false. Therefore, he took the name, "false unity," Revata.

13. PILINDAVATSA

This Venerable One's name means "left-over habits,"[1] referring to habits of many ages and many lifetimes which he had not gotten rid of. Once, he wished to cross the river; because he had certified to the fruit of Arhatship and had spiritual penetrations, he could demand that the river spirit stop the current so he could walk across. To the river spirit, who was a woman, he said, "Little Slave, stop the current."

Because she was an Arhat, the river spirit had to comply. Although she dared not say anything, she was extremely displeased. This happened repeatedly until finally the river spirit complained to the Buddha. "Your disciple Pilindavatsa," she said, "hasn't the least bit of respect for me. He came to the river and said, 'Little Slave, stop the current!' He's entirely too rude."

The Buddha said, "When he returns I'll have him apologize to you." When Pilindavatsa arrived, the Buddha said, "When you were crossing the Ganges why did you say, 'Little Slave, stop the current?' You really shouldn't have done that. Now, you had better hurry up and apologize to her."

Pilindavatsa immediately went to the river spirit with his palms joined and laughingly said, "Little

---

[1] 餘習 -*yü hsi*.

Slave, don't take offense." He had been instructed to apologize for having called her 'Little Slave,' but in apologizing he also addressed her that way! Needless to say, she was furious.

"See that!" she said. "He stands right here in front of the Buddha and calls me Little Slave again!"

"You didn't know this," said the Buddha, "but five hundred lifetimes ago, you were Pilindavatsa's servant and at that time he called you Little Slave when he gave you orders. Although you are now a river spirit, his habits have not changed and because of your previous master-servant relationship, he still calls you Little Slave."

Because of such heavy habits from the past, he was called "left-over habits," Pilindavatsa.

14. VAKKULA

This Venerable One's name means "good bearing."[1] In the past, thoughout limitless kalpas, he exclusively cultivated the precept against killing. His cultivation of that precept was not like that of us ordinary people at all. His mind did not even give rise to the *thought* of killing. Not only did he not kill outwardly, inwardly he was spotlessly clean in that he never killed a single living creature. Because of this, he received five kinds of non-dying retribution.

When he was born, he was able to speak. He smiled and laughed and said, "Mama" and "Papa," and was very playful. His mother thought, "What on earth! I've never heard of a child who could talk and joke at birth. It must be a monster." Since she was rather cruel and not compassionate, she put him in a frying pan and tried to fry him. But he wouldn't fry. It was as if nothing was happening. The pan was red hot, but Vakkula was just as happy. "All right," she said, "you may be fireproof, but you're certainly not water-proof!" and she tossed him in a pot of rapidly boiling water, but he still didn't die. Then she tried to drown him by holding him under the water, but he couldn't be drowned. Do you think this is strange or not?

She left him in the ocean and he was gulped down by a fish and he went right into the fish's stomach , escaping the fish's teeth. Just then, strangely enough, the fish was caught in a fisherman's net and the fisherman cut the fish open with a knife. Vakkula was not

---

[1] 善容 -*shan jung*.

harmed by the knife, either, and jumped right out of the fish's belly. Thus, he received the five kinds of non-dying retribution: the fire didn't burn him; the water didn't boil him; the ocean didn't drown him; the fish didn't chomp him to death; and the fisherman's knife didn't cut him. He received these five as a response from his observance of the precept against kllling and among the Buddha's disciples he was the foremost in longevity.

15. MAHAKAUSHTHILA

The Venerable Kaushthila's name means "big knees"[1] because big knees was a family trait. This Venerable One was Shariputra's maternal uncle. As previously related, he made a bet with the Buddha that if he won in debate, the Buddha would allow his nephew, Shariputra, to leave the ranks of the Sangha and return with him but if he lost, he would cut off his head. Although he lost the debate, the Buddha convinced him it would be more constructive to join the Sangha himself than to cut off his head, and Mahakaushthila did so. He was a gifted and an eloquent debator. He was one of the Buddha's constant followers, and the foremost disciple noted for eloquence.

16. NANDA

There are three disciples with the name of Nanda: Nanda, Ananda, and Sundarananda. Nanda is known as "Nanda the Cowherd."

Nanda's name means "wholesome bliss."[2] As a cowherd, he heard the Buddha speak the Eleven Matters of Tending Cows, using the tending of cows as an analogy for cultivation of the Way; Nanda, realizing that the Buddha was possessed of all-knowledge, resolved to leave home and soon attained to the fruit of Arhatship.

On one occasion the Buddha instructed Nanda to preach to a group of five hundred Bhikshunis. Hearing him speak, they all attained Arhatship. In the past, the five hundred Bhikshunis had been the concubines of a single king. The king, a great Dharma protector, built a large pagoda in honor of a Buddha. The concubines believed in the Buddha and made offerings at the pagoda, vowing that in the future they would all obtain

---

[1] 大膝 -*ta hsi.*

[2] 善歡喜 -*shan huan hsi.*

liberation with the king. The king was a former incarnation of Nanda.

17. SUNDARANANDA

Sundarananda was named after his wife, Sundari, because he loved her so intensely. Sundari means "good to love,"[1] or "attractive."[2] The two of them were never out of each other's sight. Why did he love her? Because she was the most beautiful woman in all of India. She was absolutely stunning. Stunned, Sundarananda was beguiled by her beauty so that he never left her side. It was as if they were magnetized or glued together; walking, standing, sitting, and reclining, they were an inseparable couple.

Shakyamuni Buddha wanted him to leave home. Sundarananda was the Buddha's little half-brother. When the Buddha saw that his causal affinities were mature enough that he could leave home, he also knew that Sundarananda couldn't give up his wife to do it. Thus, The Buddha decided to apply an expedient measure. One day when Sundarananda and his wife were eating lunch he went to the palace to beg for alms.

When Sundarananda saw his older brother he wanted to offer him some food, but the Buddha said, "Take it to the Jeta Grove."

"How can I do that?" said Sundarananda. "How can I leave my wife home alone?" He didn't dare contradict his brother's orders; so he asked his wife: "The Buddha said I should take the food to the Jeta Grove. Is it all right if I go?"

"Yes, on one condition," she said. "I am going to spit on the floor; you must return before that spit is dry. Otherwise, you needn't bother coming in the door because I won't let you in."

"All right," said Sundarananda, thinking he would easily make it back in time, but when he arrived, the Buddha wouldn't let him go! He ordered him to shave his head and leave home. Sundarananda spent all day trying to figure out a way to sneak back home to see his wife because he simply couldn't let her go.

One day all the Bhikshus went out to beg and Shakyamuni Buddha told Sundarananda, "Stay here today and watch the door. You're not going anywhere, today.

---

1 好愛 -*hao ai*.

2 端正 -*tuan cheng*.

Sweep the floor and clean the place up. We're going out to beg, and we'll bring some food back for you."

Sundarananda was ecstatic. "Finally! A chance to escape!" he thought. He planned to sweep the floor, wash the windows, and run. Strangely enough, as soon as he got one end of the hall swept, dirt would collect on the other side. He swept all morning until he was perspiring with exhaustion, but he still couldn't get the floor clean. As soon as he closed one window, another would blow open and the sweepings would fly around the room; then, when he shut that window, yet another would fly open. He was getting more and more frustrated the later it got. The morning was slipping away; the Buddha would return soon, and he would have missed his chance. Finally, in desperation, he ran.

He knew if he met the Buddha, he would have to return to the Jeta Grove. He also knew that the Buddha always travelled by the main roads, and so he took a side road and who do you think he ran into? The Buddha! He was returning from his alms round. Sundarananda jumped behind a big tree and, as he backed around the tree, the Buddha followed him. The Buddha would reverse his direction and Sundarananda would do so as well. Finally, they met face to face and the Buddha said, "What are you doing?"

"I waited for you until I couldn't wait anymore," said Sundarananda. "I decided to come and escort you back to the Jeta Grove."

"Good," said the Buddha, "let's go back."

Since he had no other choice, he returned with the Buddha and after he had eaten lunch, the Buddha asked him, "Would you like to go out sight-seeing with me today? I'll take you out to play."

Sundarananda thought, "I don't have the heart to go play. I'm only concerned with running home. I really don't have the spirit, but if the Buddha wants me to go I can't refuse," and he forced himself. They went to a mountain where there were a lot of monkeys. The Buddha asked him, "Tell me, which is more beautiful, Sundari or these monkeys?"

"Why, of course my wife is more beautiful. How can you compare these ugly monkeys with my wife? What an insult!"

The Buddha said, "You are truly intelligent; you can tell the good from the bad. Now, let's return."

By now, Sundarananda was obsessed with thoughts of his wife. Several days passed and no opportunity to run away presented itself. The Buddha said to him,

"You seem so depressed every day. I can't imagine what's on your mind. Let me take you up to the heavens for a look around."

"I wonder what the heavens are like?" thought Sundarananda. They ascended into the heavens, and there they saw a lovely heavenly palace filled with exquisite heavenly maidens. The Buddha said, "Who do you say is more beautiful, the maidens or Sundari?"

"The heavenly maidens!" said Sundarananda. "Compared to these goddesses, Sundari looks like a monkey! There's no comparison." As they went on their way, Sundarananda lagged behind and stole a word with one of them. "Who is your master?" he asked.

"Our master is the Buddha's little brother, Sundarananda. He has now left home under the Buddha and cultivates the Way. Next life, he will be reborn in heaven and we are to be his servants."

Delighted at the prospect, Sundarananda resolved to cultivate. Forgetting all about Sundari and thinking only of goddesses, he cultivated to be reborn in the heavens. When he had cultivated for a long time, the Buddha, seeing that he was no longer thinking of Sundari but only of the maidens, thought: "I think I'll show him something unusual." "Sundarananda," he said, "You've been to the heavens, but you've never seen the hells. Would you like to accompany me there?"

Since the Buddha taught that the hells were most unpleasant, Sundarananda wondered what would be the use of going there, but agreeing to go and take a look, he followed the Buddha there. They saw the hells of the mountain of knives, the hell of sword trees, the hell of boiling oil, the hell of the fire-soup--all the hells. In one of the hells he saw a pot of oil that was barely simmering. Two ghosts who were supposedly tending it, were nodding off, and the fire was on the verge of going out. One of the ghosts, in fact, was even lying down, sound asleep! Two truly lazy ghosts, neglecting the pot for their nap. Sundarananda asked, "Hey, Old Friend, who's your boss? How can you get away with sleeping on the job?"

The ghost sighed in exasperation and rolled his eyes. "What's that you say?" he replied.

"I said I want to know why you are loafing on the job," Sundarananda said. "Pots of oil have to boil, you know."

"What do *you* know?" said the ghost. "The person destined to undergo punishment in this pot isn't due here for a long time."

"What do you mean?" asked Sundarananda.

"The Buddha's little brother, Sundarananda, has already left home under the Buddha. He cultivates the blessings of the heavens and in the future will be reborn there. When he has used up his heavenly blessings, the five signs of decay will manifest. He will then fall into the hells to be boiled in this very pot of oil, because he did not cultivate the Way properly. He's still got several hundred years, however, so why should we busy ourselves boiling the oil now? Our jobs are quite soft; we can sleep all day if we like."

When he heard this, Sundarananda's entire body broke out in a cold sweat.

"That pot's intended for *me*," he moaned. "What am I going to do?"

The Buddha took Sundarananda back to the Jeta Grove and spoke to him of the Dharma-door that birth in the heavens is bound up with suffering, emptiness, impermanence, and non-self. He cultivated the Buddhadharma and certified to the fruit of Arhatship. Sundarananda was hopelessly in love with his wife, and yet he fell out of love as soon as he saw women more beautiful than her. Then, because he saw the sufferings in the hells, he decided truly to cultivate the Way, something he never would have done otherwise. The name Nanda also means "bliss," but this Nanda is different from the one discussed previously. He takes his name from his wife, Sundari, because he was "Sundari's Nanda."

18. PURNAMAITRAYANIPUTRA

Purnamaitrayaniputra takes his name from a combination of his father's name, Purna, meaning "full"[1] and from his mother, Maitrayani, which means "compassionate woman."[2] Putra means "son."[3] Among the Buddha's disciples he was the foremost expounder of the Dharma. Just as he was born, an auspicious rain of jewels fell from the heavens upon his house.

19. SUBHUTI

Subhuti's name means "empty-born"[4] because when he was born the family treasuries were discovered to be

---

1 滿 -*man*.

2 慈 -*tz'u*.

3 Hence 滿慈子.

4 空生 -*k'ung sheng*.

empty. His father consulted a diviner who told him this was an extremely auspicious sign and so he was also known as "good and auspicious."[1] Then, exactly seven days after he was born, the wealth reappeared in the treasuries and he became known as "good appearance."[2] Of the Buddha's disciples, he was foremost in understanding emptiness.

20. ANANDA

Ananda was the Buddha's first cousin and his attendant. He also compiled and edited the Sutras. His name means "rejoicing"[3] because he was born on the day the Buddha realized Buddhahood. Rejoicing, his father gave him the name, and the entire country celebrated the Buddha's enlightenment. With his flawless memory he was able to remember all the Sutras the Buddha spoke and was the foremost of the Buddha's disciples in erudition.

21. RAHULA

Rahula was the Buddha's son. The Buddha is said to have had three wives. The senior was Gopika, the next was Yashodhara, and the junior was Mrgadava. Rahula was the son of Yashodhara. When he was born, the people of the palace were outraged because the Buddha had already left home for six years. They all said, "She's certainly been up to no good. The Buddha has already been gone for six years. How could she legitimately have a son?"

In truth, Rahula had dwelt in his mother's womb for six long years, but no one believed it; it was too improbable. The angry populace wanted to punish her, to put her to death, and the evil rumors spread through the streets and all over the countryside. Soon everyone knew that the Buddha had been absent for six years and his wife had given birth to a son. One of Yashodhara's servants spoke to the King on her behalf saying that she had not done anything untoward and that the child really *was* the Buddha's, but no one believed her because it's simply impossible to carry a child for six years. They prepared a pit of fire and decided to throw her in. At that time, she made a vow. "If I

1善吉 -*shan chi*.

2善現 -*shan hsien*.

3慶喜 -*ch'ing hsi*, or歡喜 -*huan hsi*.

have violated the rules of conduct, then, when I jump into the pit, my son and I will burn. If I am blameless, then the heavenly dragons and the spirits will protect us, and we will not burn." Holding Rahula in her arms, she threw herself into the flaming pit; miraculously, it turned into a pool of water, and a lotus emerged to catch them. Seeing this, the King and everyone else realized they had made a mistake. They knew that the situation with Yashodhara and her son was very special, and they stopped slandering her.

Rahula's name means "obstacle."[1] In a former life, as a child, he had plugged up a mousehole with a piece of wood and waited six days before he removed it. As a result, he received the retribution of having to dwell in his mother's womb for six years. Everyone should think it over: The network of cause and effect is indeed severe! Rahula was the Buddha's son, and even he had to undergo six years of retribution.

"Obstacle" also refers to the fact that he created a lot of trouble for Yashodhara--he was quite an obstacle.

Ultimately, where did the Buddha's son come from? Was he actually Shakyamuni Buddha's son?

Yes.

Did Shakyamuni Buddha have his son in the manner common to ordinary husbands and wives?

No. Before the Buddha left home, Yashodhara expressed her desire to have a son. The Buddha merely pointed his finger at her, and she became pregnant. This may sound like a myth, but it is only one of many such occurances within the Buddhadharma. It is an inconceivable realm. If you want to research and verify it, there is no way to do so except by working hard and cultivating until you reach the level where you will know that the realm of the Buddha is miraculous, subtle, and hard-to-conceive--inconceivable.

...GREAT ARHATS SUCH AS THESE WHOM THE ASSEMBLY KNEW AND RECOGNIZED.

SUCH AS THESE refers to the above-mentioned twenty-one great Arhats whom the great assembly KNEW. KNEW means that in their hearts, they understood them. RECOGNIZED means that they had seen them with their own eyes. To understand by means of the mind and eyes is called "know and recognize."

---

[1]覆障 -*fu chang*.

In Chinese, the phrase "know and recognize" also means "sense." Those with good sense have wisdom. However, you can look at it from the opposite angle: if you can truly be without "sense," that is genuine wisdom. If you can truly be without "sense," then you can also be without "thought or schemes." "Without thought or schemes" your own inherent wisdom will certainly manifest and this is your genuine "sense" and wisdom. So, in explaining doctrines, you must explain the opposite angles as well as the doctrines themselves. Thus these GREAT ARHATS were known and recognized by the assembly.

GREAT ARHATS are not small Arhats. What are small Arhats like? He's a Little High Master and he goes around laughing and joking from morning to night. He's very innocent and he won't accept any offerings from people at all. If he does accept something he immediately gives it away to someone else. So everyone calls him the "Little Arhat."

GREAT ARHATS accept offerings from men and gods according to the meaning of their name, "ones worthy of offerings." They have also "slain the thieves" and undergo no more birth. As I previously mentioned, not only have they slain the thieves, they have slain the non-thieves as well.

"But that really sounds unreasonable to me," you say.

What makes you think the Great Arhats are reasonable? They have spiritual powers and transformations. If you want to reason with them, it simply can't be done. They have also slain the non-thieves. What at the level of the Arhat are not taken to be thieves, at the Bodhisattva level are still seen as thieves and so they must kill the "non-thieves." In going from the Small Vehicle to the Great Vehicle, the non-thieves must also be slain.

Sutra:

MOREOVER, THERE WERE THOSE WITH FURTHER STUDY AND THOSE BEYOND STUDY, TWO THOUSAND IN ALL.[F2] THERE WAS THE BHIKSHUNI MAHAPRAJAPATI WITH HER RETINUE OF SIX THOUSAND, AND RAHULA'S MOTHER, BHIKSHUNI YASHODHARA, ALSO WITH HER RETINUE.[E2]

Outline:

F2. the lesser known
E2. the Bhikshunis

Commentary:

Not only were there great Arhats present, but there were two thousand of those WITH FURTHER STUDY. The position of those with further study is that previous to attainment of the fourth fruit of Arhatship--they still have more to learn. The state BEYOND STUDY is the fourth level of Arhatship. Altogether, there were TWO THOUSAND of them. They represent the Ten Suchnesses which will be discussed later. To simply name them, they are:

1. The suchness of the marks;
2. The suchness of the nature;
3. The suchness of the substance;
4. The suchness of the powers;
5. The suchness of the function;
6. The suchness of the cause;
7. The suchness of the condition;
8. The suchness of the effect;
9. The suchness of the retribution; and
10. The suchness of the ultimate equality of the beginning and end.

Each of the ten Dharma Realms contains the other nine, making one hundred Realms. Each of the hundred Realms contains all ten of the Suchnesses, 10 X 100 making a thousand Suchnesses. Thus, the use of the word THOUSAND--TWO THOUSAND IN ALL.

THERE WAS THE BHIKSHUNI MAHAPRAJAPATI WITH HER RETINUE OF SIX THOUSAND...MAHA means "great." PRAJAPATI means "love of the Way."[1] "Great love of the Way" was the sister of the Buddha's mother. Seven days after the Buddha was born, his mother died and was reborn in the Trayastrimsha Heaven;her sister, Mahaprajapati, raised the Buddha as her own. Not only did she do so for Shakyamuni Buddha, but she was the aunt and foster mother of a thousand Buddhas. ... WITH HER RETINUE OF SIX THOUSAND refers to her relatives, friends, and such.

RAHULA'S MOTHER, THE BHIKSHUNI YASHODHARA...The Buddha's wife, Yashodhara, later left the home-life as the Buddha's disciple to become a Bhikshuni. A Bhikshuni is a woman who has left home. The word also has the same three meanings as the word Bhikshu, that is, a mendicant, a frightener of Mara, and a destroyer of evil. WITH HER RETINUE, also a great many people. All assembled at the speaking of the *Dharma Flower Sutra*.

---

[1]大愛道-*ta ai tao.*

Sutra:

THERE WERE EIGHTY-THOUSAND BODHISATTVAS, MAHASATTVAS,[D2E1] ALL IRREVERSIBLY ESTABLISHED IN ANUTTARA-SAMYAKSAMBODHI. ALL HAD OBTAINED DHARANI AND THE ELOQUENCE OF DELIGHT IN SPEECH AND TURNED THE IRREVERSIBLE WHEEL OF THE DHARMA. THEY HAD MADE OFFERINGS TO LIMITLESS HUNDREDS OF THOUSANDS OF BUDDHAS AND IN THE PRESENCE OF THOSE BUDDHAS HAD PLANTED THE ROOTS OF VIRTUE. THEY WERE CONSTANTLY RECEIVING THOSE BUDDHAS' PRAISE. THEY CULTIVATED THEMSELVES IN COMPASSION AND WERE WELL ABLE TO ENTER THE WISDOM OF THE BUDDHAS. THEY HAD PENETRATED THE GREAT WISDOM AND ARRIVED AT THE OTHER SHORE. THEIR REPUTATIONS EXTENDED THROUGHOUT LIMITLESS WORLD REALMS, AND THEY WERE ABLE TO CROSS OVER COUNTLESS HUNDREDS OF THOUSANDS OF LIVING BEINGS.[E2]

Outline:

D2. the Bodhisattvas
E1. statement of category & number
E2. statement of position & praise of virtues

Commentary:

Bodhisattvas enlighten living beings. MAHASATTVAS are great Bodhisattvas, with Seven Qualities discussed below. Bodhi means "enlightenment" and sattva means "being." A Bodhisattva is an enlightened being who enlightens other sentient beings. Bodhisattvas are also known as "living beings who have great hearts for the Way." They are also living beings, but they have great, large hearts for the Way. They are also called "beginning knights."

MAHASATTVAS are the great Bodhisattvas. The Mahasattvas have Seven Qualities:

1. They are complete with great roots. Their extremely deep foundation is a kind of greatness. They are great in that they have, as the Sutra text states, "planted the roots of virtue." For many lives and throughout many kalpas, they have sent down and nurtured roots of goodness which are now extremely deep.

Good roots are called "roots of virtue," and they are the basis of the Way of virtue. They have sent down the roots of the virtuous nature. How many of them? A limitless and boundless number. "Planted" indicates their great quantity.

As the *Vajra Sutra* says, "You should know that such people will have planted good roots with not just one Buddha, two Buddhas, three, four, or five Buddhas, but will have planted good roots with measureless millions of Buddhas." The Mahasattvas have planted their good roots, their roots of virtue, in the presence of as many Buddhas as there are grains of sand in limitless, boundless, hundreds of thousands of tens of thousands of Ganges Rivers. So, they are complete with great roots.

2. They possess great wisdom. Where did they acquire this great wisdom? It came as a result of having brought forth the great Bodhi heart. Bringing forth the great Bodhi heart, they resolve to cross over all living beings. However, although they cross over all living beings, they do not become attached to the mark of having crossed them over. As the *Vajra Sutra* also says, "All Bodhisattvas, Mahasattvas, should subdue their hearts with the vow: 'I must cause all living beings--those born from eggs, those born from wombs, those born from moisture, those born by transformation, those with form, those without form, those with thought, those without thought--to enter Nirvana Without Residue and be taken across to extinction. Yet of the immeasurable, boundless numbers of living beings thus taken across to extinction, there is actually no living being taken across to extinction.'"

Although the Buddha saves countless beings, in actuality there are no beings that he saves. Living beings save themselves. This is called, "Crossing over living beings but not attaching to the mark of doing so." Mahasattvas are not like us ordinary people who do a good deed and then say, "I have caused X-number of people to leave the home-life," or "I have caused X-number of people to believe in Buddhism. So and so is one I saved. So and so is one I convinced to believe in the Buddhadharma. So and so is one I introduced to the Buddhadharma. Ah! Ordinary people are attached to so many marks! They should separate from all marks, and then they may attain anuttarasamyak-sambodhi. If one does not separate from all marks, one is not a Bodhisattva. Mahasattvas have great wisdom.

3. The third quality of a Mahasattva is: They believe in the great Dharma. What is the great Dharma? The great Dharma is the Dharma of the Great Vehicle. You must believe in the Dharma-doors of the Great Vehicle. You must deeply believe in Prajna. You must deeply believe in cause and effect, and you must deeply believe in the Dharma-door of the Great Vehicle's actual mark. You need a heart of such great belief because the Buddhadharma is as vast as the sea and can be entered only by means of faith. Without faith, although the Buddhadharma is vast, you will not be crossed over by means of it. Why? Because you have no faith. So it says,

> Faith is the source of the Way
> and the mother of virtue, because
> it nourishes all good roots.

Where do good roots come from? They come from faith. They grow out of the heart of faith. Faith is the mother of the merit and virtue which you cultivate. Therefore, belief in the great Dharma is the third quality of a Mahasattva. Great Bodhisattvas believe in all the great Dharmas. They have faith in the supreme, wonderful Dharma; they believe especially deeply in the *Wonderful Dharma Lotus Flower Sutra*. Thus, they believe in the great Dharma.

If we have genuine and great faith in the Buddhadharma, then we *are* Bodhisattvas, Mahasattvas, too. The *Vajra Sutra* says, "All who hear these phrases and produce even one thought of pure faith are completely known and completely seen by the Tathagata." Only one single thought of the most pure, firm faith brings blessedness and virtue which surpasses that of one who has made enough offerings of the seven precious things to fill the Great Trichiliocosm. The Thus Come One is certain to know your thought; your faith will not have been in vain. Students of the Buddhadharma should bring forth hearts of genuine faith, and then they will be able to obtain a response.

For example, there are those in this Sutra assembly who have taken ill with the flu and who have coughs. I had intended to tell them to rest, but they still grit their teeth and insist on listening to the Sutra lectures. This proves that they have genuine faith. Belief in the Buddha and the Dharma should be as genuine as that. When I was young, listening to the Sutras, I too was sometimes ill, but I never failed to attend a Dharma meeting. I made up my mind that, as long as I had a breath of air, I would study the Dharma. I would not rest unless I was totally bed-ridden or unable to move. I never would have thought that now I would meet so many who "know my sound," and who also listen to the Dharma, illness and all. However, one shouldn't force things. If you are too uncomfortable, it is all right to rest.

4. They understand the great principle. What is the great principle? Above, it said that one must have great faith. In order to understand the great principle, one must do so by means of faith. In the *Avatamsaka Sutra* one speaks of the four circuits of faith, understanding, practice, and certification. First of all you must believe, then you must understand. After you understand, you must put your understanding into actual practice. Through actual practice, you may gain certification.

What is the great principle? I will tell you: you must understand that all living beings basically are Buddhas. *That* is the great principle. This refers to the first of the Six Levels of Identity with the Buddha, that of Identity with the Buddha in Principle. In principle every one of us *is* a Buddha. However, in order to realize Buddhahood you must cultivate. If you fail to cultivate and yet say, "I am the Buddha, the Buddha, Buddha, Buddha..." that's useless. It's like calling yourself the Emperor, saying, "I am the Emperor. I am the Emperor." But do you have subjects and ministers who are loyal to you? Do the people support you? No.

Of what use is a self-proclaimed Emperor? If you say that you are the Buddha, in *principle* you are correct. But you must specifically cultivate, otherwise you will be unable to return to the root, go back to the source, and recognize your original face.

Why must one understand that all living beings are basically Buddhas? It is because the Real Mark wisdom is not separate from the hearts of living beings. The wisdom of the Real Mark is complete within the hearts of all of us. Therefore, the fourth is to understand the great principle.

5. Cultivate the great conduct. Which Dharma-doors should one cultivate? One must diligently cultivate the Six Paramitas and the Ten Thousand Conducts. What are the Six Paramitas?

a. Giving. First of all, one must give. Giving means to give to others, not to instruct others to give to you. Some people talk a lot about giving by telling other people to give to them, but they don't give to others. Not only are they not Bodhisattvas, they aren't even as good as Arhats.

Giving has been discussed many times. There are three varieties of giving: 1) the giving of wealth, 2) the giving of Dharma, 3) the giving of fearlessness.

The giving of wealth includes both inner and outer wealth. Outer wealth refers to one's kingdom and treasures, to one's wife and sons. Those who practice the Bodhisattva Way have no thought at all of self or others and so they think, "What is mine is yours, and what is yours, I don't necessarily want." They have no mark of other and no mark of self, and so they are able to give away their kingdoms, their homes, and even their wives and sons. Shakyamuni Buddha, for example, should have become a king, but he chose instead to become a monk. He had three very beautiful wives, but he didn't want them; he renounced them and let them go their way. Relinquishing the glory of royalty, he went to the Himalayas to cultivate the Way.

Inner wealth refers to: Your head--if someone wants your head you give it up without a second thought; Your eyes-- if someone wants your eyes, you also give them up. You give your brains and marrow in the same way. Head, eyes, brains and marrow, skin, blood, flesh, sinews and bones--all can be given to others.

What is meant by the giving of Dharma? It is to speak the Dharma to benefit beings, to teach and transform all living beings by explaining the Buddhadharma to them.

Of all offerings,
The Dharma-offering is supreme.

The offering of Dharma is to propagate the Buddhadharma for the sake of all beings. Thus, students of the Buddhadharma should learn how to lecture on the Sutras. Do not hoard a lot of wealth and fail to come to the aid of the starving masses. Those who understand the Buddhadharma must introduce it to others. They should think, "If I understand one percent, I will explain one percent to others. If I know 100 percent, I will explain 100 percent." This is the gift of Dharma.

The third is the giving of fearlessness. When someone encounters disasters or calamities which terrify them, at that very moment you should go to reassure them saying, "Don't be afraid. It's not important. You'll certainly evoke a response because your heart is so good; certainly nothing terrible will come of it." Having dispelled their fear, you have given the gift of fearlessness.

Thus, there are three kinds of giving.

2. The second perfection is that of morality. There are many different sets of moral precepts. There are the five precepts, the eight precepts, the ten precepts, and the ten major and forty-eight minor Bodhisattva precepts. There are also the two-hundred and fifty precepts for Bhikshus and three hundred and forty-eight for Bhikshunis. We should hold the precepts.

3. Patience. Patience is a fine quality indeed. If you are able to be patient, you possess a treasure. Haven't I said before:

> Patience is a priceless treasure
> Which few know how to mine.

Patience is a priceless jewel but no one knows how to use it. People may be patient once, or, pushing it, even twice. But on the third time, they blow up. "Just what do you think you're doing, bullying me like that? Do you really think I'm afraid of *you*? Hah! I've stood for this just about long enough. Once, twice, three times--I have had all I can take. This is really too much!!!" and the fight is on. These things happen when one loses patience.

Once there was an old cultivator of patience. He wrote out a sentence on a piece of paper and tacked it on his door. It said, "My nature is like ashes." That is, his nature was like burnt out ashes and had not even a spark of fire in it. He never got angry; he worked hard and cultivated until he was very mellow, just as flexible and yielding as water. Then, along came a Bodhisattva to test him. He looked at the sign and said, "What does that sign say?"

"It said, 'My nature is like ashes,'" replied the cultivator.

A few minutes later, he again asked, "What does that sign say?"

"My nature is like ashes," came the reply.

A moment later: "What does that sign say? I can't remember clearly..."

"My nature is like ashes."

He asked the question several thousand times, and finally the old cultivator ignited. "It says my nature is like ashes. MY NATURE IS LIKE ASHES! What are you trying to do anyway? What are you trying to prove? I'm cultivating the Way. Just who are *you* to come and stir up trouble!!"

"Oh?" came the reply. "It would seem that the ashes have a bit of fire in them after all," and so saying he ascended into empty space. Who was he? He was Kuan Shih Yin Bodhisattva and he had come to test the cultivator. But, after several decades of cultivating a nature like ashes, he flunked the test. Kuan Yin Bodhisattva said, "You'd better cultivate some more. I'll be back in another twenty years to see you again."

See? It's not easy. Patience means that you have no temper. When I was a disciple, I never dared get angry, whether I was in my teacher's presence or not. Why? Because my teacher was not mean like I am. He was very compassionate. If I got angry, he would refuse to eat. He'd say, "I haven't done a good job teaching my disciple, so I won't eat." Because of this, I didn't dare get angry.

Did I have a temper? My temper was huge, bigger than anybody's, but because I had left home to cultivate, I learned to control it. So now, in America I have just accepted three Americans as left-home disciples. Before they left home, they weren't bad-tempered, but now that they have, they haven't learned anything except how to get angry. They have mastered the art of blowing their tops. Yesterday, two of them came complaining to me. One said that the other had gotten angry and the other said that the first one had gotten angry. In the end, who *did* get angry? I don't care. But, I decided to establish a rule which I announced yesterday and announced again last night and will repeat once again this evening: I don't care who gets angry, who is in the right or who is in the wrong, but whoever gets angry must kneel in front of the Buddhas for a day and a night, twenty-four hours. During this time they are not allowed to rise, either to go to the bathroom, eat, drink, or sleep. That's my rule and if you don't kneel before the Buddhas, I will do it for you myself. Try it and see.

But not only does the one who gets angry have to kneel, all of the disciples, that is, the three Americans, all have to kneel together, which means that the two who did not get angry also have to kneel.

"But that's unjust!" you say. "If only one gets angry why should the other two also have to kneel?"

If you are worried about justice, you should be informed that there simply is no justice in this world. If you're afraid, then don't get angry. Don't think you can get away with getting angry when I'm not around either, because you'll be punished all the same. You may think I don't know, but for all you know I may have a secret information service, or someone may tell me and you'll have to kneel all the same. Is that clear? Patience: Why will you have to kneel without eating, drinking or sleeping? So that you can cultivate patience. If you get angry, that means you must cultivate patience and learn to bear the pain in your knees as you kneel. Did you hear that clearly? If so, the law goes into effect immediately.

A number of people who were thinking of leaving home are suddenly afraid. The Master is really stern! I don't think I'd dare leave home under him."

If you're afraid, then just don't get angry, and everything will be all right. I didn't invent this law; it's an old-established custom. But whether or not you kneel is up to you, not me. Why did I establish the rule? If I didn't, then as I accepted more disciples, they would constantly be fighting and bringing their silly arguments to me. There wouldn't be enough hours in the day to pass judgments on their stupid cases. How can cultivators of the way get angry? They can't. If, as a teacher, you get angry at your disciples, that's permissible. But to get angry at one's peers is not.

Patience is a princeless gem
Which few know how to mine;
But if you can master it
Everything works out fine.

If you've mastered patience, then everything goes well. If you haven't, everything goes wrong.

4. The fourth perfection is that of vigor. Last summer, one of my disciples spoke about vigor and now he is being vigorous because he has come to the lecture, illness and all.

There are two types of vigor: bodily and mental. Bodily vigor refers to bowing to the Buddhas, reciting Sutras, and holding mantras, working hard at cultivation and never ever relaxing--sleeping less, too. It's no easy matter to be a monk. You can't just sleep all day. Vigor by day and vigor by night. Those who vigorously apply genuine effort do not just put on a show for other people. They cultivate vigorously whether anyone is looking or not. The work of cultivation is done for oneself; it is not done as a show. You must be vigorous.

5. The fifth perfection is Dhyana samadhi. This refers to cultivating skill in investigating Dhyana meditation. Perfection of mental vigor lies in constant mindfulness. Mental vigor is the diligent cultivation of precepts, samadhi, and wisdom and the eradication of greed, hatred, and stupidity--evicting thoughts of greed, hate, and stupidity from your heart. Then, once you are

vigorous, you can cultivate the investigation of Dhyana mediation. Dhyana meditation needs the aid of vigor. If you are not vigorous, it's like setting something in the sun for one day and then freezing it for ten. You shouldn't be one who is fond of the lotus today and fond of the sandalwood flower tomorrow--in other words, fickle. If you heat something in the sun for one day and then freeze it for ten, what use has it? Don't cultivate for one day and rest for ten. In Chinese both words sound the same:

修 --cultivate one day, (*hsiu*),

休 --rest one day (*hsiu*).

You'll never obtain skill in Dhyana samadhi that way.

6. The sixth perfection is Prajna. Prajna is the most important of the perfections. Roughly, it means "wisdom". In cultivating one must have wisdom. Without wisdom, there is no way to cultivate. Stupid people may cultivate and try to make progress, but they never get anywhere. Those with wisdom can apply effort in any situation because they have genuine Prajna.

Of the green bamboo
and yellow flowers,
None is not Prajna.

Everything's a manifestation of wisdom. For example, one of my disciples told me that another one said, "Every time he (the disciple who told me this) talks to me, he scolds me." *Who* is he scolding? Isn't that stupid? If one was intelligent, how could he receive a scolding? Even if he *was* scolding you, if you had wisdom you wouldn't accept his scolding and it would revert right back to him. In the *Sutra of Forty-two Sections* it says that someone once scolded the Buddha, but the Buddha made no reply. The Buddha said, "You insulted me but I didn't respond and so the insult reverts to you. It is like trying to spit at the sky: The spit will fall right back into your own face." So even if he *does* scold you, if you don't react, it's just as if he hadn't. If he scolds you, pretend he is singing you a song or that you don't understand him because he is speaking Japanese, or Chinese, or French. If you can't understand him, then, there's no problem whatever. This is genuine wisdom. If you do understand him and think, "He's scolding me!" well, then, ultimately, *who* are you? Bodhisattvas do not have the mark of self, others, living beings, or a lifespan. How can they hold onto an "I"? Those who have left home especially must take their "selves" and throw them into the Pacific Ocean. Get rid of them! Have no self and then everything will be okay.

This has been a discussion of the fifth of the Seven Qualities of a Mahasattva: They cultivate the great conduct, that is, the Six Perfections and the Ten Thousand Conducts.

We have been discussing the Seven Qualities of a Mahasattva and have discussed the first five: they are complete with great roots, they possess great wisdom, they believe in the great Dharma, they understand the great principle, and they cultivate the great conduct.

Within the cultivation of the great conduct we have talked about the Six Perfections. The Ten Thousand Conducts indicates many practices. To speak of them in detail, there are not merely ten thousand, but eighty-four thousand. However, because of the limitations of time, we cannot discuss each one in detail.

Now, we will discuss the Three Phases of Thought.

> Bodhisattvas sweep away the
> Three Phases of Thought,
> And annul the Four Marks.

They sweep away the Three Phases of Thought as one would sweep the dirt up off the floor. What are the three phases of thought? They are: 1) past thought, 2) present thought, and 3) future thought.

What is past thought? It is thought which has already gone by. Having already gone by, it's in the past.

Present thought: You may say, "This is the present," but just as you say it it passes and becomes the past. The present does not stand still and the past has already gone by. The present does not stay. If you say *this* is the present, it's already gone by. It's turned into the past. So present thought cannot be obtained.

And what about future thought? Future thought has not yet arrived. Since it hasn't arrived, where are you going to find it? So it is said, "past thought cannot be obtained, present thought cannot be obtained, and future thought cannot be obtained." If these three, the past, present, and future phases of thought are entirely unobtainable, what is there to be attached to? There *is* nothing to be attached to. When there is no attachment, *that* is the attainment of liberation. The attainment of liberation--*that* is genuine freedom.

Bodhisattvas also cultivate the Four Methods of Conversion: 1) giving, 2) kind words, 3) helpfulness, and 4) cooperation.

Bodhisattvas should be resolved to give, to make gifts of wealth, Dharma, and fearlessness to all living beings as discussed above. Kind words: Bodhisattvas must practice affectionate speech. But only Bodhisattvas can do this; those who are not Bodhisattvas cannot. Bodhisattvas use kind, affectionate words which spring from the compassionate affection they hold for all living beings. How did they become compassionate? Bodhisattvas have no mark of self. They see all living beings as identical with themselves. Not only do they see all living beings as identical with themselves, but they see themselves as identical with all living beings, not only identical but as a unity. They make no distinctions between "him and me." So they like to rescue living beings because it is the same as rescuing themselves. They do so by means of compassionate and kind words to all living beings.

Helpfulness: All living beings like to receive benefit. You should benefit them, help them out in their affairs. There are many ways to help others: but in general, Bodhisattvas do deeds which cause others to obtain advantage.

Cooperation: Bodhisattvas can transform themselves into thousands of millions of bodies. When they see a living being, they determine which kind of body they will need to assume to save them. They then transform to that kind of body to teach it. For example, when Shakyamuni Buddha was practicing the Bodhisattva way, he turned into a deer in order to teach and transform the deer.

Practicing the Bodhisattva Way, you must practice what is hard to practice. If it's basically difficult, you have to do it. That's the Way of the Bodhisattva. They must give up what is hard to give up. If it's hard to renounce, you must renounce it. The harder something is to give up--your riches for example--the more genuine the renunciation becomes. You must bear what is difficult to bear. Things which are difficult to endure must be endured. This is the duty of one who practices the Bodhisattva Way. What is hard to yield, you must yield. If it is difficult to yield in a given situation, you must be able to do so. I often say:

You must
eat what others cannot eat and
bear what others cannot bear.

This is not to say "eating what others cannot eat" means that you rush in and eat all the good food before anyone else gets a chance to have any. It doesn't mean that one eats the most delectible delicacies in the world, those which others have never tasted. It means that one eats those things which others do not like to eat. Bodhisattvas can eat such things.

I will tell you something: I am not a Bodhisattva, but I can eat the things which others do not like to eat. When I was seventeen years old, in Manchuria there was a Way Virtue Society which exclusively taught the Way, virtue, humaneness, and righteousness. I joined the Society when I was sixteen. When I was seventeen, I became the head instructor of about sixty or seventy people. I was very young and the students were men and women in their 40's, 50's or 60's. The Society advocated thrift and economy to the point that we even ate our potato skins. People would usually throw the skins away, but in the Way Virtue Society we talked about Way Virtue and eating what others do not like to eat. So I said to the students, "When everyone eats their potatoes they shouldn't spit the skins out. Force them down. This will show that we actually do eat what others cannot eat.

I said it, and I ate my own potato skin, but the students for the most part let my words blow past their ears like the wind and spit the skins out on the tables or on the floor. When we ate, no one was allowed to talk. I had already told them not to spit out the skins so I didn't pay any attention to what they did. After lunch I went around the tables with a bowl, picked up all the potato skins that the students had spit out on the tables on the floor, and I stood in front of them and ate them. The students were very aghast and embarrassed. From that time on, not a single student dared to spit out his potato skin. They never spit them out again. If I hadn't actually practiced what I preached with my own example, I could not have influenced the students to change. They spit the skins out of their mouths and I put the skins in my mouth and ate them. They were greatly ashamed. This is called "eating what others cannot eat and bearing what others cannot bear."

Bearing what others cannot bear: What is it that people cannot bear? Temper! If you bully a person a little bit, he will get angry. If you can bear others' anger, perhaps by pretending that they are singing you a song or speaking a foreign language, it is as if nothing happened. Bearing, enduring, yielding, and renouncing are all primary prerequisites of those Bodhisattvas who cultivate the great conduct.

6. The sixth Quality of a Mahasattva is that they pass through great kalpas. How great are the great kalpas which they pass through? I will tell you: One kalpa is 139,600 years. One thousand kalpas is a small kalpa. Twenty small kalpas is a middle kalpa. Four middle kalpas is a great kalpa.

How many great kalpas does the Bodhisattva pass through? Three great uncountable numbers of kalpas. The Bodhisattva traverses three great *asankhyeya* kalpas. *Asankhyeya* is a Sanskrit word which means "uncountable." Think it over: what does it add up to? Three great *asankhyeya* kalpas--how long would you say this was?

So, it's not easy to be a Bodhisattva. It takes a long, long time. You must pass through many, many great kalpas to be a Bodhisattva Mahasattva.

7. The seventh quality of a Mahasattva is that he seeks the great result. What is the great result? The result of Anuttara samyaksambodhi, that is, of supreme equal and proper enlightenment, the result of the realization of Buddhahood.

A Bodhisattva who has all seven qualities is therefore called a Mahasattva, a Great Being.

How many Mahasattvas were present at the speaking of the *Lotus Sutra* ? There were eighty thousand of them, all of whom had entered the path towards certification to the supreme equal and proper enlightenment. Once on the path, they only made forward progress. So the text says,

ALL WERE IRREVERSIBLE WITH RESPECT TO ANUTTARA-SAMYAKSAMBODHI. There are Three Kinds of Irreversibility: 1) Irreversibility of Position. As Great Vehicle Bodhisattvas, they would never retreat to the position of the Two Vehicles. 2) Irreversibility of thought. Bodhisattvas are ever-mindful in their practice of the Bodhisattva Way, in the practice of the Six Perfections and the Ten Thousand Conducts. In every thought, they think only of going forward; they never retreat. It would never occur to them, "Ah, I'm not going to practice the Bodhisattva Way anymore. I'll go back to the Two Vehicles and be an independent Arhat instead." It would never happen because they are irreversible. (3) Irreversibility of Practice: They only go forward; they do not retreat. Thus, there are Three Kinds of Irreversibility: Position, thought, and practice.

ALL HAD ATTAINED DHARANI: Dharani is a Sanskrit word interpreted as meaning "unite and maintain,"[1] or "suppressing and holding."[2]

"Unite" means that they unite all Dharmas. "Hold" means that they hold limitless principles. The Dharmas spoken by the Buddha contain an unlimited number of principles and the irreversible Bodhisattvas had all obtained Dharani, the uniting of all Dharmas and the holding of all principles.

Dharani also means "spell" or "mantra."[3] It means suppressing and holding because Dharanis give rise to goodness and eradicate evil. They suppress evil and uphold the good. They suppress evil and cause good deeds to be practiced. It also carries the meaning of "doing no evil and respectfully practicing all good acts," which is the meaning of the term "morality." However, there is a slight difference in that the moral precepts must be upheld by you yourself. With the Dharani, you recite a spell which helps you to sever evil and cultivate goodness. The power of the spell aids you.

There are many kinds of Dharanis. The Sutra text states, ALL HAD ATTAINED DHARANI AND THE ELOQUENCE OF DELIGHT IN SPEECH. This could also be interpreted to mean that they had attained the Dharani of the Eloquence of Delight in Speech.

AND TURNED THE IRREVERSIBLE DHARMA WHEEL. The Bodhisattvas turn the Wheel of Dharma to teach and convert living beings. What is meant by turning the Dharma Wheel? There is the common phrase, "The Dharma Wheel Forever Turns." The eternal turning of the Dharma Wheel refers to the irreversible Dharma Wheel. What is meant by the turning of the Dharma Wheel? For example, here we lecture on the Sutras and speak the Dharma. We are also translating the Sutras into English, and introducing the Buddhadharma to all people and this, too, is turning the Dharma Wheel. There are not just one, but many different types of work involved in propagating the Buddhadharma, all of which are considered to be the turning of the Dharma Wheel to teach living beings. Therefore, as disciples of the Buddha,

---

1 總持-*tsung ch'ih.*

2 遮持-*che ch'ih.*

3 咒 -*chou.*

we must take the work of turning the Dharma Wheel as our own work, as our duty and responsibility. We should do whatever work we can do to turn the Wheel of the Buddhadharma.

For example, now in the scientific age, we have a wet-copier and every day we put out typescript copies of the English translation of the previous night's lecture so that everyone can have a copy. This is called turning the Dharma Wheel. Turning the Dharma Wheel is the circulation of the Buddhadharma so that it flows like water and never stops.

When I was young, I also did the work of propagating the Buddhadharma. At first, before I was able to lecture on the Sutras, I printed Sutras. Whenever someone was printing a Sutra, I would contribute enough money for the printing of a few hundred or a few thousand copies. Then I would give them to my friends or relatives, perhaps at New Year's or some other holiday, or on their birthdays I would make them a present of a copy of a Buddhist Sutra. The Chinese like red paper, so I wrapped them in red paper so that they made beautiful gifts. I would say, "I am giving you the most important gift there is. Why? Because it can save your life, the life of your wisdom and your Dharmabody. Because you are my friend, I am giving you that which I like most--the Buddhadharma." I spoke to them very sincerely and earnestly and they could not but read them. Once they read them, they would become interested in the Buddhadharma and come to me saying, "Where did you get those Sutras? I have some friends I would like to give copies to. Can you give me a few more?" and I was in business, distributing books. No matter who was printing Sutras, I would subscribe. While I was in Manchuria, my wealth consisted of nothing but Buddhist Sutras. I had more Sutras in my room in Manchuria than there are in this entire lecture hall--a whole lot. Wherever I go, I have a lot of Sutras.

In Hong Kong I spent the most money on Sutras. I probably printed more than a million dollars HK worth of Sutras. When I was about to come to America I gave away over several hundred thousand dollars worth of Buddhist Sutras; I would give each person a big package of them as gifts. I had planned to give them away gradually, but because I was going to America, I hurried up and gave them away because I had no place to store them.

The thing I liked to do most was to print Sutras. So now that you are making copies of the lectures and this is also a very good way to spread the Dharma, it pleases me a great deal. This is how I turned the irreversible Dharma Wheel; I hope that everyone will exert themselves vigorously in this regard.

THEY HAD MADE OFFERINGS TO LIMITLESS HUNDREDS OF THOUSANDS OF BUDDHAS...Not only did they turn the irreversible Dharm Wheel, but they made offerings to all the Buddhas, limitless numbers of them, an uncountable number. How many? Hundreds of thousands of Buddhas.

AND IN THEIR PRESENCE HAD PLANTED THE ROOTS OF VIRTUE...These Great Bodhisattvas throughout limitless kalpas and in the presence of limitless Buddhas had sent down and nourished the roots of the virtuous nature. How did they plant them? How did they nurture them? By making offerings to the Triple Jewel and turning the irreversible Dharma Wheel. If you can make offerings to the Triple Jewel, that is to nourish and nurture the roots of your virtuous nature.

AND WERE CONSTANTLY BEING PRAISED BY THE BUDDHAS. The eighty-thousand Mahasattvas were constantly, at all times, receiving the praise and commendation of all the Buddhas who said to them, "Good men! You are truly fine! Good Men! You practice the Bodhisattva way and are irreversible in your practice of the Bodhisattva way and you are not bad at all. The Buddhas all praise the Bodhisattvas.

THEY CULTIVATED IN COMPASSION...They had always used a compassionate heart to teach and transform beings, and they cultivated compassion in their own persons.

AND WERE WELL ABLE TO ENTER INTO THE BUDDHAS' WISDOM. They were quite capable of attaining the Buddhas' wisdom.

THEY HAD PENETRATED THE GREAT WISDOM, AND ARRIVED AT THE OTHER SHORE. They had penetrated the greatest wisdom there is, that is, the understanding of the Buddhas. Great Wisdom is the Buddhas' wisdom, the Buddhas' wisdom is the great wisdom. Having attained the great wisdom of the Buddhas, they were then able to arrive at the other shore. The "other shore" refers to the Sanskrit word, "Paramita," perfection.

THEIR REPUTATIONS EXTENDED THROUGHOUT LIMITLESS WORLD REALMS. The eighty thousand Bodhisattvas' Mahasattvas' names had been heard by all living beings who were constantly aware of them. In all the limitless worlds...

AND THEY WERE ABLE TO CROSS OVER COUNTLESS HUNDREDS OF THOUSANDS OF LIVING BEINGS. They could save and transform an uncountable number of hundreds of thousands of tens of thousands of them.

Sutra:

THEIR NAMES WERE: THE BODHISATTVA MANJUSHRI, THE BODHISATTVA WHO CONTEMPLATES THE WORLD'S SOUNDS, THE BODHISATTVA WHO HAS ATTAINED GREAT MIGHT, THE BODHISATTVA CONSTANT VIGOR, THE BODHISATTVA UNRESTING, THE BODHISATTVA JEWELED PALM, THE BODHISATTVA MEDICINE KING, THE BODHISATTVA COURAGEOUS GIVING, THE BODHISATTVA FULL MOON, THE BODHISATTVA GREAT STRENGTH, THE BODHISATTVA UNLIMITED STRENGTH, THE BODHISATTVA WHO HAS TRANSCENDED THE THREE REALMS, THE BODHISATTVA BHADRAPALA, THE BODHISATTVA MAITREYA, THE BODHISATTVA JEWEL ACCUMULATION, THE BODHISATTVA GUIDING MASTER --- AND OTHER BODHISATTVAS, MAHASATTVAS SUCH AS THESE, EIGHTY THOUSAND IN ALL. E3

Outline:

E3. partial listing of their names

Commentary:

What were the names of the eighty-thousand Mahasattvas? Since there were eighty-thousand of them, if we were to list every name, *The Lotus Sutra* would be too long. So only a few of the leaders have been listed to represent the rest.

listed.THEIR NAMES WERE: THE BODHISATTVA MANJUSHRI... Manjushri, a Sanskrit word, is interpreted as "wonderful virtue"[1] or "wonderfully auspicious."[2] Of the Bodhisattvas, Manjushri has the greatest wisdom and so he is known as "The Greatly Wise Bodhisattva Manjushri." Among the Bodhisattvas he holds the highest

---

[1] 妙德 -*miao te.*

[2] 妙吉 -*miao chi.*

rank and so he is listed first, before The Bodhisattva Who Contemplates the Sounds of the World. There are four great Bodhisattvas: Bodhisattva Manjushri, the Bodhisattva Who Contemplates the Sounds of the World (Sanskrit--Avalokiteshvara, Chinese--Kuan Shih Yin), The Bodhisattva Universal Worthy (Sanskrit--Samantabhadra, Chinese--P'u Hsien) and Earth Store Bodhisattva (Sanskrit--Kshitigarbha, Chinese--Ti Tsang)

Bodhisattva Manjushri dwells in China on Wu T'ai Mountain where his Bodhimandala is located. His efficacious responses are marvelous beyond all reckoning. He realized Buddhahood long ago and was called Buddha of the Race of Honored Dragon Kings. After realizing Buddhahood, he "hid away the great and manifested the small," in order to practice the Bodhisattva way, and teach and transform living beings, and help the Buddha propagate the Dharma. His spiritual penetrations and miraculous functions are inconceivable.

In China, the great contemporary late elder master, the Most Venerable Hsü Yün, made a vow to bow once every three steps to Mount Wu T'ai to pay reverence to the Bodhisattva Manjushri. He bowed from Mount P'u T'ou, an island in the South China Sea, one thousand miles to Mount Wu T'ai in Shansi. Every time he took three steps, he made one full prostration to the ground. Then he rose, took three steps, and bowed again. He was bowing to the Bodhisattva Manjushri, seeking a response so that he might open his wisdom and become greatly wise just like that Bodhisattva. The distance was approximately a thousand miles. At one bow every three steps, how long would you say it took him? A long time. If you want to know the details, see The Elder Master Hsü's *Nien P'u* or *Hua Chüan* (biographies).

When The Venerable Hsü Lao had reached the Yellow River it was winter and snowing. He took refuge from the storm in an old vendor's straw hut beside the Yellow River. The snow fell unceasingly and the Venerable Hsü Lao was right on the verge of dying from the cold and hunger.

Just then, an old beggar came by. He melted some snow in a pan and made some yellow rice gruel and gave it to the Elder Master. When the Elder Master had eaten it, he felt revived and asked the beggar his name.

"My name is Wen," the beggar said.

"And what is your other name?" the Master asked.

"I am called Wen Chi," the beggar replied, and he asked the Master, "Where are you from?"

"I have come from Mount P'u T'ou in the South China Sea," the Master replied.

At daybreak, Wen Chi took some snow to make rice gruel. Pointing to the contents of the pan, he said, "Do you have this in the South China Sea?"

The Master replied, "No."

"Then what do people drink there?"

"Water."

By this time the snow had melted into water. The beggar pointed at it and asked, "Then what is this?"

The Master was speechless.

The two of them decided to journey together to Mount Wu T'ai. The beggar didn't bow; he carried the Master's pack. Without the heavy pack to carry, his bowing and walking was much easier. Before, it took great effort to bow and rise. Now he was able to bow faster. When Master Hsü Lao was bowing, the Master asked Wen Chi, "Where are you from?"

"I come from Mount Wu T'ai," said the beggar, "and all the monks there know me. They are all my good friends."

They continued their journey. Sometimes they stayed in monasteries along they way, and the monks would gang up on the beggar and scold the Master. "If you are making a pilgrimage, make one. If you're bowing you should just bow. Why have you got an attendant? What kind of show are you putting on?" they jeered.

Everywhere they went, the two of them were harassed. Sometimes people wouldn't even allow them to stay in the temples, but would immediately throw them out. They underwent a great deal of harsh treatment.

Although the beggar had been able to endure a lot of abuse, when the two of them had nearly reached Mount Wu T'ai, he finally decided he had suffered enough at the hands of the monks and he told the Master, "Up ahead someone will come to help you, but I am going to leave now," and he took his leave.

The Master went on ahead and sure enough, he soon met an official from Hunan with a horsecart. The official put the Master's pack in the horse cart and the Master continued to bow once every three steps.

When they arrived at Mount Wu T'ai, the Master asked the monks if they knew a beggar named Wen Chi. But no one, not a single monk on Mt. Wu T'ai, knew of such a beggar. Later, someone asked the Master, "What was the beggar's name?

"Wen Chi," the Master replied.

"Oh! That's Manjushri Bodhisattva! 'Wen' stands for 'Wen Shu Shih Li' (the Chinese transliteration of Manjushri) and 'Chi' stands for 'auspicious.' The beggar was the Bodhisattva Wonderfully Auspicious, Manjushri."

So, the Venerable Master Hsü Lao had bowed all the way to Mount Wu T'ai seeking a magical response from Manjushri Bodhisattva and he moved the Bodhisattva to come and carry his backpack for him. Master Hsü Lao made the tremendously difficult journey of over a thousand miles to pay reverence to Manjushri Bodhisattva and Manjushri was walking right along with him for ever such a long time but he didn't recognize him. When, later, he realized that it was Manjushri Bodhisattva, he was nowhere to be seen.

So the wonderful occurrences of Manjushri Bodhisattva are indeed inconceivable.

Because the Bodhisattva is wonderful, he transformed himself into a beggar. He could have transformed himself into a wealthy elder with a horse and carriage to help the Master, but instead he went with the Master on foot, and shared his hardships. There are many such incidences of his magical deeds, but we won't go into them now.

The Bodhisattva Manjushri, "wonderful virtue," or "wonderfully lucky," is a very special Bodhisattva. When he was born, ten kinds of extraordinary events occurred which show that he was different from other Bodhisattvas. Manjushri is known for his great wisdom.

"But the Venerable Shariputra is also known for his wisdom," you may ask. "What is the difference between the two types of wisdom?"

The wisdom of Shariputra is "provisional" wisdom and the wisdom of Manjushri is "real" wisdom. The wisdom of Shariputra is the Hinayana wisdom; the wisdom of Manjushri is the Mahayana wisdom.

What were the ten auspicious signs which manifested at Manjushri's birth?

1. The room was filled with bright light. The light, brighter than the light which could be made by any number of light bulbs, represents the Bodhisattva's great wisdom.

2. The vessels were filled with sweet dew. Sweet dew is miraculous; drinking it will cure all the sicknesses in the world. Then, instead of having to undergo birth, old-age, sickness, and death, you'll only have birth, old-age, and death to deal with.

3. The seven jewels came forth from the earth. The seven jewels are gold, silver, lapis lazuli, crystal, mother-of-pearl, red-pearls, and carnelian.

Why did the jewels appear?

Manjushri has cultivated the Six Perfections and the Ten Thousand Conducts to such a high level of perfection that in response, wherever he goes, precious gems appear.

4. The gods opened the treasuries. Manjushri Bodhisattva's great spiritual powers caused the earth to open up and expose the many treasures it contains. This differs from the third, in which the seven jewels welled up out of the earth. Here, the treasures were exposed when the earth opened up.

5. Chickens gave birth to phoenixes. Even more unusual than the gods opening the treasuries was the fact that chickens gave birth to phoenixes. Basically, of course, chickens only give birth to chickens. But because Manjushri's birth was such a special occasion, they gave birth to phoenixes.

6. Pigs gave birth to dragons. This is even more unusual than chickens giving birth to phoenixes. And, if you think that's something, look at number seven.

7. Horses gave birth to unicorns.

Does anyone know what number eight is? Of course you don't because I haven't told you yet. But after I tell you, you should remember it.

8. Cows gave birth to white *tsai*. The white *tsai* is an extremely rare and auspicious animal. It's not like an ox and it's not like a horse. It's not like anything at all. It looks like a horse, but it has the hooves of an ox. It's in a special category all of its own.

9. The grain in the granaries turned to gold. Do you think this is strange or not? Some of you probably think it's so strange that you don't even believe it. If you don't believe it, it's because you don't understand it. If you don't understand it, it's no doubt because you've never encountered such a thing before. So how could you possibly believe it?

However, the world is a very big place and what we have seen and heard is extremely limited. Therefore it is not strange that there are unusual phenomena which we have not seen or heard. When the grain turned to gold, it could no longer be used as food, but then just a few grains could be exchanged for a lot of food.

And what was number ten?

10. Elephants with six tusks appeared. As we know, elephants usually have only two tusks. At the time of Manjushri's birth, however, they appeared with six. Is this or is this not strange?

These ten special signs occurred at the time of the Bodhisattva's birth and represent Manjushri's rare eloquence in speaking all dharmas. Manjushri speaks the Dharma with superb eloquence. In fact, were you to hear him speak, you wouldn't care to hear me speak anymore, because there's simply no comparison. You may say, "We like to listen to you speak the Dharma, and we think you speak quite well." But if you heard Manjushri, you would know that he is incomparable.

When he speaks Dharma, Manjushri Bodhisattva does not discriminate among the dharmas. Although he does not discriminate among the dharmas, he nevertheless does not *not* distinguish all dharmas. The wonder lies right at this point, and that is why he is known as "wonderful virtue,"--Manjushri.

An Upasaka asks: Why were there six tusks on the elephants?

That's a very good question and I'm glad you asked it. The six tusks stand for the Six Perfections and the elephants stand for the Ten Thousand Conducts. The Six Perfections are: giving, morality, patience, vigor, concentration, and wisdom. They have already been explained, and so there is no need to go into them at this time.

THE BODHISATTVA WHO CONTEMPLATES THE WORLD'S SOUNDS...In Sanskrit, the Bodhisattva's name is Avalokiteshvara. In Chinese, it is Kuan Shih Yin, "contemplator of the world's sounds," and Kuan Tzu Tsai, "contemplator of self-mastery." We should all recognize this Bodhisattva. Because he is very compassionate, no one fears him and everyone knows him. This Bodhisattva is like a compassionate mother who grants the wishes of all living beings according to what they seek. There is a popular saying in Chinese,

Home, home, Kuan Shih Yin;
Everywhere, Amitabha.

Kuan Shih Yin Bodhisattva is Amitabha Buddha's chief disciple. Amitabha Buddha is the teaching host in the Western Land of Ultimate Bliss. To his left stands the Bodhisattva Kuan Yin and to his right, the Bodhisattva Who Has Obtained Great Might. They are known as the Three Sages of the Western Direction. When Amitabha Buddha steps down as teaching host, the Bodhisattva Kuan Yin will succeed him. Bodhisattva

Kuan Yin will in turn be succeeded by the Bodhisattva Who Has Obtained Great Might.

Because the Bodhisattva Who Contemplates the World's Sounds can manifest in countless forms to relieve beings of their suffering, he is known as the Greatly Compassionate Kuan Shih Yin. With a thousand eyes he views living beings tossing in the sea of suffering, and with a thousand hands he reaches down to pull them out.

The twenty-fifth chapter of *The Dharma Flower Sutra* deals with the Bodhisattva's miraculous powers. We shall wait until then to discuss them further.

THE BODHISATTVA WHO HAS OBTAINED GREAT STRENGTH... Whenever this Bodhisattva takes a step, the entire great trichiliocosm quakes in six different ways. This is why he is called "Great Strength."

What are the Six Types of Earthquakes?

The first three refer to movement:

1. shaking,
2. rising,
3. surging;

The following three refer to sounds:

4. banging,
5. roaring,
6. crackling.

These movements are much more severe than those which could be caused by our biggest bombs. However, unlike modern weapons which wreak havoc, the six types of quakes couldn't possibly hurt anyone.

The Bodhisattva Who Has Obtained Great Might is also known as the Bodhisattva of Boundless Light because one who sees the light of but one of the Bodhisattva's hairpores will see as well the pure, subtle light of the Buddhas of the ten directions.

THE BODHISATTVA CONSTANT VIGOR..."Constant"means he never quits. He never quits being vigorous in his cultivation. There are two kinds of vigor: bodily vigor and mental vigor. This Bodhisattva cultivates practices to teach and transform living beings. He is not like some of us who may start a project and then, as soon as the problems start to arise, abandon it in favor of taking a nap. The Bodhisattva Constant Vigor never sleeps, he just keeps working.

He will pass through limitless kalpas trying to teach one single living being and helping him to bring forth the heart of Bodhi. He may instruct him in countless Dharma-doors, but in all that time, he may still be unable to save him. Despite the fact that he has spent so much time and effort trying to save him, he will never grow weary or become discouraged. If we would like to save living beings, we should follow his example. If, in this life, we are unable to save someone, we should resolve to try again in the next life, or the life after, or the life after that, until we finally succeed.

On the other hand, if you notice that someone has been following you around, trying to teach and transform you, you should hurry up and take their teaching to heart and bring forth faith. That person may very well be the Bodhisattva Constant Vigor who has gone to so much trouble, life after life, just trying to teach you! You shouldn't just go on ignoring him. Listen to him!

Mental vigor means that you never become discouraged, you never think, "It's too hard!" and you never feel that there are simply too many difficulties involved in teaching and transforming others. Constant vigor is unflagging diligence.

THE BODHISATTVA UNRESTING...You may wonder, "Just what is the difference between Constant Vigor and Unresting? Aren't the two concepts pretty much the same? Why do we need two separate Bodhisattvas?"

Actually, it is not known how many Constant Vigor Bodhisattvas there are. They are numberless. We also cannot calculate the number of Bodhisattvas Unresting there are. In other words, if you are constantly vigorous in your cultivation of the Buddhadharma, then you, yourself, are the Bodhisattva Constant Vigor. If you pursue your study of the Dharma without resting, then you, yourself, are the Bodhisattva Unresting. It should be clear that there are an incalculable number of these Bodhisattvas.

"But what is the difference between the two?"

Although they are basically the same, if you want to speak of their differences, the Bodhisattva Constant Vigor continually enters the paths of rebirth in order to save living beings; the Bodhisattva Unresting passes through an enormous amount of time without ever becoming tired.

"Not getting tired" means that one does not fear fatigue. If one is bowing to the Buddha or reciting Sutras, one does not rest the moment one feels a bit tired. No matter what one does, one never rests. The Bodhisattva Unresting is always extremely busy, but he never gets upset because no one is helping him or because no one knows that he's doing good deeds. He would never advertise his own merit. There was a layman who used to come here and advertise his merit, praising himself for having worked for the temple or given money. His propaganda didn't get him very far, however, because more and more Americans came to the temple and his English wasn't very good. He was quite the reverse of Unresting Bodhisattva who, for as many kalpas as there are sand grains in the River Ganges, did not rest at all and never took a break. The days turned into months and the months into years; the years turned into hundreds of thousands of tens of thousands of millions of kalpas, and the Bodhisattva Unresting did not rest at all.

THE BODHISATTVA JEWELED PALM...Jewels, gems, refer to Dharma jewels. Palm is the palm of the hand. This Bodhisattva takes his name from his practices and from his original vows. What is meant by "practices?" They are the Dharma-doors which he cultivated. What are "basic vows?" They are the vows he made in the causal ground, when he was just beginning his cultivation. Some say he takes his name from his virtuous practices, and Way Virtue; others say he takes his name from his capability.

The Bodhisattva Jeweled Palm holds many different kinds of Dharma jewels. The first is the As-You-Will Pearl Dharma Jewel. With the As-You-Will Pearl, everything is "as your heart wishes" and you get what you seek. The second jewel he holds is the Lariat Hand and the third is the Jeweled Bowl Hand. The fourth is the Jeweled Sword Hand, the fifth, the Vajra Hand and Eye. The Sixth is the Jeweled Pestle Hand. The Seventh is the Bestowing Fearlessness Hand. The Bestowing Fearlessness Hand dispels all fear.

In the causal ground, the Bodhisattva Jeweled Palm cultivated the Forty-two Hands and Eyes of the Thousand Handed, Thousand Eyed Bodhisattva Who Contemplates the Sounds of the World. Thus he obtained the name Jeweled Palm, because all his palms hold all manner of gems, Dharma Jewels. So he is called Bodhisattva Jeweled Palm.

THE BODHISATTVA MEDICINE KING...Medicine King Bodhisattva and Medicine Superior Bodhisattva were explained in the Shurangama Sutra in the passage which discusses methods used by the twenty-five Sages to obtain perfect penetration.

There is an account in Buddhism about Medicine King Bodhisattva. Long ago there was a Wheel-turning Sage-King who had a thousand sons. The thousand sons all made vows to leave home and cultivate. Accordingly, they are to become the thousand Buddhas of the present age, called the Worthy Kalpa. Of the thousand Buddhas, four have already become Buddhas, Shakyamuni Buddha being the fourth to appear in the Worthy Kalpa.

The Wheel-turning King also had a concubine by whom he had two additional sons. The elder made a vow to protect and support the Dharma of his thousand older brothers, that is, to protect and support a thousand Buddhas. Whenever a Buddha appears in the world, he acts as their protector.

The second son, seeing that his brother had vowed to be a Dharma Protector, vowed that whenever any one of his thousand brothers became a Buddha, he would be the first to make offerings to him, but not just once, he would continue to make offerings all during the time that Buddha dwelt in the world. And he would not make offerings to just one older brother, but to all thousand of them, each as they became Buddhas.

After those Buddhas each enter Nirvana and the Dharma-ending age descends, the younger brother has vowed to rescue living beings. Using various kinds of medicines, he cures the illnesses of living beings. At the end of the kalpa, there occur the three disasters of flood, fire, and wind as well as the disasters of war and pestilence. In epidemics, those who contract the disease will die immediately. But the Bodhisattva Medicine King has vowed to save all sick living beings. This is Bodhisattva Medicine King's past life history. He concentrated exclusively on curing the illnesses of living beings. Not only did he cure the illnesses which plagued their bodies, but he cured as well their mental illnesses. He cured the sicknesses of their hearts and bodies so that afterwards they could cultivate.

BODHISATTVA COURAGEOUS GIVING...Courage is bravery. One must have courage in order to give. If one has no courage, one will be unable to give. The Ten Thousand Conducts take the Six Perfections as their mainstay, and the Six Perfections take giving as their mainstay. Thus, the other Perfections and the Ten Thousand Conducts are all included within the practice of giving.

If you give with courage and bravery, the merit and virtue you will obtain is inconceivable. If, in giving, you use an inconceivable spirit and energy, the reward you obtain will also be inconceivable.

For example, we may intend to give, but as soon as we have a thought of ourselves our good intentions vanish. "If I give my money to him, what am *I* going to do? If I give away my clothing, what am *I* going to wear? If I give away my house, where am *I* going to live?" This is an example of a lack of courage. As soon as one thinks of oneself, one will lose one's courage and fail to give.

Take food and drink: You may have thought to give it away, but then it occurs to you, "If I give this away, what will *I* eat?" The moment you think of yourself, your courage dissolves along with the spirit of courageous giving.

The Bodhisattva Courageous Giving thinks to give and, without further ado, he gives. "He's in trouble," he thinks, "I'll help him out. I'll give him a hundred dollars to buy some clothes and something to eat." He gives and that's all there is to it. Once you think of yourself, you will lose your courage. This Bodhisattva gives with courage; he gives wealth, Dharma, and fearlessness in the most vigorous and energetic fashion and so he is called The Bodhisattva Courageous Giving.

THE BODHISATTVA JEWELED MOON...takes his name from the jeweled moon. THE BODHISATTVA MOONLIGHT...who takes his name from the light of the moon which dispels the darkness of the night. THE BODHISATTVA FULL MOON...The three Bodhisattvas Jeweled Moon, Moonlight, and Full Moon take their names from firmly holding the moral precepts. As it says in the *Shurangama Sutra*, "They sternly upheld the Vinaya and were a vast model for the Three Realms." The Vinaya is the moral code. The three Bodhisattvas held the precepts until their light shone as brightly as the full moon. Although the names differ, they all come from the pure holding of the precepts. In reality, the Bodhisattva Jeweled Moon is just the Bodhisattva Full Moon ahd the Bodhisattva Moonlight is just the Bodhisattva Jeweled Moon. It is said,

> Purely holding the precepts
> One is like the full moon;
> With purity of body and of mouth,
> All darkness disappears.

When the karma of body, mouth and mind is pure, all darkness vanishes. Thus, the three Bodhisattvas take their names from having sternly held the precepts over a long period of time.

THE BODHISATTVA GREAT STRENGTH...The Bodhisattva Great Strength is especially powerful. His great strength is equal to that of the Bodhisattva Who Has Obtained Great Might.

THE BODHISATTVA LIMITLESS STRENGTH...Great Strength is not limitless strength. This Bodhisattva's strength surpasses that of the Bodhisattva Great Strength. Actually, great strength is just limitless strength and limitless strength is great strength.

THE BODHISATTVA WHO TRANSCENDS THE THREE REALMS... the realm of desire, the realm of form, and the formless realm. How does he transcend them? It is by means of his great strength and also by means of his limitless strength. The Bodhisattvas Great Strength, Limitless Strength, and The Bodhisattva Who Transcends the Three Realms all cultivate the same practice, the Perfection of Vigor. They go forward with heroic vigor. How do we know that they cultivate vigor? Their great strength, limitless strength, and the transcending of the three realms is proof. The three names are actually the same. Great Strength is Limitless Strength. Limitless Strength is the One Who Transcends the Three Realms. Without limitless strength, one could not surpass the three realms. So the three Bodhisattvas cultivate the practice of vigor and they have great, limitless strength and the courage and spirit to surpass the three realms. Therefore, they are always vigorous and they always go forward--that's what their names mean.

THE BODHISATTVA BHADRAPALA...There are three ways of interpreting this Bodhisattva's name. The first is "Good Protector."[1] The second is "Worthy Leader."[2] The third is "Worthy Guardian."[3]

What is meant by "Worthy Protector?" This Bodhisattva is able to protect the Buddha's work and so he is called "Good Protector." He is one of the Great Bodhisattvas, one of the leaders, a leader of men and gods--a "Worthy Leader." His name also means Worthy Guardian, for among the sages and worthies, he is able to guard and support living beings. Thus, the word Bhadrapala has these three meanings.

1善守 -*shan shou*.

2賢首 -*hsien shou*.

3賢護 -*hsien hu*.

THE BODHISATTVA MAITREYA...Maitreya means "compassionate clan."[1] He is also known as Ajita, "Invincible,"[2] because no heavenly demons or externalists can be victorious over him. Maitreya Bodhisattva dwells in the inner court of the Tushita heaven and cultivates the "compassionate heart samadhi." Everyone who meets him brings forth a compassionate heart. Because he is compasionate towards all beings, all living beings are fond of him and loyal to him.

Bhadrapala Bodhisattva cultivates the Perfection of Dhyana Samadhi. The Bodhisattva Compassionate Clan, or Invincible, cultivates the "compassionate heart samadhi," which is also called "the patience samadhi." When Shakyamuni Buddha steps down as teaching host of the Saha world, Maitreya will succeed him. When will this happen? Many externalists say, "Maitreya Bodhisattva has come; Maitreya Bodhisattva has appeared in the world," but they are speaking in a dream. Why do I say this? Shakyamuni Buddha stated very clearly when Maitreya would come:

This present world kalpa is now in a period of decrease. Every hundred years, man's average lifespan decreases by one year and his height by one inch. When man's average lifespan is ten years, the period of increase will begin again and every hundred years man's height will increase one inch and his average lifespan will increase by one year. When man's lifespan has reached eighty-four thousand years, the period of decline will begin again and, when man's lifespan has decreased to eighty-thousand years, Maitreya Bodhisattva will appear in the world. He will come to teach and transform living beings in the "Three Dragon Flower Assemblies." So those present-day externalists who do not understand the Buddhadharma are simply indulging in confused prattle. The time of Maitreya Bodhisattva's appearance has been definitely fixed.

According to the calculations within the Buddhadharma, man's average lifespan at present is between sixty and sixty-five years. When the average lifespan has decreased to ten years it will begin to increase again. How much time will that take? Then, it will increase to eighty-four thousand years. How long will

---

1慈氏 -*tz'u shih.*
2無能勝-*wu neng sheng.*

that be? Then it will again decrease until it reaches eighty-thousand years and Maitreya Bodhisattva will then appear in the world. So those people who presently speak dream-talk are truly pitiable.

THE BODHISATTVA JEWEL ACCUMULATION...This Bodhisattva has accumulated many treasures. What are they? He has accumulated limitless, boundless merit and virtue. The merit and virtue which he has amassed is like a precious treasure, Dharma treasure.

THE BODHISATTVA GUIDING MASTER...What is a guiding master? To guide is to lead; a master is a teacher. He is the guide and teacher of living beings and he shows them the Way. Now we have tourist buses which take people out on tours and this is called "touring". The Bodhisattva Guiding Master leads people to return to the proper road, to return to the Buddha path. Who does he lead? He leads those who have fallen into the hells. When people have fallen into the hells, they do not think to bring forth the heart of Bodhi. As they undergo punishment and torment, they do not know to repent and reform. So the Bodhisattva Guiding Master uses all manner of expedient devices to lead them to bring forth again the heart of Bodhi and to cultivate the Way to Bodhi. This is the meaning of Guiding Master Bodhisattva's name.

...AND OTHER BODHISATTVAS, MAHASATTVAS SUCH AS THESE...as the ones listed above, there were Bodhisattvas, Mahasattvas, to the number of EIGHTY THOUSAND IN ALL. When I lectured the *Ti Tsang Sutra* and when I lectured *The Dharma Flower Sutra*, I explained the Seven Qualities of a Mahasattva and I shall now give a test. Whoever remembers them should explain them for us:

1) They plant good roots, 2) they possess great wisdom, 3) they have great belief, 4) they understand the great principle, 5) they cultivate the great conduct, 6) they pass through great kalpas, 7) they preach the great truth.

Sutra:

AT THAT TIME, SHAKRO DEVANAM INDRAH WAS PRESENT WITH HIS RETINUE OF TWENTY THOUSAND GODS. AMONG THEM WERE THE GOD MOON, THE GOD UNIVERSAL FRAGRANCE, THE GOD JEWELED LIGHT, AND THE FOUR GREAT HEAVENLY KINGS WITH

THEIR RETINUES, TEN THOUSAND GODS IN ALL. THERE WAS THE GOD COMFORT, AND THE GOD GREAT COMFORT, WITH THEIR RETINUES, THIRTY THOUSAND GODS IN ALL.[D3E1]

Outline:

D3. other members of the assembly
E1. desire realm heaven gods

Commentary:

AT THAT TIME...At what time? At the time when Shakyamuni Buddha spoke the *Dharma Flower Sutra*, and the eighty-thousand Bodhisattvas had all arrived at the Bodhimandala to join the assembly. The eighty-thousand Bodhisattvas were great Bodhisattvas; they were the sons of the Buddha. The Buddha is the Dharma King and the Bodhisattvas are Dharma Princes. Therefore, in *The Amitabha Sutra* it says, "Manjushri, the Dharma Prince..." In *The Dharma Flower Sutra* the great Bodhisattvas all were Dharma Princes.

The Buddha has three kinds of sons: 1) true sons, 2) initiate sons, and 3) uninitiate sons.

Who are the Buddha's true sons? They are the Bodhisattvas, the Dharma Princes who are the Buddha's external retinue as they protect and support the Buddha on the outside. The initiate sons are the Bhikshus and Arhats who act as the inner retinue. The uninitiate sons are the common people, living beings in general. They have not studied the Buddhadharma, and so they are "uninitiate"--they stand on the outside. One could also say that uninitiate sons are those within the Buddhadharma who, although they study the Buddhadharma, they have not certified to the fruit, and they remain on the level of the common person and are not at the position of the worthy sages.

The Buddha's three kinds of sons include the Bodhisattvas, Arhats, and all living beings in the six paths. The beings in the six common realms and those in the three sagely realms, that is, beings in the nine Dharmarealms are all included among the Buddha's sons.

SHAKRO DEVANAM INDRAH...is a Sanskrit word which means "able to do." [1] Able to do what? Able to be the heavenly lord. Shakra is the one many revere as "the Lord on High," or "Old Father in Heaven," or "the Heavenly Host"---in other words, God. He is the one

---

[1] 能作 -*neng tso*.

whom the externalists worship. In the Shurangama Mantra, he is referred to as "Yin two la ye," in the line which reads "Na mwo yin two la ye." "Yin two la ye," the King ,is just Shakro Devanam Indrah.

Shakra is the ruler of the Heaven of the Thirty Three, the Trayastrimsha Heaven, which is the second of the six desire realm heavens. He is revered by the Chinese as the Great Jade Emperor, an Emperor in the heavens. But he still ranks in the six common realms; he has not yet reached the level of the sage. In Buddhism he is regarded as a Dharma protector. Although he protects the Buddhadharma, he is not even given a place to sit in the assembly of the Buddha; he has to stand.

If he doesn't even have a seat in the assembly, why do so many people worship him? Why do they believe in him and regard him as the only true lord of heaven and earth?

Although he doesn't even have a seat in the Buddhadharma and although he is forced to stand and act as a Dharma protector, within his own territory, he is the one and only mighty leader. There is an apt analogy for this situation:

There was a small country village located deep in a mountain valley which had no communication with the outside world. The mayor often went to the big cities where he was recognized merely as a small-town mayor. But to his citizens, country folk who had never been out, he said, "I am the world's greatest ruler! Everyone must obey my commands. I am the Emperor. I am the President. I am the world-ruler." Because he was their leader, they assumed that he was telling the truth. They didn't know that above the mayor stood the Governor, the Senators, and the President, or perhaps the Emperor. Why didn't they know? Because they had never communicated with the world beyond their small isolated mountain village. As far as they knew, the mayor is the highest personage, the greatest in the world, and they all respected him and trusted him.

The Heavenly Lord is just like the small-town mayor. Those who do not understand the Buddhadharma are like the poor mountain people who have never been to the big city and know nothing about the big, wide world. The country folk think that the mayor is the highest ruler and common people who do not understand the Buddhadharma only know that there is a Lord on High, a Heavenly Lord. They don't know that above him are the Buddhas and Bodhisattvas. They don't know because the Lord doesn't want his subjects to know, just like the mayor doesn't want his citizens to mingle with the outside world because if they did, they would quickly realize that he was simply a small-time mayor, and they wouldn't put quite so much faith in him. Shakra is that way, too.

Where did Shakra come from?

Long ago, after the Nirvana of Kashyapa Buddha, Shakra was a woman. Not only was he a woman, he was a poor woman. Not only was he a poor woman, he was a beggar-woman. One day, she came across an image of Kashyapa Buddha and noticed that its gold finish was cracked and peeling. She gathered thirty-two of her women friends together, and they combined their efforts to raise funds in order to have the temple rebuilt and the image regilded. The merit and virtue they acquired from this act caused them to be reborn as heavenly lords, each in her own heaven. The woman who organized the project was reborn as Shakra in the heaven in the center, located on the peak of Mount Sumeru. Her thirty-two friends were born as rulers in thirty-two heavens surrounding it, eight on each of the four sides, making thirty-three heavens in all. Thus, we have the name "Heaven of the thirty-three."

Ultimately, how many heavens are there?

There are an uncountable number. However, the Heaven of the Thirty-three is located on the peak of Mount Sumeru and is the second of the six desire realm heavens. The Heaven of the Four Great Kings is located half-way up Mount Sumeru and is the lowest of the six desire realm heavens.

Shakro Devanam Indrah was present WITH HIS RETINUE, those of his own kind, TWENTY THOUSAND GODS, AMONG WHOM WERE THE GOD MOON, THE GOD UNIVERSAL FRAGRANCE...who is fond of fragrance and so emits fragrance from his person continually which perfumes the Dharma Realm. THE GOD JEWELED LIGHT is fond of jewels and consequently emits jeweled light. These three are considered Shakra's inner officials, likened to cabinet officials.

THE FOUR GREAT HEAVENLY KINGS... dwell in the lowest desire realm heaven. It is half-way up Mount Sumeru. One king dwells on each side. In the east dwell Dhrtarashtra,"the king who maintains his country." In the south dwells Virudhaka,"increasing and growing." In the west dwells Virupaksha,"broad eyes". In the north dwells Vaishravana,"erudite." They are known as the Four World-Protecting Kings because they endeavor to protect living beings of this world from ghosts and spirits who would harm them. They are considered to be Shakra's outer-officials, similar to military officials.

EACH WITH HIS RETINUE, TEN THOUSAND GODS IN ALL. They all came to the Dharma assembly to hear the *Wonderful Dharma Lotus Flower Sutra*.

Although the God Universal Fragrance is fond of fragrance and the God Jeweled Light is fond of jewels, it's not that they like these things for themselves. The God Universal Fragrance knows that all living beings like fragrance and so he emits a fragrance which pervades the world. If it wasn't for the fragrance this God emits, the world of human beings would reek with an unbearable stench. The fragrance he emits wards off those foul odors.

The God Jeweled Light knows that all beings are greedy for valuable objects. He radiates a jeweled light to fulfill the wishes of living beings. Once their wishes have been fulfilled, they can bring forth the heart of Bodhi. The God Universal Fragrance does not emit fragrance because he likes to smell it but because he knows all beings like good smells. The God Jeweled Light does not radiate jeweled light because he likes jewels, but because he knows all beings like them. The gods emit fragrance and light because they wish to cause living beings to awaken to the fact that such inconceivable states do exist in the world, and so that they will then bring forth the supreme heart of Bodhi.

THE GOD COMFORT...Extremely comfortable, he dwells in the fifth of the desire-realm heavens, the Nirmanarati Heaven, which is the "heaven of transformational bliss." The bliss in this heaven is created through transformation.

THE GOD GREAT COMFORT...is from the sixth desire-realm heaven, the Paranirmitavashavartin Heaven, "the heaven of the comfort derived from the transformations of others." The gods of this heaven do not find their comfort within their own heaven, but they take as their own the transformations created by the other gods in the other heavens.

WITH THEIR RETINUE, THIRTY THOUSAND GODS IN ALL. So many! More than the gods above. Shakra only had twenty thousand. These gods had ten thousand more.

Sutra:

THERE WAS THE GOD KING BRAHMA, RULER OF THE SAHA WORLD, AS WELL AS THE GREAT BRAHMA SHIKIN AND THE GREAT BRAHMA BRILLIANCE, AND OTHERS, WITH THEIR RETINUES, TWELVE THOUSAND GODS IN ALL. E2

Outline:

E2. gods of the form realm heavens.

Commentary:

The SAHA WORLD...What is the Saha World? Saha is a Sanskrit word. The Saha World is the "sweet world," the sweetest place there is.

"Dharma Master," you say, "I've been listening to your lectures on the Sutras for a long time, and you haven't made a mistake yet. This time, however, you're definitely wrong. "Saha" is interpreted from the Sanskrit as "patiently endured"[1] because it is a place where suffering is undergone. If anything, Saha means "bitter," not "sweet."

Really? Then if you know it is bitter, why do you cling to it? Why are you still unable to part with this world? Why do I explain Saha as sweet? Just because I see that you are unable to give it up. If you can't bear to part with it, it must be sweet, don't you think? If it were bitter, you would have let it go long ago.

You say, "Well, Dharma Master, if you put it that way, there's not much I can say."

There may not be much you can say, but I have something to add: This world is not bitter; it is also not sweet. It is a tasteless world--utterly blank. But, despite its lack of taste, it's full of trouble. What kind of trouble? It's real pain. So, Saha, may be interpreted as "sweet." It also means "patiently endured," for in this world beings are forced to undergo a great deal of suffering, both internal and external.

They endure the Three Sufferings: the suffering within suffering, the suffering of decay, and the suffering of process. They endure the Eight Sufferings: the suffering of birth, old age, sickness, and death, the suffering of being separated from what one loves,

---

[1] 堪忍 -*k'an jen.*

the suffering of being around what one hates, the suffering of not getting what one wants, and the suffering of the raging blaze of the five skandhas.

So much suffering! And yet they patiently endure it saying, "It is truly unbearable; how can it be endured?" Basically, it's simply unbearable and yet still you are able to bear it, and what is more, within this state of extreme suffering you cling tenaciously to existence in the Saha World. You can still patiently endure it; you are still unable to let go of this world. This is why I say that this is a "sweet" world. Most people think it's as sweet as an apple. Actually, once they've tasted it, they know that this world is bitter, as bitter as *huang lien*, the bitterest of medicinal herbs. In fact, it's even more bitter. Knowing the bitterness of this world, and yet still being able to bear and undergo it, is very difficult.

If you were able to taste as much bitterness in cultivating the Way, you would certainly become a Buddha. In Manchuria, my disciple Kuo Hsün said, "When I was a prisoner in a Japanese labor camp, I never had enough food to eat, I didn't have enough clothes to keep me warm, and I never got enough sleep. If those who cultivate the Way could endure one half of the suffering endured by labor camp prisoners, they would most certainly accomplish Buddhahood." After he left the home-life, he ate only one meal a day, before noon, and never ate at other times. Day and night he sat in Dhyana, never lying down to sleep. Of all my disciples, he was foremost in the cultivation of ascetic practices.

Later, Kuo Hsün didn't want to remain in the Saha World, and so he set himself on fire. After he had burned to death, his body remained sitting in full-lotus posture. When the people went to examine him, they reached out and touched his body and it crumbled into ashes. This proves that he had samadhi power. If he had not had the skill to enter samadhi, the fire certainly would have caused him to jump. If ordinary people get burned, they invariably jump away. But when the fire had gone out, Kuo Hsün's body remained in sitting posture and he hadn't moved an inch--proof of his samadhi power.

So if anyone says that he has samadhi power and can enter samadhi, you can test him out. Burn him. If he doesn't move, then he really does have samadhi power. If he's still sitting there when the fire goes out, then his samadhi is genuine. If your samadhi power isn't up to that, then don't brag that you have samadhi. So I don't dare say that I have samadhi power. If I said I did, I might get tested out.

The Saha World...

WORLD includes the three periods of time--past, present, and future, as well as space.

THE GOD KING BRAHMA RULER OF THE SAHA WORLD... RULER is one who is the boss. BRAHMA is the GOD KING BRAHMA who is the king of the Great Brahma Heaven.

THE GREAT BRAHMA SHIKHIN...SHIKHIN is Sanskrit. It means "crown curls"[1] because his head is covered with curls.

THE GREAT BRAHMA BRILLIANCE...There was another god named Brilliance.

AND OTHERS...more of them...WITH THEIR RETINUE, TWELVE THOUSAND GODS IN ALL.

More on the Three and Eight Sufferings

The Three Sufferings:

1. The suffering within suffering. This is the suffering of poverty and distress. One may be poor and then follows the suffering of having no food to eat, having no clothes to wear, and no place to live. Would you call this suffering or not? It is suffering within suffering.

2. The suffering of decay. One may have food, clothes, and a place to live, in fact one may live in a fabulous penthouse apartment--one may not only have clothes to wear, but one may own the most fashionable, beautiful garments--one may not only have food to eat, but one may eat the world's rarest and tastiest delicacies, things no one else has ever tasted--but it's all too good to last, and the good times are soon over. Perhaps one's house catches on fire, or one is robbed, or has some kind of accident and, although one once enjoyed wealth and honor, one's happiness decays and falls apart. This is the suffering of decay.

3. The suffering of process. If one does not undergo the suffering within suffering or the suffering of the decay of wealth and honor, one must still undergo the suffering of process. From youth to the prime of life, from the prime of life to old age, from old age to sickness, from sickness to death--in every

---

[1] 頂髻 - *ting chi.*

thought there is shifting and changing, like the waves on water which follow one another without cease. No one can avoid this process of aging which continues unceasingly. This is the suffering of process.

The Eight Sufferings:

1. The suffering of being separated from what one loves. Through circumstances, you may be forced to separate from that person whom you love the most, the one you cannot bear to be separated from. This kind of suffering is extreme.

2. The suffering of being around what one hates. Perhaps you really hate someone. "I can't stand him," you say. "I'm leaving. I don't want to be around him." So you go somewhere else and meet someone exactly like him, whom you hate just as much. You think you can just walk out and that will be the end of it, but wherever you go, you run into someone just like him. This is the suffering of being around what you hate.

3. The suffering of not getting what one wants. When you wish for something and long for it but there's no way you can obtain it, that is suffering.

4. The suffering of the raging blaze of the five skandhas. This suffering is even more extreme than the above. The five skandhas, form, feeling, thinking, activity, and consciousness are never more than a step away. They are right with you, walking, standing, sitting, and reclining.

The five skandhas are like a raging fire, a blazing conflagration.

To the above four sufferings, add the sufferings of birth, old age, sickness, and death, and you've got the Eight Sufferings.

Sutra:

THERE WERE EIGHT DRAGON KINGS: THE DRAGON KING NANDA, THE DRAGON KING UPANANDA, THE DRAGON KING SAGARA, THE DRAGON KING VASUKI, THE DRAGON KING TAKSHAKA, THE DRAGON KING ANAVATAPTA, THE DRAGON KING MANASVIN, AND THE DRAGON KING UTPALAKA, AND OTHERS, EACH WITH HIS RETINUE OF SEVERAL HUNDREDS OF THOUSAND FOLLOWERS.[E3]

Outline:

E3. the dragons

Commentary:

Long ago, there were many dragons, and everyone could see them. In the present day, however, they do not appear. Why? Because there are too many people, and the dragons out of fear do not dare show themselves. Dragons belong to the class of animals, but they are not like ordinary animals because they have spiritual penetrations.

What spiritual penetrations do they have? They can make themselves big or small. They can manifest so that people can see them, and they can also make themselves invisible by means of the transformations of their spiritual penetrations.

And how did they become dragons? You shouldn't look down on them just because they are animals, for in previous lives, dragons were people who cultivated the Way. However, they were "quick with the Vehicle and slow on the precepts," that is, they cultivated the Great Vehicle practices with vigor, but neglected the precepts. They cultivated the Way with great intensity, but they did not keep the precepts. They did not sever their thoughts of desire, specifically thoughts of sexual desire. Because they did not cut off their thoughts of desire, they did not keep the precepts. Thus, although they cultivated the Way and worked very hard, investigating the Great Vehicle Buddhadharma, because they did not keep the precepts and were very negligent about them, they fell into rebirth in the bodies of dragons. On the one hand, because they didn't keep the precepts, they were born in the bodies of dragons. On the other hand, because they cultivated the Great Vehicle and were very vigorous in cultivating the Buddha Way, they obtained spiritual penetrations, even though they were animals. I explained this principle when I lectured on the *Shurangama Sutra*, but I was afraid you might have forgotten and so I have repeated it. "Quick with the Vehicle but slow with the precepts," they fell to rebirth in dragon bodies.

There are those who are "quick with the precepts but slow with the Vehicle." They keep the precepts very sternly but are not vigorous in cultivating the Great Vehicle Dharma. Such cultivators are born as humans, as wealthy and honored people. They are, however, not very bright. Although they are very wealthy and honored, they are very stupid. Because they uphold the precepts very strictly, they are wealthy and honored. Because they did not read or recite the Great Vehicle Sutras or investigate the Buddhadharma, they lack wisdom. Thus, they are rather stupid--not totally stupid, but not overly intelligent either.

Others are "quick with the Vehicle and quick with the precepts." While making speedy progress in their cultivation of the Great Vehicle Buddhadharma, they keep the precepts well. They are extremely dedicated in their investigation of the Buddhadharma. Such people can perhaps certify to the fruit or, if they don't certify to the fruit, they can be reborn in the heavens and enjoy divine blessings.

Still others are "slow with the Vehicle and with the precepts." They don't cultivate the Great Vehicle Buddhadharma, and they don't keep the precepts. All day they are lazy as can be. Some who have not left the home-life do not investigate Buddhism or practice it and are very lazy. There are even those who have left home who do not investigate the Buddhadharma and are extremely lazy. In the morning they sleep in until ten o'clock. Then they rise. And at night they retire early.

They say,

'Tho the sun has risen three-hundred feet
the monk has still not risen;
But scheming for name and fame is not
as good as doing nothing.

The sun is high in the sky, but the monk is still sound asleep in bed. But seeking for name and plotting for fame is not as good as just being lazy and not doing anything at all. Laziness is better by far!

Lazy, they are slow with the Vehicle and with the precepts. They don't keep the precepts and don't investigate the Buddhadharma. They claim to have left home; it's only a name because they don't actually cultivate--they don't work hard. They may be fond of sneaking off to take it easy. The minute there's work to do they retreat. But if there's something good to eat, they are the first ones to sneak a bite. They are good at eating but lazy in doing. In this way they fall into hell; they run off to the hells. There, since they love to eat, they are free to eat from morning to night. What do they eat? Pills of hot iron. You'd rather not work or study? You won't have to do anything there at all, except undergo punishment. Perhaps you'll be fried in oil, thrown on a mountain of knives, on the sword-trees, or into the cauldrons of boiling-oil--and you can have a taste of *that*. Why?

Because you're lazy! We'll see if you're still lazy once you get there. This is what happens to people who neglect both the Vehicle and the precepts.

In *The Dharma Flower Sutra* assembly, there were eight dragon kings present. There were also a great many small dragons.

This reminds me of when in Manchuria my disciple Kuo Hsün, the disciple who set himself on fire, was quick with the Vehicle and with the precepts. He maintained the precepts and cultivated the Great Vehicle Buddhadharma. He built a small grass hut, about eight by eight. When he asked me to perform the opening ceremony, called "opening the light," or "opening the eyes," I went with several of my disciples, Kuo Neng, Kuo Chih, Kuo Tso, and Kuo Ying. That night, I stayed in the hut and ten dragons came by asking to take refuge with the Triple Jewel.

As the weather had been extremely hot and there hadn't been any rain for a long time, I asked the ten dragons, "Dragons are in charge of the rain. Why haven't you made it rain? And you want to take refuge?"

The dragons replied, "Before it can rain, we have to have an order from God Shakra, that is Shakro Devanam Indrah. Without his order, we wouldn't dare just casually make it rain."

So I said to the dragons, "You go tell Shakra that I am asking for rain within a thirteen mile radius of this hut. If you persuade Shakra to permit rain tomorrow then the day after tomorrow I shall transmit the Three Refuges to you and accept you as disciples of the Buddha."

Sure enough, the next day it rained in, as a matter of fact, a radius of just thirteen miles around the hut where I was standing. No rain fell outside of a thirteen mile radius. On the following day, I transmitted the Refuges to the ten dragons. After taking refuge, they began to cultivate.

I gave the dragons the name "Hurry and Cultivate" and "Quickly Cross Over." All ten of the dragons had the same name. "Hurry and Cultivate" means hurry up and cultivate in order to "Quickly Cross Over" all the other dragons. That's their work at present: teaching and transforming other dragons.

Because on the day before they took refuge, the dragons had brought rain, I gave Kuo Hsün's hut the name "Dragon Rain Cottage." After it rained, I conducted the Refuge Ceremony for them. So, although you may not be able to see them, dragons are around all the same.

Now, this may sound like a myth, but in reality there is nothing in the least mythical about it. It was my own personal experience.

Dragons can undergo an infinite variety of transformations by means of their spiritual penetrations.

Present at *The Dharma Flower Sutra* assembly were eight dragon kings: The first was NANDA. NANDA is Sanskrit and means "bliss."[1] UPANANDA means "wholesome bliss."[2] These two dragon kings were brothers. In the past, they were very unruly. Later, they met and were tamed by Mahamaudgalyayana.[2A] Now they have become Dharma protectors who have come to *The Dharma Flower Sutra* assembly to listen to the Sutra. The two dragon brothers, Bliss and Wholesome Bliss, guard Magadha, regulating the winds and rain and insuring good crops, benefiting the population greatly.

THE DRAGON KING SAGARA...SAGARA means "ocean."[3] He is a dragon king who lives in the sea.

THE DRAGON KING VASUKI...VASUKI means "many heads."[4] A single dragon body may have nine heads, twelve heads, fifteen heads--three or seven heads. VASUKI means "many heads."

THE DRAGON KIND TAKSHAKA...TAKSHAKA means "putting forth poison."[5] He puts forth many lethal vapors

THE DRAGON KING ANAVATAPTA...ANAVATAPTA means "no heat."[6] THE DRAGON KING MANASVIN...His name means "large-bodied,"[7] because he is very big. THE DRAGON KING UTPALAKA, which means "blue lotus."[8] AND OTHERS... Not only were these eight dragon kings present, but there were also a lot more. EACH WITH HIS RETINUE OF

---

1 歡喜 -*huan hsi.*

2 善歡喜 -*shan huan hsi.*

2A see page 201.

3 鹹海 -*hsien hai.*

4 多頭 -*to t'ou.*

5 現毒 -*hsien tu.*

6 無熱 -*wu je.*

7 大身 -*ta shen.*

8 青蓮華 -*ch'ing lien hua.*

SEVERAL HUNDREDS OF THOUSANDS OF FOLLOWERS. Each dragon king brought along a flock of dragon sons and dragon grandsons, lots of little dragons, several hundreds of thousands of them in their train.

Sutra:

THERE WERE FOUR KINNARA KINGS: THE KINNARA KING DHARMA, THE KINNARA KING FINE DHARMA, THE KINNARA KING GREAT DHARMA AND THE KINNARA KING UPHOLDER OF DHARMA, EACH WITH HIS RETINUE OF SEVERAL HUNDREDS OF THOUSANDS OF FOLLOWERS. E4

Outline:

E4. the kinnaras

Commentary:

Not only were there dragons present in the assembly, but there were also KINNARA KINGS. Kinnaras are one of the Eight Classes of Supernatural Beings: gods, dragons, yakshas, gandharvas, asuras, garudas, and mahoragas. "Kinnara" means "doubtful spirit,"[1] because they resemble human beings, but they have a horn on their head.

Because of the horn on their heads, one might think they were spirits, but because they look just like people, one might not. They look like people, but they've got a horn which makes people doubtful as to whether or not they are spirits.

Therefore they are called "doubtful spirits."

Kinnaras are musicians in the court of the Jade Emperor (Shakra).

THE KINNARA KING DHARMA...There was a doubtful spirit called Dharma who has many "dharmas" or "methods" of making music and many methods of causing people to study the Buddhadharma. The music he makes is subtle and wonderful causing those who hear it to resolve to study and practice the Buddhadharma.

THE KINNARA KING FINE DHARMA...not only has many "dharmas" for making music, but they are extremely fine. His music is such that it impresses all who hear it. Not only do they resolve to study and practice

---

1 疑神 -*i shen*.

the Buddhadharma and to see how fine and subtle it is, but it also expresses the greatness and expansiveness of the Buddhadharma.

THE KINNARA KING UPHOLDER OF DHARMA...Not only leads people to want to cultivate and to see how fine and great the Buddhadharma is, but he leads them to bring forth hearts which delight in cultivating according to Dharma, to receive and uphold the Dharma.

EACH WITH HIS RETINUE OF SEVERAL HUNDREDS OF THOUSANDS OF FOLLOWERS. Each kinnara king was accompanied by a lot of followers, several hundreds, or several thousands, or perhaps several tens of thousands of them in their train.

Sutra:

THERE WERE FOUR GANDHARVA KINGS: THE GANDHARVA KING MUSIC, THE GANDHARVA KING MUSICAL SOUND, THE GANDHARVA KING BEAUTIFUL, THE GANDHARVA KING BEAUTIFUL SOUND, EACH WITH HIS FOLLOWING OF SEVERAL HUNDREDS OF THOUSANDS OF FOLLOWERS.[E5]

Outline:

E5.the gandharvas

Commentary:

GANDHARVAS are also musical spirits in the Jade Emperor's court. Hearing that the kinnaras and gandharvas are musicians, we should not become attached to the fact and say, "In Buddhism there are the kinnara kings and the gandharva kings who make music," and then take up the study of music. You should know that they made music for the Jade Emperor. It was not made within the Buddhadharma. After taking refuge with the Buddha, they became Buddhism's Dharma protectors and are listed with the Eight Classes of Supernatural Beings, some of which are ghosts and some spirits who protect the Buddhadharma. This is not a recommendation that you study music.

THERE WERE FOUR GANDHARVA KINGS...Gandharva, a Sanskrit word, means "incense inhalers,"[1] because they particularly like the smell of incense. When the Jade Emperor wishes them to make music, he just burns some ox-head chandana incense, and when the gandharvas smell it, they come to make extremely fine music.

---

1 臭香 -*hsiu hsiang*.

The first was the GANDHARVA KING MUSIC, a talented musician. The GANDHARVA KING MUSICAL SOUND made even better music than the Gandharva King Music. THE GANDHARVA KING BEAUTIFUL...His music was exquisitely beautiful, not only melodic, but elegant as well. THE GANDHARVA KING BEAUTIFUL SOUND was the last of the four gandharva kings.

EACH WITH HIS RETINUE OF SEVERAL HUNDREDS OF THOUSANDS OF FOLLOWERS...with other little gandharvas in their train, and also lots of little kinnaras--all came to hear the Buddha speak the Dharma

Now, just because you've found out about the celestial musicians, you shouldn't get "sticky" about music. Don't be like a certain singer who goes around chirping like a bird and singing a song for everyone he sees. Don't be like that. What is more, that person always makes excuses for himself to me saying, "Of the eighty-four thousand Dharma-doors, this is one!" He says that making music is one of the Dharma-doors, but he's utterly shameless. He himself is attached to and caught up in music, and so he tries to snag others into becoming attached to it as well. It's truly pitiful.

Sutra:

THERE WERE FOUR ASURA KINGS: THE ASURA KING KHARASKANDHA, THE ASURA KING VEMACHITRIN, AND THE ASURA KING RAHU, EACH WITH HIS RETINUE OF SEVERAL HUNDREDS OF THOUSANDS OF FOLLOWERS.[E6]

Outline:

E6. the asuras

Commentary:

ASURA is a Sanskrit word which is interpreted "without wine,"[1] for they have no wine to drink. It is also interpreted as "ugly,"[2] because they have a very repulsive appearance. This applies only to the men, because the women are very beautiful. It also means "not gods,"[3] because they have the blessings

---

[1] 無酒 -*wu chiu.*

[2] 無端正 -*wu tuan cheng.*

[3] 非天 -*fei t'ien.*

of the gods but not the authority of the gods. Asuras may be found in the realms of the gods, people, hungry ghosts, and animals.

Asuras are of a hostile temperament; they relish fighting. They like to wage and win wars. In the heavens a group of asuras are especially war-like and are constantly battling with the heavenly generals. As I have told you many times before, the asura king VEMACHITRIN had a beautiful daughter named Shachi to whom the Jade Emperor became engaged. Why did he want to marry her? The Jade Emperor still has a body with thoughts of desire. Because he has not severed thoughts of sexual desire, he likes beautiful women. One day, catching sight of the beautiful asura girl, he became enamored of her and asked the asura king for his daughter's hand in marriage. The asura king thought, "The Jade Emperor's got a lot of power. I'd best not cross him."

After they were married, the Jade Emperor liked to listen to an immortal speak the Dharma. Because he went to lectures every day, the asura girl soon grew suspicious. "He goes out every day and never gets home until late at night. Most likely he's out playing around with other women." Finally, she confronted him, "Just where do you go every day? You wouldn't be conducting some improper business on the side, would you?"

"No," said the Jade Emperor. "I go to lectures on the Sutras every day and that's why I'm always home late. You shouldn't be suspicious."

The asura girl, not believing he was going to Sutra lectures, decided he must certainly be up to no good. The asura girl had a certain amount of spiritual power and was able to make herself invisible. She could be standing in one spot and ordinary people with mortal eyes, or even the Jade Emperor, with his heavenly eyes, couldn't see her.

So, one day when as usual the Jade Emperor got in his chariot and headed for the lecture, the asura girl made herself invisible and rode along. Upon arriving, the Jade Emperor got out of the chariot and so did the asura girl. Then, she materialized.

"What are you doing here?" asked the Jade Emperor in surprise.

"What are *you* doing here?" she snorted, looking around at the beautiful goddesses in the assembly.

"I've come to listen to the Sutra lecture," he said.

"Well, so have I," she countered.

Now, the Jade Emperor is still a common mortal; he's not a certified sage by any means, and so he sometimes gets afflicted. This time, he picked up his flower whip and lashed the asura girl. The asura girl was furious and went directly to her father.

Previously, when the Jade Emperor was about to be married, he had invited the Asura King to a banquet. As a gesture of respect to his new father-in-law, he sent out his generals and troops to welcome him. However, the asura king was suspicious of the welcoming party. He felt intimidated and was displeased at the Jade Emperor's show of power. Now his daughter returned with the report that the Jade Emperor was not following the rules at all. "Every day he goes out with other women," she said. "And today, when I tried to talk to him about it, he struck me!" At this, the Asura King became enraged. "Jade Emperor," he stormed, "this means war! We're going to fight to the finish," and he mobilized the asura troops against the Jade Emperor.

Strangely enough, the Jade Emperor lost battle after battle and could find no way to overcome the Asura King. Finally he had no recourse but to ask the Buddha for help. The Buddha told him to instruct his troops all to recite "Mahaprajnaparamita!" As they went into battle, they recited the phrase--"Mahaprajnaparamita!"--the asuras lost battle after battle until they had retreated as far as they could and were backed up into a lotus root.

Why was the Asura King unable to withstand the "Mahaprajnaparamita?" It's very simple: Before they recited it, they would win a battle and then lose a battle; after they recited the phrase the Buddha taught them, they won continuously. Previously, the asuras and the heavenly troops had been more or less equal in strength. Neither side had any wisdom to speak of, and their battles were utterly chaotic. When the heavenly troops recited "Mahaprajnaparamita," they attained great wisdom while the asuras still had none. When those without wisdom fight those with wisdom they invariably lose. So the asuras were very stupid and the heavenly troops were very wise. When the wise battle against the stupid, sooner or later, the stupid ones always lose. Such was the situation between the asuras and the heavenly troops.

More than anything, asuras like to fight. We can take a look at the people in the world: whoever likes to fight is an asura. Asuras aren't necessarily found only in the heavens. Human beings who like strife and war are transformation bodies of asuras. They liked to fight when they were in the heavens, and they continue to do so as people.

Here, there were FOUR ASURA KINGS: THE ASURA KING BALIN...BALIN means "fettered"[1] because he was tied up. Who tied him up? He was tied up by the Jade Emperor's heavenly troops.

THE ASURA KING KHARASKANDHA...KHARASKANDHA means "broad shoulder blades"[2] because his shoulders were especially broad, and he was very powerful.

THE ASURA KING VEMACHITRIN...VEMACHITRIN was the asura king just mentioned who fought the Jade Emperor. Although he was terribly ugly, his daughter was remarkably beautiful. After his battle with the Jade Emperor, he ended up retreating into a lotus root. His name means "sea water wave sound."[3]

THE ASURA KING RAHU...RAHU means "obstructing and holding,"[4] for when he raises his hand he can blot out the light of the sun and the moon. One could explain his name in many ways. You might say he can obstruct afflictions, you might also say that he is obstructed by afflictions. If you say he can obstruct afflictions, then he has no afflictions; that's one explanation. You could also say that he has been obstructed by afflictions so that all day long he gets angry and wants to pick a fight.

EACH WITH HIS RETINUE OF SEVERAL HUNDREDS OF THOUSANDS OF FOLLOWERS. Each asura brought along a great many followers.

Sutra:

THERE WERE FOUR GARUDA KINGS: THE GARUDA KING GREAT MAJESTY, THE GARUDA KING GREAT BODY, THE GARUDA KING GREAT FULLNESS, AND THE GARUDA KING AS YOU WILL,

---

1 被縛-*pei fu.*
2 廣肩胛 -*kuang chien chia.*
3 海水波音-*hai shui po yin.*
4 障持 -*chang ch'ih.*

EACH WITH HIS OWN RETINUE OF SEVERAL HUNDREDS OF THOUSANDS OF FOLLOWERS.[E7]

Outline:

E7. the garudas

Commentary:

THERE WERE FOUR GARUDA KINGS: What's a Garuda King? Those of you who have heard Sutras explained, will know. Those who haven't will know after I explain it. Garuda is Sanskrit. It means "the great golden-winged p'eng bird."[1] They are not born from eggs, but from transformation. Their bodies are immense and they have a wingspread of 300 yojanas, a yojana being 80 *li*, a *li* being about one-third of a mile. When he flaps his wings, the entire ocean dries up, exposing all the dragons who live in its depths. The p'eng then eats the dragons, one by one, just like we eat noodles.

Chickens and birds eat worms, and worms belong to the same category as dragons. In fact, most insects recognize dragons as their rulers. The small birds eat small worms; the big birds eat big worms--that is, the p'eng birds eat dragons. Dragons are simply big worms. Well, the p'engs had been eating the dragons for quite a while, until finally the dragons were on the verge of extinction. The reason we don't see dragons around in this world anymore is because, for the most part, they were eaten by the p'eng birds. If, however, the dragons became extinct, the p'eng birds would have nothing to eat and would also starve. This is why we don't see many p'eng birds around either. As the dragons disappeared, the p'engs lost their sustenance and began to diminish as well. So, if we in the world have nothing to eat we will also become extinct.

Finally, the dragons went to the Buddha pleading for help. "The race of dragons is facing extinction," they said, "because we are truly no match for the p'eng birds. With their spiritual strength, they can cause the oceans to dry up with a single mighty flap of their wings. Because we have no place to hide, they are eating us so fast that soon the race of dragons will entirely disappear."

Then Shakyamuni Buddha took one of his old precept sashes--not a new one--and said, "Take this back with you and give one thread of it to each dragon to wear, and the p'eng birds will not be able to see you." The dragons returned and followed the Buddha's instructions, and sure enough, the next time the p'engs flapped at the ocean, they saw no dragons on the bottom. When they figured out that the Buddha had helped the dragons, they went to the Buddha to argue their side of the case.

"You've helped the dragons," they said, "but now we have nothing to eat and we're going to starve to death. What's to be done?"

Shakyamuni Buddha said, "You won't starve. Don't eat the dragons. After this, I will instruct my disciples to send out, every day at noon, part of their meal for you to eat."

This is why, when we perform the noon meal offering, when we send out a bit of food for them, we recite this verse:

> The great p'eng, the golden-winged bird,
> And all the ghosts and spirits in the wilds,
> The rakshasa ghost-mother and her children--
> May they all be filled with sweet dew.

And we give the p'eng birds their food.

From that time on, the p'eng birds did not eat the dragons. Nevertheless, they managed to eat most of them and now only a few dragons remain. There are only four or five dragons left, one in each ocean or so, and they are rarely seen. The great p'eng birds took refuge with the Triple Jewel, and you may have seen their pictures in various books. However, although the p'eng birds are huge, they have spiritual penetrations and can make themselves small. They are more or less like the dragons in that respect. Dragons can perform transformations themselves and they are p'eng bird food, so of course the spiritual penetrations of the p'engs must be inconceivable. Don't think that the spiritual penetrations of dragons are so special, because those of the great p'eng are even greater.

THERE WERE FOUR GARUDA KINGS: THE GARUDA KING GREAT MAJESTY...He soars into empty space and fills the heavens and covers the earth with his majestic, awe-inspiring presence.

THE GARUDA KING GREAT BODY...Garuda kings are big enough to begin with. But this one is massive, bigger than the average garuda. Even he is not as big as THE GARUDA KING GREAT FULLNESS...He's so big that when he lands on the ocean, he displaces every drop of water in it, completely filling it.

There was yet another GARUDA KING called AS-YOU-WILL...as you like it, just as your heart wishes it to be, everything's just the way it should be. If he wants to eat dragons, they jump right into his beak. He doesn't even have to flap his wings at the ocean to get his dragon meals because as soon as he thinks about eating a dragon they pop right into his mouth. He just says, "Here! Here! I want to eat you!" and the dragons obediently comply for the Garuda King As-You-Will.

EACH WITH HIS RETINUE OF SEVERAL HUNDREDS OF THOUSANDS OF FOLLOWERS...a great number of them, and they all came to join the Dharma Flower Assembly.

Sutra:

THERE WAS VAIDEHI'S SON, THE KING AJATASHATRU, WITH HIS RETINUE OF SEVERAL HUNDREDS OF THOUSANDS OF FOLLOWERS.[E8] EACH MADE OBEISANCE TO THE BUDDHA'S FEET, WITHDREW TO ONE SIDE, AND SAT DOWN.[C2]

Outline:

E8. the humans
C2. summation

Commentary:

VAIDEHI is Sanskrit and means "consider."[1] Vaidehi was the wife of King Bimbisara of Magadha and their son was named AJATASHATRU. Ajatashatru means "hated before birth."[2] Before he was born, many inauspicious events took place. His name also means "fingerless,"[3] because when he was born his mother hated him so intensely that she bit off one of his little fingers.

Ajatashatru committed every evil deed, including all of the Five Rebellious Acts--that is, unpardonable offenses. He: 1) killed his father, 2) killed his mother, 3) killed an Arhat--a certified sage--4) shed the Buddha's blood--one time he threw a rock at the Buddha and it hit him on the foot and drew his blood--and 5) broke up the harmony of the Sangha. Those of you who have read the *Sutra of Sixteen Contemplations* will know the causes and conditions surrounding these events.

As a Prince, Ajatashatru was Devadatta's friend. Although Devadatta was the Buddha's cousin, he did everything he could to slander and ruin the Buddha,

---

1 思惟 -*ssu wei.*

2 未生怨 -*wei sheng yüan.*

3 無指 -*wu chih.*

behaving in an entirely strange and sinister fashion. Knowing that the Prince was heir to the throne, he cultivated his friendship and then persuaded him to kill his own father and mother so that the Prince could become King. Then, as King, he could have the Buddha killed, too, and Devadatta would be proclaimed as the "new Buddha." As the "new King" and the "new Buddha," the two of them could then together rule the world. So, despite the Buddha's awesome virtue, his own cousin was his bitter enemy.

Acting on Devadatta's ill advice, the Prince had his father imprisoned in a dungeon surrounded by seven walls. One had to pass through seven doors in seven walls to get in. It was impregnable, stronger than even iron or brass. He denied him food and water until he was on the verge of starvation. Such were the Prince's commands, and, with the King in jail, no one dared protest them.

Because Vaidehi loved her husband very much, she managed to sneak in to see him. In those days, women wore head ornaments studded with hollow beads. Vaidehi filled the beads with grape juice. Wearing them on her head, she stole in to see her husband and gave him the juice to drink.

What kind of a son had they given birth to who would want to starve his own father to death?

When the King had drunk the grape juice, the two of them sat there in the jail cell and began to cry. The King thought, "Shakyamuni Buddha is a greatly enlightened one, complete with all-knowledge. He certainly knows how I have been suffering here in jail. He should rescue me!" Just as he thought of the Buddha, the Buddha knew, and he sent Great Maudgalyayana, his disciple, to transmit the eight precepts to him. The Buddha also sent the Venerable Purnamaitrayaniputra to speak the Dharma to him every day, and teach him how to cultivate, and apply effort.

After twenty-one days, the King, despite his wretched condition, was peaceful and full of bliss from having heard the Dharma. When King Ajatashatru inquired of the jailor as to his father's condition, the jailor told him what had been going on. The Prince was furious with his mother, and having cursed her violently, he picked up a sword and was about to kill her. He was stopped by two court ministers who said, "We have read that many evil kings have killed their fathers and enthroned themselves, but we have never heard of a single one who has killed his mother. Such a deed would defile the caste of the Kshatriyas we cannot remain standing behind someone who would commit such an act. Great King, take heed! Do not kill your mother!"

Hearing this, the King was sorry and put his sword away, but he nevertheless went ahead and locked his mother in jail. She suffered greatly and bowed in the direction of Mount Grdhrakuta, where the Buddha resided. Then the Buddha himself came to see her and she wept saying, "This world is too full of suffering. I don't wish to dwell in it any more. I want to find a better world where I won't have to undergo so much pain. My own son wants to kill me. What is the good of remaining in this world?" She asked the Buddha to point out a bright road for her rebirth in another world. The Buddha spoke the *Sutra of Sixteen Contemplations* which are sixteen methods of contemplation teaching one how to seek rebirth in the Western Land of Ultimate Bliss by reciting the name, "Namo Amitabha Buddha." Vaidehi and her husband cultivated that Dharma accordingly, and later were reborn there.

King Ajatashatru killed his mother and father, created disharmony within the Sangha, killed Arhats, and shed the Buddha's blood. These Five Rebellious acts basically cannot be repented of. There is no way to save one who has committed them. However later, realizing his mistakes, he stood before the Buddhas, wept bitter tears, and brought forth deep repentance. Because he completely reformed himself, the Buddha relieved him of his offenses. Thus he was able to attend the Dharma Flower assembly. King Ajatashatru was the foulest and most evil of men, but he later reformed his faults and went towards the good. He came to the assembly with HIS RETINUE OF SEVERAL HUNDREDS OF THOUSANDS OF FOLLOWERS, kings, great ministers, and the common people, all of whom came to hear the Sutra.

EACH BOWED WITH HIS HEAD AT THE BUDDHA'S FEET, WITHDREW TO ONE SIDE, AND SAT DOWN. The above-mentioned gods, dragons and the entire eightfold division, as well as all the people, bowed to the Buddha. Then they returned to their proper places and sat down.

Sutra:

AT THAT TIME THE WORLD HONORED ONE, HAVING BEEN CIRCUMAMBULATED BY THE FOUR-FOLD ASSEMBLY, PRESENTED

A2B1C1D1

WITH OFFERINGS, HONORED, VENERATED, AND PRAISED...

Outline: A2.specific explanantion of roots and branches of Sutra
B1.branches division: opening provisional to reveal real,(from here up to and including Chap 14).
C1.intro. section (from here to end Chap 1.)
D1. gathering of the assembly

Commentary:

Bhikshus, Bhikshunis, Upasakas, and Upasikas are the four assemblies of disciples. It may also be said they are 1)the initiating assembly, 2) the interlocutory assembly, 3) the influential assembly, and 4) the assembly which creates affinities.

Bhikshus, men who have left home, and Bhikshunis, women who have left home, are the two assemblies of left-home disciples. Upasakas are male lay people; Upasikas are female lay people. Together they make up the two assemblies of those at home. These are the four assemblies of disciples. Upasaka and Upasika are Sanskrit words which mean "men closely related in affairs," and "women closely related in affairs," respectively. They draw near the monasteries and the temples and the Triple Jewel to aid and assist them in their affairs. They make up the two "outer assemblies,"--the Dharma Protectors.

Bhikshu has three meanings: 1) mendicant, 2) frightener of Mara, and 3) destroyer of evil. Bhikshuni also has these three meanings. They are the two "inner-assemblies"--the Buddha's retinue, the assembly which practices the Dharma.

As to the second set of four assemblies, the first, the initiatory assembly understands the Buddha's purpose. Their causal affinities have already matured so that they initiate through their questions the Buddha's explanation of points of doctrine. They have wisdom and the ability to devise provisional methods, that is, the wisdom to set up clever expedient devices. They have a mirror-like wisdom which enables them to "reflect" the potentials of beings present and to know the appropriate time a given Dharma should be spoken. Then they take the initiative and ask the Buddha to speak Dharma, acting as the initiatory assembly.

The second is the interlocutory assembly. These are the ones whom the Buddha directly addresses in speaking the Dharma. For example, in the *Vajra Sutra*, Subhuti is the interlocutory assembly. In the *Amitabha Sutra*, Shariputra is the interlocutor, along with all the other Great Bodhisattvas and Great Arhats. The other Sutras all have their interlocutory assemblies as well. In the *Shurangama Sutra,* for example, Ananda is the interlocutor, along with the twenty-five sages.

The third is the influential assembly. Those in this assembly already understand the Buddhadharma, and they do not necessarily need to hear it preached. These great Bodhisattvas have already frequently heard the Buddha speak Dharma, but they still come to support the Dharma assembly and act as an influence on the others who see them and think, "The great Bodhisattvas have come to hear the Sutra," and so they too delight in listening. Without the great Bodhisattvas in the audience, they might have thoughts of disbelief. "Nobody comes to listen to the Sutra," they might think. "Probably the Sutras the Buddha speaks are meaningless." But when the great Bodhisattvas come to hear the Sutra, the Arhats, the Bhikshus and Bhikshunis, Upasakas and Upasikas see them and think, "The great Bodhisattvas have come!" Their hearts grow faithful and sincere. They stare unblinkingly; their spirits are in rapt attention and they clean out their ears and listen respectfully. Their eyes don't turn away; their spirits are fixed attentively, and they listen to the Buddha preach the Dharma as if they had just washed their ears clean--with the utmost reverence. Why? Because they have been influenced by the influential assembly which has secretly aided them in bringing forth the resolve to listen.

The fourth is the assembly which creates affinities. They feel that they have no Dharma-affinities with people to speak of, and so they go to the Dharma Assembly to create them.

What is meant by "creating affinities?"

In America there are few Dharma Assemblies, but in China Sutras are lectured in many Dharma Assemblies. People will buy candy and give each member of the audience perhaps three pieces, or five, or ten, dividing it between them; and then they all eat candy. Or they may buy cookies for everyone. First, they offer them to the Buddha, next to the Dharma, then to the Sangha; they save some for everyone giving it to them in order to create affinities. Others buy fruit or other things which people like to eat in order to establish this connection.

Why do they wish to create affinities?

It is because they feel they have no affinities with people. They don't get along with their relatives, and their "friends" don't care for them. Nobody likes them at all in fact and so they want to create affinities with others by giving them food or small gifts.

Some give money. In China, the audiences consist mainly of those who have left home, not lay people. The lay people may buy cloth or other necessities to present as offerings to those who have left home. This is the assembly which creates affinities with those in the Dharma Assembly, the last of the Four-fold assembly of disciples.

In the Dharma Flower Assembly, the Four-fold Assembly was present in its entirety.

HAVING CIRCUMAMBULATED...What is meant by "circumambulated?"

In Chinese it is made up of two words which means "to encircle" and "to wind around." It means to walk around something in a circle as we did when we installed the Buddha image and then walked around it reciting, "Namo Amitabha Buddha." In Buddhism, as a matter of ceremony, one circumambulates the Buddha three times, keeping the Buddha to one's right, in other words in a clockwise circle.

And after this, everyone should remember that when we have a gathering we should stand in line and progress clockwise in an orderly fashion when serving ourselves lunch. If everyone goes in opposite directions, collisions will occur and everyone will feel crowded and pushed. If everyone procedes clockwise in an orderly fashion, no one will bump heads.

After the Buddha realized Buddhahood, people did not know how to pay reverence to him. So then some gods from the Five Pure Dwelling Heavens transformed into people and appeared before the Buddha. They circumambulated him three times to the right, bowed in worship, retreated to one side, and then sat down in order to serve as an example--to show the humans how to properly worship the Buddha. This is the meaning of "circumambulate."

HAVING BEEN PRESENTED WITH OFFERINGS...Not only did they circumambulate the Buddha and bow before him, but they also made offerings to him. So many people! What did they give him? They presented him with an offering of a true, respectful heart. So it says, HONORED, VENERATED. HONORED means that they put their five limbs--knees, elbows and forehead--on the ground, prostrating themselves in worship. In Buddhism , bowing in this way is the highest form of paying respect.

They venerated the Buddha and they also PRAISED

him. We are praising the Buddha when we recite Sutras or verses, as for example, the verse in praise of Amitabha Buddha which begins, "Amitabha's body is the color of gold./The splendor of his hallmarks has no peer..."

Another verse goes,

> In the heavens and below there is
> no one like the Buddha;
> In the worlds of the ten directions
> he is without equal.
> I have seen everything in the world
> that there is to see,
> And there's nothing in it
> that compares with the Buddha.

All the praises of the Buddha, the World Honored One, lauding him as most venerable, honored and esteemed, are spoken to praise and laud him.

To say a few more words about creating affinities: It is extremely important to do so, for if you do not, no matter how well intended you are towards someone they will be displeased with you. Why is this? Because no affinity exists between you.

Long ago, there was an extremely intelligent Dharma Master would could memorize the Sutras after simply reading them once. He was not as dull-witted as I am; I have to read them three times before I remember them. He could remember them after the first reading. He could also lecture on all the Sutras; he did it so well that, because of his unobstructed eloquence, even the gods came to hear him. However, although the gods came, no people came to hear him. Why did the gods attend? Because his lectures were just too wonderful. Why didn't any people show up? Because he simply had no affinities with people. Since he was wise, he understood the reason, the workings of cause and effect behind it, and he went to live in the mountains. He bought a lot of rice and sat in the mountains and fed the birds. From morning to night he recited the Great Compassion Mantra and the Shurangama Mantra over the rice and contemplated all the birds thinking, "All the birds who eat my rice shall in their next life become people, casting off their beast and bird bodies."

He continued to spend his days feeding all the birds on the mountain and the birds spread the word among themselves that there was food. The news passed down the grapevine and soon they came in great flocks to eat the rice. He did this for twenty years and then went back down the mountain and began lecturing on Sutras again. This time, things were entirely different. The young people in the area flocked to listen to his lectures. Not only did they listen, but they were extremely respectful of him and honored him with five-point prostrations. They were obedient and did exactly as they were told, completely faithful to him.

And where did the young people come from?

They were the birds who had cast off their bird-bodies and become humans. Because they had been nourished by the Dharma Master's Dharma food and obtained such benefit, as people, they did not forget the kindness he had shown them and came to support him.

Here, we have three masters--four including myself--and when I lecture, I don't care if anyone listens or not. But in the future if no one comes to listen to your lectures, you can go feed the birds. After you've fed them, there will be plenty of people to listen to you.

Because the Dharma Master created affinities with the birds, when the birds became people they came to hear the Buddhadharma. So everyone should pay attention to this point and seek to create affinities with everyone. This is why you should not lose your tempers or rage at people. If you do that, you will have no affinities with them and you'll turn into "loner" Dharma Masters. No one will believe in you, and wherever you go, no one will make offerings to you. In the future, you may even starve to death, but it's not for sure.

Today, I will explain "making offerings." Offerings should be made with a true heart, with a sincere heart.

What is a true heart? And what is a sincere heart?

With a true heart, you give up that which you cannot give up. That's the true heart. It means giving up that which you love most. If you can renounce it, that's the true heart.

What is a sincere heart? A sincere heart is an unscattered heart. With a sincere heart, when you do something you do it straightforwardly, with great earnestness. It also means to "turn your thoughts to one," to have a single heart--not two hearts--when making offerings.

Long ago there was a beggar who saw that everyone made offerings to the Triple Jewel in order to foster merit and virtue. He thought that, although he didn't have much money, he would use all the money he had to buy a pint of oil and present it as an offering to the permanent dwelling, the temple, the Triple Jewel--the Buddha, Dharma, and Sangha.

The Abbot of the temple had attained the Penetration of the Heavenly Eye, and when the beggar arrived at the temple gate, the Abbot was there to greet him. He escorted him back to the temple, inviting him to his own quarters, and was most attentive to him. He even asked him to stay for lunch.

Not long after that, another man who was very rich sent a *lou* of oil, about two or three hundred pounds, several hundred times the amount the beggar had given as an offering to the Triple Jewel. However, the Abbot merely sent the Guest Prefect to greet him and did not go himself. The monks and novices did not understand his actions and asked him, "Why did you go to escort a poor beggar who gave only a pint of oil and ask him to your own quarters to eat lunch, and then when someone else sent three hundred pints, three hundred times the beggar's gift, you did not attend to him yourself? We are quite puzzled about this and would ask you, Abbot, please to explain."

The Abbot said, "You don't understand. The poor man who gave one pint as an offering used all the money he had to buy it. Would you say he was sincere or not? The one who bought three hundred pints was wealthy. He not only could have bought three hundred pints, but 30,000 pints, or even more, and so for him, the offering was nothing special at all. The poor man with a true heart renounced that which is difficult to renounce. He exhausted his entire worldly resources to make the offering. If he were not a great Dharma Protector, could he have done something like that? That is why I went to greet him and invited him to lunch. The other man was terribly wealthy and his gift of three hundred pints was just like one hair from nine cows. Why should I have looked after him?"

From this we can see that in making offerings to the Triple Jewel you must renounce what is hard to renounce and give what is hard to give, then the merit and virtue accrued is great. Those who are wealthy did not gain their wealth in this present life only. Because in previous lives they were able to renounce that which is hard to renounce and do what is hard to do, they are wealthy in their present life."

This is what the Abbot said to the novices and monks by way of explanation, and after that they understood the principle that when making offerings to the Triple Jewel, one must use a sincere and true heart.

HONORED...One does honor with both the body and the mind. It should not be that the body does honor and the mind does not. Nor should it be that the mind does honor and the body does not. Both the body and mind must do honor, within and without--a unity. That is what is meant by "honored." VENERATED means not to treat with disrespect. PRAISE means to laud the Buddha with verses--ten million of them, telling how rare the Buddha is.

Sutra:

...FOR THE SAKE OF THE BODHISATTVAS, SPOKE A GREAT VEHICLE SUTRA NAMED THE LIMITLESS PRINCIPLES, A DHARMA FOR INSTRUCTING BODHISATTVAS OF WHICH THE BUDDHA IS PROTECTIVE AND MINDFUL.[D2E1F1]

Outline: D2. manifestation of portents
E1. six portents in this world system
F1. portent of speaking Dharma

Commentary:

FOR THE SAKE OF THE BODHISATTVAS he SPOKE A GREAT VEHICLE SUTRA. The Sutra was titled *The Sutra of Limitless Principles*. The Buddha spoke it before he spoke *The Dharma Flower Sutra*. He spoke *The Sutra of Limitless Principles* as a DHARMA FOR INSTRUCTING BODHISATTVAS, OF WHICH THE BUDDHA IS PROTECTIVE AND MINDFUL. At that time Six Portents were manifest.

What were the Six Portents?

1. The portent of speaking Dharma;
2. The portent of entering samadhi;
3. The portent of the raining of flowers;
4. The portent of the shaking of the earth.
5. The portent of the rejoicing of the assembly; and
6. The portent of emitting light.

Most likely, these are the Six Portents. I may be mistaken, but I don't believe I am. I don't think my memory is quite that bad. So those are the Six Portents and we are now discussing the first, the Portent of the Speaking of Dharma.

Someone may ask, "But the Buddha very often speaks the Dharma and enters samadhi. Why have such common occurrences suddenly become auspicious portents?"

This speaking of Dharma differs from that of other times. This time, after he spoke the Dharma, the Buddha entered samadhi. Having entered samadhi, there was a rain of flowers. After the rain of flowers, there was an earthquake. After the earthquake, everyone rejoiced and the Buddha emitted the white hair-mark light. These all betoken an extraordinary circumstance; thus, they are called the Six Portents.

FOR THE SAKE OF all the great BODHISATTVAS, SPOKE A GREAT VEHICLE SUTRA..."The Bodhisattvas" refers to the eighty-thousand Mahasattvas present in the Dharma Flower Assembly. They were all great Bodhisattvas who listened to a Great Vehicle Sutra.

What is a Great Vehicle Sutra?

These are the Seven Qualities of the Great Vehicle, as cultivated by Great Vehicle Bodhisattvas:

1. The greatness of the Dharma. The entire Tripitaka, with its Twelve Divisions of Sutra Texts, is contained within the Great Vehicle Sutras. The Small Vehicle does not include the Great Vehicle, but the Great Vehicle does include the Small Vehicle. So, first of all, the Dharma is Great.

2. The greatness of the heart brought forth. What is meant by bringing forth the great heart? It is to bring forth the great heart of Bodhi, not the small heart of Bodhi, so that, from the level of a common person, right up until the realization of Buddhahood, one never retreats. An unretreating heart is a great Bodhi heart.

3. Understanding the Great Storehouse. This refers to understanding the doctrines contained within the Great Vehicle Bodhisattva Storehouse. The Great Storehouse is the Bodhisattva Storehouse. Understanding the doctrines of the Bodhisattva Storehouse and cultivating according to the Dharmas of the Bodhisattva Storehouse is to understand the Great Storehouse.

4. The greatness of purity. Bodhisattvas who study the Great Vehicle can see the Way and their hearts are great, immaculate, pure, and clear.

5. The greatness of the adornment. With what do they adorn themselves? Blessings and wisdom. They adorn themselves with blessings and virtue, wisdom and intelligence.

6. The greatness of the time. They pass through three great asankheya kalpas. The sixth may also be

explained as the greatness of the cause.

7. The greatness of the perfection. Perfection refers to the fulfillment of the Six Perfections and the Ten Thousand Conducts. They adorn themselves with the characteristics and obtain the fruit of Bodhi. So this may also be explained as the greatness of the fruit or result.

Because of these seven qualities, it is called the Great Vehicle.

Everyone says, "The Great Vehicle? Why that's just Mahayana!"

"Well what is Mahayana anyway? How big is it?" I ask. "How many qualities of greatness are connected with the Great Vehicle?" And they don't know.

Having heard the Seven Qualities of the Great Vehicle, we should note that they differ somewhat from the Seven Qualities of a Mahasattva which were previously enumerated. So it's the Great Vehicle spoken for the sake of the Bodhisattvas. SPEAK means to expound. SUTRA is a text. The word Sutra has already been discussed; it is a Sanskrit word which is interpreted as a "tallying text" for it tallies above with the principles of all the Buddhas and below with the opportunities for teaching living beings. It also has many other meanings which need not be reiterated here.

CALLED THE LIMITLESS PRINCIPLES. Before Shakyamuni Buddha spoke *The Dharma Flower Sutra,* he spoke a Sutra called *The Limitless Principles*. Limitless Principles means that the principles are uncountable. However,

> "Where does the limitless come from?"
> It comes from the limited.
> "And where does the limited come from?"
> From the one principle.
> "Where does the one principle come from?"
> It comes from the markless.
> "Where does the markless come from?"
> It comes from the Actual Mark.

Therefore it is said, "The Actual Mark is unmarked." The limitless principles come from the limited principles and the limited principles come from the one principle, the primary principle.

"Where does the one principle come from?"

It comes from the markless, the markless principle. The markless principle comes from the Actual Mark principle.

The Actual Mark is unmarked. Which mark does it not have? It has no mark of birth-and-death. The Actual Mark is also not unmarked, for it has no mark of Nirvana. Without the marks of birth-and-death or Nirvana, it is the Actual Mark.

However, there is nothing which is not marked by it. Everything, for example, the limitless principles, all come from it, from the Actual Mark. For this reason, *The Sutra of Limitless Principles* is also *The Sutra of the Actual Mark Principles.*

Previously, I have explained the word "all," as "one." Why? For this reason: The one is limitless and the limitless is one. In fact, there isn't even *one*. That's the Actual Mark.

"Where does the one come from?"

It comes from the absence of one.

Basically, there isn't a "one," but people deliberately stick another head atop their heads and come up with a "one." When there's nothing to do, they go out and find ways to be busy. Basically, there is no problem at all, but people fuss around and find problems to take care of.

What is the function of THE SUTRA OF LIMITLESS PRINCIPLES which the Buddha now speaks? It is A DHARMA FOR INSTRUCTING Great Vehicle BODHISATTVAS, a method for teaching and transforming them, instructing Bodhisattvas in the methods used to practice the Bodhisattva Way. The Bodhisattvas study the Great Vehicle Dharma, OF WHICH THE BUDDHA IS PROTECTIVE AND MINDFUL. Basically the Buddha had no intention of speaking this Dharma, and he remained silent for a long time not discussing it. Why? Because the Buddha is PROTECTIVE AND MINDFUL of this Great Vehicle Dharma. He had no intention of speaking it. If he did speak the Great Vehicle Dharma, it might cause all living beings to disbelieve it; certainly, it would not be appropriate to their potentials. Since it was inappropriate, the Buddha waited a long time before speaking this dharma.

This has been a discussion of the first of the Six Portents: The speaking of Dharma.

Sutra:

AFTER THE BUDDHA HAD SPOKEN THIS SUTRA, HE SAT IN FULL LOTUS AND ENTERED THE SAMADHI OF THE STATION OF

LIMITLESS PRINCIPLES, BODY AND MIND UNMOVING. F2

Outline:

F2. portent of entering samadhi

Commentary:

This is the second portent, that of Entering Samadhi.

AFTER THE BUDDHA HAD SPOKEN THIS SUTRA, after Shakyamuni Buddha had spoken this Sutra...

"Which Sutra? Was it *The Wonderful Dharma Lotus Flower Sutra?*"

No. It was *The Sutra of Limitless Principles*, which is the Dharma for instructing Bodhisattvas of which the Buddha is protective and mindful. Since he had spoken the Sutra, one might expect him to take a rest. He did not rest, however. HE SAT IN FULL LOTUS...The lotus posture may be a full-lotus or a half-lotus, depending on whether both or only one of the legs are pulled up over the opposite thigh.

"Why sit in full-lotus?"

It aids you in your cultivation of the Way. The lotus position is also called the "vajra sitting."

No doubt you have all heard me relate the account of the "ghost-pressured Dharma Master" and so I need not repeat it now, but I will talk about the full-lotus position.

When practicing Ch'an, if you sit in full lotus, then you are less likely to doze off. That's the first advantage.

"What is meant by dozing off?"

It means that you sit there and sleep! When you sit in full lotus, you won't fall over as it creates a solid balance beneath you. It promotes the easy development of your samadhi power. One meditates with the hope of obtaining samadhi power; the lotus position is helpful in this regard. When your samadhi power comes forth, your wisdom power will be increased, because wisdom power comes from samadhi power. Samadhi power comes from precept power. When you sit in full-lotus, upright and sedate, that is your own inherent precept substance. From the precepts comes samadhi, from samadhi comes wisdom. Precepts, samadhi and wisdom, the Three Non-outflow Studies, are born from full-lotus sitting.

Another thing: When you sit in full-lotus, all the gods and dragons and the rest of the eight-fold division protect you. With the gods, dragons and others of the eight-fold assembly protecting you, the deviant demons, outside ways, weird demons and strange ghosts--all the demon kings retreat far into the distance; they run far away. Therefore the Vajra full-lotus sitting is a most important factor in cultivating the Way.

When I was in Manchuria the following event occurred: there was a dharma teacher of an outside-way who had over three thousand disciples, but he knew that he himself had no Way-karma, no Way-power. For this reason, he went everywhere, seeking the Way. He didn't dare let his disciples know what he was doing, because if they knew he did not have the Way, they would no longer believe in him. He transmitted an outside-way dharma-door and at the same time traveled everywhere looking for the Way. He looked for two or three years but still did not meet a bright-eyed learned advisor.

Later, he met me. How did that happen? I had known him some time previously, but had not seen him for a long time. He had heard of me when I was sitting beside my mother's grave as an act of filial piety. He had heard of me, but he had never met me. One day, I went to his house.The night before, his nephew had had a dream in which he saw me, even though he had never actually met me and did not know me. When he saw me in his dream, he didn't know why, but he sought the Way from me. His name was Kuan Chan Hai. He heard me say, "You can't seek the Way; you can't cultivate the Way. Why? Because you are wearing a skin of foul retribution on your body; you have a skin of offense karma."

He persisted in asking me for the Way, and then, I reached out my hand, and from the top of his head, pulled an entire layer of skin off of him. I threw it on the ground and when he looked at it, he saw it was the skin of a pig. Then in his dream I said, "Now that I have pulled off your skin of foul retribution, you can cultivate the Way."

The day after the dream, I went to his house, for I knew his uncle, Kuan Chung Hsi. He said, "Uncle, who is he? I dreamt last night that he came here and pulled a pig skin off of my body."

The uncle said, "He is the one who cultivates filial piety from La Lin, Hsi Huang Ch'in. He's well known as the Filial Son." The nephew was delighted and related to his uncle the particulars of his dream. His uncle had the Way uppermost in his mind and he too, rejoiced. "The Way has been sent to our home!" he said. "We should quickly seek the Way from him!" The two of them knelt before me and refused to get up; they wanted me to accept them as their teacher. I was 23 or 24 at the time, twenty-three.

I said, "I can't be anyone's teacher. I don't have the Way; I am seeking the Way myself at present."

"Be compassionate," they pleaded. "We both know that you are a cultivator of the Way and we must bow to you as our teacher!"

I said, "Don't be nervous. I will take you around everywhere to seek for the Way. When you meet someone you feel is qualified to be your teacher, you may bow to him. Don't bow to me as your teacher," and I refused to accept them.

Today, we will just speak this far.

Yesterday we were talking about sitting in full lotus. Kuan Chung Hsi and his nephew Kuan Chan Hai had sought the Way from me. Kuan Chung Hsi had over three thousand disciples, but he had no method by which to end his own birth and death. He very nervously went everywhere seeking the Way. After several years, probably about three, he had not found it. When I went to his home, his nephew had had a special dream, and so he knew who I was. The two of them knelt before me begging me for the Way.

I said, "I don't have the Way, but I can help you find it. Come along with me and we shall search everywhere for it--in all the temples and monasteries, or wherever there are cultivators, and when you meet someone who suits you, you can take him as your teacher. They came along with me, and we traveled to all the well-known places where people cultivated the Way. I introduced them to the cultivators, but in all cases they were not satisfied with them and returned again to seek the Way from me.

I said, "I don't have the Way. All I can do is instruct you in a method of cultivation. What method? The full-lotus sitting. Try it out and see if you can sit in full-lotus."

When the uncle tried it, his right leg stuck straight up in the air, over six inches off the bench. This was because he was one of the native mountain people and they had the peculiar trait of having very large kneecaps. They were known as "big kneecap bones." Although it was very difficult, still, he could get into that position and sit, so I told him to practice sitting that way and then I left.

Over seventy days later I returned to his house. His kneecaps had been quite large to begin with, but now they had swollen even bigger. They were so swollen that he couldn't even walk. In Manchuria, iron wheeled carts are used for transportation, and the wheels are about two inches wide. They make two-inch ruts in the roads. Kuan Chung Hsi was unable to step over a cart rut, his legs were so swollen. Seeing this, I felt the practice was too severe, so I said to him, "You shouldn't practice sitting in full-lotus. It's something you probably just can't manage. You can stop practicing it."

He said, "Only if I die will I discontinue practicing this sitting. As long as I haven't died, I don't care how swollen my legs get, I shall continue to practice, because if in cultivating the Way one is not able to bear pain, how can one possibly expect to succeed? If I can't even discipline myself to sit in full-lotus, how can I possibly cultivate the Way? I am determined to accomplish it."

I said, "If you're going to be that way, I won't pay any attention to you. If you practice, practice! If you don't, don't. Do as you please," and I left.

After one hundred days--the previous time it had been seventy days--I again returned to his house and saw that he could now walk. His legs were no longer swollen. I asked him, "Have you quit practicing the full-lotus position?"

"No," he said, "and now, not only has the swelling gone down, but my legs no longer hurt. Both my legs lie on the bench, they don't stick up in the air anymore, and they don't hurt."

I said, "Those with determination know success. Your strong resolve brought about your accomplishment." I then taught him the methods used to cultivate Dhyana. He practiced them, cultivating the skill of sitting in Dhyana meditation.

His nephew, Kuan Chan Hai, had traveled with his uncle everywhere seeking the Way. He sought it for three years, and then two more--five years in all--and still had not found a teacher. He was extremely well-disposed toward me and always gave me gifts on New Year's and other holidays, perhaps good things to eat or other things, a great many of them. I knew he thought well of me.

Once, I took him to the Three Conditions Temple where I was staying, to meet the Abbot. I had assumed he would bow to the Abbot as his teacher, but he didn't. We started out for his house. About half-way there, we passed through a small forest. Suddenly, he grabbed my sleeve and knelt down. I said, "What are you doing?"

He said, "I have traveled for so many years and of all the people I have seen, I believe in you the most. Now I must bow to you as my teacher."

Seeing him in such a state, tugging at my sleeve, I pretended to get angry. I jerked my arm away, turned around, and stomped off. I walked about a quarter of a mile and turned around to see him still kneeling there. He hadn't risen and tears were rolling down his face. I walked back and stood before him. "What are you doing?" I said.

"You *must* accept me as your disciple," he sobbed, "otherwise, I'm not going to get up. I'll stay here kneeling until I die."

"Oh? Well, kneel until you die; that would be the very best thing you could do!" I said. "If you want to die kneeling, go ahead, but nobody's ordering you to do it. Kneel all you want, but I am leaving," and I left again. I walked about one third of a mile and turned around to see him still kneeling; he hadn't risen. At that point my heart felt a slight twinge, and I returned and said, "Very well, I'll accept you." He was the first disciple I received in Manchuria.

Before taking refuge, he was a vegetarian. After taking refuge, he practiced sleeping sitting up. He never lay down, never allowed his ribs to touch a mat or bed. He also never ate after noon.

After his uncle had been cultivating for roughly five years, he knew himself on what day he was going to go to rebirth (die). He addressed the members of his household saying, "On such and such a day I am going to leave. You must not cry or grieve. Most of all, I would like to see the Filial Son. If he could come, that would be the very best. But I do not know where he is at present and have no way to send him a letter. Everything else, I can let go of, but this one wish alone remains unfulfilled."

When the day arrived, he sat upright, and without any illness he died sitting. After his death, many people in his village had a very strange dream: they all dreamt that they saw two young lads dressed in dark robes, in front of him, leading him off to the West. This is what his wife later told me.

Sitting in full-lotus is a most important factor in cultivation of the Way. If you can master it, it will be extremely beneficial for you in your cultivation.

Having finished speaking *The Sutra of Limitless Principles,* Shakyamuni Buddha SAT IN FULL LOTUS AND ENTERED THE SAMADHI OF THE STATION OF LIMITLESS

PRINCIPLES, that sort of samadhi. To enter into the SAMADHI OF LIMITLESS PRINCIPLES is also just to enter into the Actual Mark Samadhi, where only the Real Mark remains.

BODY AND MIND UNMOVING...Someone may ask, "When the body does not move, we can observe this, but how can one know if the mind is unmoving?"

If your body does not move, then your mind may also be unmoving. Once your body moves, your mind moves as well. Therefore, those who have entered samadhi do not move either in body or mind. The mind, or heart, being discussed here (in Chinese "mind" and "heart" are represented by the same character) is not the lump of flesh within your chest. Whether or not you enter samadhi it is unmoving. So the text says, BODY AND MIND UNMOVING. Why is it unmoving? Because the Buddha has entered samadhi. His body and mind have obtained the realm of the clear pure basic source. For this reason, the body and mind are unmoving. This has been a discussion of the second, the Portent of Entering Samadhi.

Sutra:

AT THAT TIME THERE FELL FROM THE HEAVENS A RAIN OF MANDARAVA FLOWERS, MAHAMANDARAVA FLOWERS, MANJUSHAKA FLOWERS, AND MAHAMANJUSHAKA FLOWERS, WHICH WERE SCATTERED UPON THE BUDDHA AND THE ENTIRE GREAT ASSEMBLY.[F3]

Outline:

F3. portent of rain of flowers

Commentary:

This passage of text is the third, the Portent of the Raining of Flowers. AT THAT TIME, when Shakyamuni Buddha had entered samadhi, body and mind unmoving, at that very same time THERE FELL FROM THE HEAVENS A RAIN, falling down out of the sky, of MANDARAVA FLOWERS. Mandarava is a Sanskrit word. Mandarava flowers are interpreted as "white flowers,"[1] or as "flowers which go along with one's wish."[2] MAHAMANDARAVA flowers are the big variety of white flowers.

---

1 白華 -*pai hua.*
2 適意華 -*shih i hua.*

MANJUSHAKA FLOWERS are "red flowers."[1] MAHAMANJUSHAKA FLOWERS are huge deep red flowers. WHICH WERE SCATTERED UPON THE BUDDHA AND THE ENTIRE GREAT ASSEMBLY..All present in the Dharma Assembly received the offering of flowers.

"What does the rain from heaven of these four kinds of flowers represent?"

They represent the Dwellings, Practices, Dedications, and Grounds. In the *Shurangama Sutra* we have already heard about the Ten Dwellings. They are represented by the Mandarava Flowers. The Mahamandarava Flowers represent the Ten Practices. The Manjushaka flowers represent the Ten Dedications. The Mahamanjushaka flowers represent the Ten Grounds. Thus, the four kinds of flowers represent these four sets of positions, the four Bodhisattva levels.

WHICH WERE SCATTERED UPON THE BUDDHA, the flowers drifted down and settled upon the Buddha and upon THE ENTIRE GREAT ASSEMBLY as well. THE ENTIRE GREAT ASSEMBLY : In cultivation everyone must pass through the Ten Dwellings, the Ten Practices, the Ten Dedications, and the Ten Grounds. This, then, has been a discussion of the third, the Portent of the Raining of Flowers.

Sutra:

ALL THE BUDDHA UNIVERSES QUAKED IN SIX WAYS.[F4]

Outline:

F4. portent of shaking of the earth

Commentary:

ALL THE BUDDHA UNIVERSES QUAKED IN SIX WAYS. This is the fourth, the Portent of the Shaking of the Earth. Why was it that all the Buddha universes quaked in six ways? It was because Shakyamuni Buddha was about to speak *The Dharma Flower Sutra*. Before he spoke *The Dharma Flower Sutra*, these various occurrences took place to indicate and point out the great significance of the Sutra. That is why all these states manifested.

ALL THE BUDDHA UNIVERSES refers to all the universes in which there are Buddhas. They all QUAKED IN SIX WAYS. The Six Types of Earthquakes have been

---

1赤華 *-ch'ih hua.*

explained many times and in fact I even quizzed you on them once. Some of you may remember one of them, some two, some three, others four or five, but nobody remembers all six. Now, I am not going to ask you if you know them, I'll just go ahead and tell you again:

The Six Types of Earthquakes are 1) banging, 2) roaring, 3) crackling, 4)shaking, 5) rising, 6) surging. The first three refer to sound; the second three refer to movement, to the visible appearance of the earth as it shakes, rises, and surges. One set is sound; the other is movement.

The Six Types of Earthquakes represent the six organs: eye, ear, nose, tongue, body, and mind. Generally speaking, there are Six Types of Earthquakes, but if one wishes to expand the explanation, there may be said to be Eighteen Types of Earthquakes by virtue of the fact that each of the six have three applications. Three times six, of course, is eighteen, and they represent the eighteen realms of sense. The eighteen realms of sense are composed of the Six Sense Organs, the Six Sense Objects, and the Six Consciousnesses.

How do each of the Six Types of Earthquakes turn into three?

Let's take the fourth, shaking, for example: the first is shaking; the second is universal shaking, and the third is everywhere universal shaking. That's three. Banging works the same way: banging, universal banging, and everywhere universally banging. There's also roaring, universal roaring, and everywhere universal roaring as another three. Crackling, universal crackling, and everywhere universal crackling are another three. Rising, universal rising and everywhere universal rising are another three. Surging, universal surging, and everywhere universal surging are yet another three. That makes eighteen in all.

"What is meant by the set of three?"

"Shaking" refers to shaking in one particular place. "Universal Shaking" is the shaking in one set of Four Continents: Jambudvipa in the south, Uttarakuru in the north, Aparagodaniya in the West, and Purvavideha in the east. When the set of four great continents shake, that is termed "universal shaking."

However "universal shaking" refers to only one set of four continents. "Everywhere Universal Shaking" refers to shaking throughout the entire three thousand great thousand worlds; they all shake. The Six Types of Earthquakes--sound and movement--taking place to the end of empty space and throughout the Dharma Realm is termed "everywhere universal shaking.

The Six Types of Earthquakes also represent the four levels: the Ten Dwellings, the Ten Practices, the Ten Dedications, and the Ten Grounds with the addition of Equal Enlightenment and Wonderful Enlightenment, a total of six positions.

What does the quaking represent?

It represents the breaking up of our ignorance, because as you pass through six levels, the six positions, you break through ignorance six times. Each time you break through it, it diminishes. Thus they are called the Six Types of Earthquakes.

Everyone who sits in Ch'an undergoes these Six Types of Earthquakes. Those who do not sit in Ch'an may also experience them. They represent the six sense organs: eye, ear, nose, tongue, body and mind. These are the six types of earthquakes.

Let's discuss the term "rising." When there is rising in the east, there is sinking in the west. The east rises and the west sinks. The movement begins in the east. The east is associated with wood and wood with the color green. In the human body, the color green is associated with the liver. Thus, the liver is associated with wood. The liver is associated with the eyes and so this deals with the eye organ.

The south is associated with the color red. The south and the color red are associated with the heart and fire. Fire is red and is associated with the human heart. The heart is associated with the tongue, the tongue is red.

The west is associated with white and metal. Within the human body, metal is associated with the lungs. The lungs are white in color. Of the six sense organs, the nose is associated with the lungs.

When the merit of the eyes arises, the afflictions of the nose are wiped away. When the afflictions of the eyes disperse, the merit of the nose arises. Each of the six organs has its own merits. The merits of the eye, ear, nose and tongue are discussed separately later in the Sutra text. They are also discussed in the *Shurangama Sutra*. So when the merit arises, afflictions are wiped away. When afflictions arise, merit is wiped away. So they interact in their quaking.

The north is associated with the color black, water. In the human body the color black is associated with the kidneys. The kidneys are associated with the ear organ. With relation to the ear and tongue: when the merit of the ear arises, the afflictions of the tongue are wiped away. When the merit of the tongue arises, the afflictions of the ear are wiped away. They interrelate with regard to merit and affliction.

The four directions are represented by the body, and the center, by the mind. The body is complete with the four organs and the mind conceptualizes through them. So the Ten Dwellings, the Ten Practices, the Ten Dedications, the Ten Grounds, Equal Enlightenment, and Wonderful Enlightenment are represented by the Six Types of Earthquakes. The eye, ear, nose, tongue, body, and mind are also represented by the Six Types of Earthquakes. The inner quakings are the six organs, the outer quakings are the levels of Bodhisattva practice. Three of the Six refer to movement and three refer to sound. A lot could be said about them, but today we will stop here.

ALL THE BUDDHA WORLDS QUAKED IN SIX WAYS. This is the fourth, The Portent of the Shaking of the Earth. The Six Types of Earthquakes represent quaking at the gates of the six sense organs. The six sense organs--eye, ear, nose, tongue, body and mind--interact to aid one another. One could also say that they have formed themselves into a party, banded together like the *lang* and the *pei*. What is meant by "banded together like the *lang* and the *pei*?" The two animals, the *lang* and the *pei* must be together in order to walk. If they are not together they can't walk. Why? Because the *lang* and the *pei* are unlike ordinary wolves. The *lang* has only fore-legs and the *pei* has only backlegs. The two of them must get together in order to walk. So it is said, "banded together like the *lang* and the *pei*." The eye, ear, nose, tongue, body, and mind--the six sense organs--are also this way. They can do evil deeds and they can also do good deeds. When they run downhill, they can drag your Dharma-body with them into hell, or perhaps into the realm of hungry ghosts, or the animal kingdom. This happens all because the eye, ear, nose, tongue, body, and mind have taken you there.

When one realizes Buddhahood, it is also because of the eye, ear, nose, tongue, body and mind cooperating with each other. They are no longer like the *lang* and the *pei*, dependent upon one another, but the function as a cooperative organization. You help them and they help you. For example, as I said last week, "When the merit of the nose arises, the afflictions of the eyes are wiped away. When the merit of the eyes arises, the afflictions of the nose are wiped away."

"What is meant by the 'afflictions of the eyes' and the 'afflictions of the nose?'"

The afflictions of the eyes: When you see things you like but cannot obtain them, then there is affliction. When you see them you give rise to a heart of greed. Your eyes see them and your heart gives rise to greed, and so this type of affliction is created because of the eyes.

"Then what is meant by the merit of the eyes?"

The merit of the eyes: When your eyes read the Sutras, you think, "The Sutras are truly find. I'm going to read them," and your eyes help your heart to understand the doctrines in the Sutras. When your eyes see images of the Buddha, you then bow to the Buddha.

Why did you bow to the Buddha?

Because your eyes saw the image of the Buddha and so you wished to pay reverence and make offerings. This came about through the merit of the eyes. The eyes can help you and so can the nose, the ears, the tongue, the body and the mind. All of the six sense organs work in the same way with the same power. They can help you or they can destroy you. It depends upon what you *do*.

If you base your actions on wholesome merit and virtue, the eye, ear, nose, tongue, body and mind will help you do acts of wholesome merit and virtue. If you operate from a base of transgression, offense and error, the eye, ear, nose, tongue, body and mind will also come to your aid in doing acts of transgression, offense and error. For this reason the *Shurangama Sutra* says, "If you fall into hell, it's because of your six sense organs; if you realize Buddhahood, it's also because of your six sense organs." Nothing else.

So when I say that stupidity is just wisdom, the principle is the same as that of the use of the six sense organs. When you've heard Sutras explained for a while, you will reach the point where, comprehending one point you will comprehend all, understanding one you will understand all, knowing one, you will know all, awakening to one, you will awaken to all.

> The self-nature is like empty space;
> It contains both the true and false.

The self-nature of human beings is just like empty space. Contained within empty space there is both true and false.

> Awaken to and fathom the basic substance:
> In one penetration, penetrate all.

Once you have understood the doctrine of the basic self-nature, then when you understand one thing, you will understand everything. Take, for example, eating: Why do we eat?

To satisfy the hunger in our stomachs. All of our food and drink, whether it tastes good or bad, is merely to satisfy our hungry stomachs. It all serves the same purpose.

Why do we wear clothes?

To keep out the cold. No matter what kind of clothes you wear, they all serve the purpose of protecting you from the cold.

Now, everyone needs to eat, wear clothes, and sleep, and we look upon these three things as extremely important. Why? Because without them our very lives are in danger. We should now look upon our study of the Buddhadharma as important as eating, as important as wearing clothes, and as important as sleeping. Without the Buddhadharma our self-natures are in danger. We must employ our six sense organs in the quest of the Supreme Way of enlightenment and then it may be said that "the great earth quaked in six ways."

Those who have not sat in Dhyana meditation will not know of this, but those who have may have experienced the sudden jerking of one of their hands, or perhaps their eyes, nose, or ears will shake. This is the manifestation of what is termed "the quaking of the six roots."

At the point of most extreme stillness,
the light penetrates through,
And another heaven appears.

When you work intensely, when your efforts reach their most extreme point, another state entirely manifests.

Last summer during the *Shurangama Sutra* sessions, someone had some experience with this. As she sat there her hand would suddenly and involuntarily jerk up into the air. This is a transformation undergone by the body. When there is movement, there is change, and with change comes transformation.

Those who have applied effort and obtained skill such as this, must still receive the guidance of a genuine bright teacher in order to avoid taking the wrong road. Without the guidance of a genuine bright advisor, a good knowing advisor, it is very easy to take the wrong fork in the road, to become frightened, and then not dare continue to apply effort. If anyone experiences these kinds of states, they should not be frightened, for they are just one of the Six Types of Earthquakes.

The doctrines in the Sutras must be applied to our own bodies and our own self-natures. What are the Sutras for? They are to point out to each one of us, personally, the road which we should walk down. That is why the Buddha spoke so many Sutras. The roads are all contained within the self-natures of each one of us. The Buddha taught eighty-four thousand Dharma-doors to cure the eighty-four thousand kinds of bad habits and faults of living beings.

We ourselves may be unaware of our faults and continue to be influenced by them in our actions. Running after our faults, turned by them, we take it as happiness. In reality, day by day, we sink lower, and are unaware of what is happening. So, in the Sutras, the Buddha clearly points out the path to each one of us. The Six Types of Earthquakes are not separate from our own six sense organs.

Why do the six sense organs quake? The quaking represents the destruction of ignorance. Why are there six? Because ignorance is broken through six times. Ignorance is broken at the First Fruit, and the Second Fruit, at the Third Fruit, and at the Fourth Fruit. Then, ignorance is broken at the level of Equal Enlightenment, and at the level of Wonderful Enlightenment. Having broken through ignorance at the level of Wonderful Enlightenment, one realizes Buddhahood. So the Six Types of Earthquakes represent these six levels, six positions: the First Fruit, Second Fruit, Third Fruit, Fourth Fruit, Bodhisattvahood and Buddhahood. This has been a general explanation of the Six Types of Earthquakes.

Sutra:

AT THAT TIME THE ENTIRE GREAT ASSEMBLY OF BHIKSHUS, BHIKSHUNIS, UPASAKAS, UPASIKAS, GODS, DRAGONS, YAKSHAS, GANDHARVAS, ASURAS, GARUDAS, KINNARAS, MAHORAGAS, BEINGS HUMAN AND NON-HUMAN, AS WELL AS THE MINOR KINGS, THE WHEEL-TURNING SAGE KINGS, ALL ATTAINED WHAT THEY HAD NEVER HAD BEFORE. THEY REJOICED AND JOINED THEIR PALMS AND, WITH ONE HEART, GAZED UPON THE BUDDHA.[F5]

Outline:

F5. portent of rejoicing of the assembly

Commentary:

This is the fifth, the Portent of the Rejoicing of the Assembly. Everyone rejoiced, everyone was happy.

AT THAT TIME, right then.

What time was that?

It was just as the six kinds of earthquakes occurred. THE ENTIRE GREAT ASSEMBLY, those present in the Dharma Flower Assembly, all the great BHIKSHUS, the BHIKSHUNIS...The word Bhikshu has three meanings, 1) mendicant, 2) frightener of Mara, and 3) destroyer of evil. A Bhikshuni is a woman who has left home; the same three meanings apply.

There was once a Ch'an cultivator who cultivated and cultivated until he became enlightened. When he got enlightened he went to find a greatly virtuous lofty member of the Sangha to give him certification. The lofty Sangha member asked him, "What have you obtained?"

"I have obtained nothing,"he replied. This is like today when the passage from the *Vajra Sutra* came up in which the Buddha questions Subhuti, "Has the Thus Come One obtained anuttarasamyaksambodhi?"

The enlightened Bhikshu said he had not obtained anything and so the Sangha member asked him, "What enlightenment have you come to?"

He said, "I know that being a Bhikshuni is something women do."

The greatly virtuous one said, "Oh...I'll grant that you are enlightened. You have truly become enlightened."

Because the greatly virtuous high Sangha member had gained the use of the Five Eyes: the Buddha Eye, the Heavenly Eye, the Wisdom Eye, the Dharma Eye and the Flesh Eye, he knew that the cultivator had become enlightened and was not lying, and so he certified his enlightenment. If any one of us were to say the same thing, would it necessarily mean that we had become enlightened?

Imitating others is not enlightenment. Imitating the words of others is not enlightenment. You must have your own individual viewpoint. To merely imitate the words of others is not an indication of enlightenment. The sentence which the cultivator spoke had never been spoken by anyone. He said, "Now, I know for sure that being a Bhikshuni is something women do," and so his enlightenment was sealed and certified. If you were to say the same thing, it would not mean that you were enlightened, and no one would seal and certify you. Why?

Because you'd just be imitating someone else and it would not be something you enlightened to on your own.

UPASAKAS, UPASIKAS...Upasakas are male lay people, upasikas are female lay people. There are two ways of explaining these terms. Translated from Sanskrit, Upasaka means "a man who is close in affairs," and Upasika means "a woman who is close in affairs." That's the first method of explanation. Sometimes they live in the temples in which case they are not called "men or women who are close in affairs," but rather "men or women who dwell nearby," which is the second method of explanation. Bhikshus, Bhikshunis, Upasakas, and Upasikas comprise the Four-fold Assembly of Disciples.

GODS are those who live in the heavens, are those who dwell in the Six Desire Realm Heavens.

DRAGONS are big worms. What do the big worms eat? They eat little worms. Since they eat little worms, the great gold-wing P'eng birds collect on their debt and keep the score even by eating the dragons, the big worms.

YAKSHAS...Yaksha is a Sanskrit word. It means "speedy,"[1]--they are extremely fast and quick. It also means "bold and sturdy."[2] These greatly powerful ghosts and spirits are extremely brave, healthy, and strong. The great yaksha ghosts and spirits can tip the mountains over into the sea. With one hand they can throw a mountain several hundred miles. They can move the mountains. We now have hydraulic jacks, but none of them can move mountains. The yaksha ghosts are so brave and strong they can throw them several hundred li with one hand and with the other they can catch them and bring them back. Would you say they were strong or not...the powerful ghosts and spirits...?

GANDHARVAS are the music-making music spirits.
ASURAS: everyone knows them as the "wineless ones" or "the ugly ones." They have the blessings of the gods but not the authority of the gods. They have no influence in the heavens. The male asuras look like one of the eight kinds of ugly monsters. They're hideous, nothing could be uglier. The female asuras are very beautiful. To say nothing of people, when even the Jade Emperor sees them, his heart moves with

---

1 速疾 -*su chi*
2 勇健 -*yung chien.*

thoughts of desire. That's why he asked the Asura king for his daughter's hand in marriage and took an asura girl as his wife.

GARUDAS are the big birds, the great gold-winged P'eng birds. You've all heard about him many times and perhaps some of you have even seen him. Some have only heard of him. Those who have seen him--what's he like? The little Shramanera knows the great gold-winged P'eng bird.

KINNARAS are also music spirits in the court of the Jade Emperor. They have a single horn on their heads and so people doubt whether they are spirits or not and they are called "doubtful spirits." They have their doubts about whether or not they are spirits, but ultimately are they spirits? There's no way to decide it once and for all. However, they do make music for the Jade Emperor; they play guitars and things like that. But they are not like people because they have a horn on their head...the "doubtful spirits."

MAHORAGAS are great boa snakes.[1] They are extremely big.

Exactly how big are they?

They are a bit smaller than dragons. If you know how big dragons are you will know how big mahoragas are. But then there are big dragons and small dragons. There are also big mahoragas and small ones.

BEINGS HUMAN are people AND NON-HUMAN are those ghosts and spirits and the rest of the eight-fold division.

AS WELL AS THE MINOR KINGS, THE WHEEL-TURNING SAGE KINGS. Had Shakyamuni Buddha left home one day later than he did, he would have become a Gold Wheel-turning King. Gold Wheel-turning kings have a great abundance of blessed retribution, because they beget a thousand sons and have seven treasures which are like the As-You-Will Pearl. Whenever they need money for their travel expenses, they just scrape off a patch of earth and take out as much gold or silver as they need. It's all as-you-will according to their wish. They have a chariot in which, in a flash they can make a circle all the way around the Four Continents--a distance greater even than from here to the moon. It takes them no time at all.

---

1 大蟒蛇 -*ta mang she.*

There are four kinds of Wheel-turning Sage Kings. The Gold Wheel-turning King watches over one set of Four Continents: Jambudvipa in the south, Purva-videha in the east, Apara-godaniya in the west, and Uttarakuru in the north. He rules them all.

The Silver Wheel-turning King watches over three continents. He does not rule over Uttarakuru but does rule over the remaining three. The Bronze Wheel-turning King watches over Jambudvipa and Purva-videha. The Iron Wheel-turning King only watches over Jambudvipa.

Someone may ask, "During the time of Shakyamuni Buddha, were such Wheel-turning Kings ruling?"

That's a good question. There were none in our world at that time.

"Then where did they come from?"

They came from worlds in other directions. You shouldn't take such a narrow view-point and see only a space as big as your own house. You have neighbors, don't you? And there are the villages and the big cities. Don't be like a country person on his first trip to the city. Although there were no Wheel-turning Sage Kings ruling in the Saha world at the time of Shakyamuni Buddha, they did come from other worlds.

"What other worlds?"

It would take a long time to investigate that question and, right now, I don't have the time.

THE ENTIRE GREAT ASSEMBLY, all those assembled whom we just discussed.

Ultimately, how many were present?

Even the Buddha didn't know; how could I tell you?

ALL ATTAINED WHAT THEY HAD NEVER HAD BEFORE, They rejoiced and joined their palms--everyone was joyful, just as now, those who understand me are laughing. Those who don't understand what I am saying think, "What are they laughing at? What's going on?" In their hearts, they want to laugh too, but they're afraid they will laugh in the wrong place and so they don't dare. Wait until the translation. Then they'll laugh.

WITH ONE HEART, GAZED AT THE BUDDHA. This is the Portent of the Rejoicing of the Assembly. They all stared unblinkingly at the Buddha. Without turning their gaze away, they looked up at him.

Sutra:

THEN THE BUDDHA EMITTED FROM BETWEEN HIS BROWS A WHITE HAIR-MARK LIGHT WHICH ILLUMINED EIGHTEEN THOUSAND WORLDS TO THE EAST, OMITTING NONE OF THEM.[F6]

Outline:

F6. portent of emitting light

Commentary:

THEN...When was that? The word "then" has the same meaning as "at that time," which was the phrase used for the six quakings of the earth. It was not the same time, however.

Then what time was it?

It was at the time when the great assembly rejoiced and with one heart gazed upon the Buddha. It was at this time that the Buddha saw that everyone in the great Dharma assembly was rejoicing and so he, too, rejoiced. He rejoiced and emitted light and so this is the sixth, the Portent of Emitting Light. The Six Portents which have just been discussed took place in this world. There are also Six Portents which occured in other worlds which will be discussed.

THE BUDDHA EMITTED FROM BETWEEN HIS BROWS, from the space in between his two eyebrows A WHITE HAIR-MARK LIGHT. If you look at the Buddha images you will see a gem between the Buddha's brows which represents the white hair-mark light. Buddha images are made of clay or wood and there is no way to show the Buddha's white hair-mark, except to represent it with a jewel. The white hair-mark projects a kind of light which can shine far away or shine closeby, like a light through a glass tube.

ILLUMINATING EIGHTEEN THOUSAND WORLDS TO THE EAST, The EAST is associated with wood and the wood with birth.

The Buddha ILLUMINATED EIGHTEEN THOUSAND WORLDS TO THE EAST. Eighteen thousand worlds are not too many; it's still a calculable number. All of the eighteen thousand worlds received the universal illumination of the Buddha's light. OMITTING NONE OF THEM, not one of eighteen thousand worlds failed to receive the light. This has been a discussion of the sixth, the Portent of Emitting Light.

Sutra:

...REACHING BELOW TO THE AVICHI HELLS AND ABOVE TO THE AKANISHTHA HEAVEN. FROM THIS WORLD WERE SEEN ALL THE LIVING BEINGS IN THE SIX DESTINIES IN THOSE LANDS...

Outline:

E2. six portents in other worlds
F1. living beings in six destinies

Commentary:

This begins a new section on the Six Portents in Other Worlds. When Shakyamuni Buddha emitted light, not only were portents seen in this world, but portents in other worlds also were seen REACHING BELOW TO THE AVICHI HELLS. "Avichi" is a Sanskrit word. It means "unspaced."[1] In the unspaced hells there is no space in the sense that, if one person is in that hell, it is full, and if many people are in that hell, it is also full. There is also no break in the space or time spent in these hells. Both time and space are uninterrupted. It is not known how long one who has fallen into these hells must stay there. So it is called "unspaced."

AND ABOVE TO THE AKANISHTHA HEAVEN. "Akanishtha" is also Sanskrit and means "the ultimate form heaven."[2] In the Realm of Form, it is the highest heaven.

FROM THIS WORLD refers to the Saha World. From the Saha World, looking eastward through eighteen thousand worlds, WERE SEEN ALL THE LIVING BEINGS IN THE SIX DESTINIES IN THOSE LANDS, the gods, people, asuras, hell-beings, hungry ghosts, and animals. These are the living beings of the six paths. Everyone could see them

---

[1] 無間 -*wu chien.*

[2] 色究竟 -*shai chiu ching.*

and could see very clearly and distinctly what retributions were being undergone by the beings in each particular path.

The living beings in the six destinies are those turning on the wheel of the six paths of rebirth. The turning wheel will be familiar to those who have listened to Sutra lectures, but those who have not will not understand this concept. So I shall explain it again:

What is meant by the living beings in the six destinies? The six destinies are:

1. the gods,
2. asuras,
3. people.

These are known as the Three Wholesome Paths.

4. the hells,
5. hungry ghosts,
6. animals.

These are known as the Three Evil Paths.

Asuras are sometimes classed in the Three Wholesome Paths and sometimes in the Four Evil Destinies, i.e., the asuras, hell-beings, hungry ghosts, and animals.

The gods are the beings who live in the heavens. How did they become gods? Through the cultivation of the five precepts and the ten good acts. The five precepts are the basic precepts which must be held by Buddhist disciples. They are:

1. no killing,
2. no stealing,
3. no sexual misconduct,
4. no lying,
5. no taking intoxicants.

One who maintains the precepts against killing for a long time will receive the reward of longevity. Why do some people live for so long and others for such a short period of time? Those who live long do so because they have received the retribution of a long life as a result of having maintained the precept against killing. Those who have a short life in the past enjoyed killing and have received the retribution of a short lifespan. Such are the retributions involved with the precept against killing.

Why should one maintain the precept against stealing? Stealing robs people of their valuables and their peace of mind as well. Stealing means that you "steal off " without anyone knowing and take other people's things without asking. What kind of retribution does one receive for this?

In the future, you will not be able to keep your wealth for very long. You may have a lot of money and property, but it will soon be stolen away from you. You undergo this retribution because in previous lives you stole from others. You failed to keep the precept, and so in your present life you will be robbed of all your own wealth. If it lasts, that's because you kept the precept. Those who remain wealthy and honored do so because they kept the precept. Those who do not keep the precept will not be wealthy and honored for long.

Sexual misconduct, lying, and taking intoxicants work in the same was as the two above. For example, if you don't keep the precept against sexual misconduct and violate others' wives, in the future others will violate your wife. That's the retribution.

Lying works the same way. If you don't deceive others, you will not be deceived by others.

You say, "In this life, I have not deceived anyone. Why have so many people deceived me?"

Didn't I just explain it? Retribution is not a matter of simply a single lifetime. It involves the past, present, and future. You may not have deceived anyone in this life, but do you know how many people you deceived in your last life?

You don't know. You don't know, and so when others deceive you, it's because you deserve it.

As to taking intoxicants, drinking wine is not a major fault to speak of. The problem is that when you drink, you tend to drink too much. It turns you upside-down so you do crazy things. In Buddhism, drinking or taking any intoxicating substance is prohibited. Wine muddles the nature. When you've been drinking and you try to talk, your tongue is so big you can't speak clearly.

There are many principles involved in explaining the five precepts, but the most important thing is to keep them, not only in your actions, but in your thoughts as well. That is genuine morality.

As to stealing, it doesn't matter whether the item is large or small, if no one has given you permission and you make use of other people's things, you have broken the precept. As a small example: Say someone buys a bottle of wine and you see it and think, "What's his is mine, and what's mine is mine," and you drink a glass. That is a violation of the precept against stealing. So, you have broken the precept against stealing and the precept against consuming intoxicants.

Now, you may think, "I don't drink, so I couldn't break that precept."

So you don't drink wine? Well, you drink milk, don't you? What about that carton of milk in the referigerator that, paying no attention to the consequences, you opened and drank. Then, when someone asks you, "Who bought the milk?" all you can say is "I don't know. I don't know! I just *drank* it!"

Now, wouldn't you say that was acting unreasonably? If you drank it without the owner's permission, you are guilty of stealing.

The same applies to other foods--things in general.

On the other hand, if someone steals from you, you should take a good look at yourself. "Why are they stealing my food? It must be that, in former lives, I stole food, and so in this life it has come back on me. Well, forget it." That's what the person who is stolen from should think. The person who stole it, however, can't say, "I'm stealing your food now, and you can go ahead and steal it back from me next life." How do you know you will have any food to be stolen in your next life? For all you know, you may not have anything at *all* in your next life, and then how could someone steal from you? So don't harbor thoughts of stealing. If you didn't buy it, you can't use it as you please. If you get the owner's permission it's okay. Otherwise,you can't go around sneaking other people's things.

If you talk about the fine points, to take even a blade of grass, a splinter of wood, a needle, or a piece of thread without asking is considered stealing. Sexual misconduct, lying, and taking intoxicants work the same way. Having explained one precept, you should be able to understand the rest of them. To say too much would waste a lot of time.

How does one get born in the heavens? Through holding the five precepts. Born in the heavens, one enjoys unlimited heavenly blessings. However, they eventually come to an end. When the Five Signs of Decay appear, one falls. Therefore, the heavens are not ultimate.

Asuras also foster merit and virtue, but they do it with afflicton.

"How can one foster merit and virtue with afflictions?" you ask.

When doing it, they concentrate solely on competing with others. They say belligerently, "I gave ten dollars to the temple. How much did you give?" They pit themselves against everyone else. "You gave five? I'll give ten. Oh? You gave ten? I'll give twenty!" They fight to be number one, and in the future they turn into asuras. They have merit and virtue all right, but they compete to get it; it's not done from their hearts.

They also fight for fame. They want people to say, "See? So and so is number one. He gave the most money." Fighting for top billing is a sure way to become an asura. In the practice of the Buddhadharma, it is essential to have a true understanding of cause and effect. Then your efforts won't get all messed up.

Some people even think, "Since I can't get famous here, I'll go somewhere else." Then everyone thinks, "See so and so? He went all the way to New York to do acts of great merit and virtue." That way everyone knows. These are the causes for becoming an asura; in the future such people will become asuras.

As soon as they start talking, they get angry. No matter what's going on, they have to be number one. To do acts of merit and virtue without cutting off affliction is merely to perform meritorious and virtuous acts which have outflows. It is not non-outflow merit and virtue. You should do merit and virtue, but don't insist that everyone recognize you as number one, or number two.

There is, however, another kind of person who "shuns" fame. He sneaks around doing merit and virtue and then secretly tells someone, "Hey, I did five thousand dollars of merit and virtue over there, and no one knows I did it. I'm just telling you." Really! They, too, are asuras, and they are even worse than the ones mentioned above. Why? Because they are *yin* asuras, not *yang*. On the surface it looks like they don't like fame, but in reality their behind-the-back self-advertising campaigns are even worse. So if you bring forth the resolve to do merit and virtue, remember that if the causal ground is not genuine, the result will be distorted. When you are planting causes, if you do not plant proper ones, when the time come to reap the fruit, it will be deformed, bad. You'll become an asura.

"What's wrong with that?" you ask.

There's plenty wrong with it! All they do is fight. Does that appeal to you?

As to the destiny of people, how does one become a human being? It is also through doing acts of merit and virtue, holding the five precepts, and cultivating the ten good deeds. They hold the five precepts and cultivate the ten good deeds on the lower level, however. Asuras perform them at the middle level, gods at the higher level. There are innumberable distinctions, but we won't go into them now. These are the causes of birth in the Three Wholesome Paths.

What about the Three Evil Paths? They come from greed, hate, and stupidity. Are you greedy? If you are too greedy, you'll turn into a hungry ghost. Why are hungry ghosts hungry? Because, when they were alive, they were greedy for food. They always had to have a little bit more of whatever it was they were eating. If you like to eat "a little more" then you can turn into a hungry ghost and have nothing at all to eat. Why were they greedy for food? Because they had already had an awakening, an enlightenment. What were they enlightened to? To the fact that in the future they aren't going to have anything to eat, that they are going to become hungry ghosts. "I'm going to turn into a hungry ghost! I'd better hurry up and eat all I can now," they think. They've got a bit of skill in predicting the future. So it is with greed.

Hatred: Do you enjoy getting angry? Fine. Keep it up, and you will end up in hell. In hell, you won't even be able to stand yourself. "I'll just try out that mountain of knives," you'll say, and in a fit of rage you'll throw yourself on it and get slashed to death. All because of anger. "Let's just see how terrible those knives are!" Or you may throw yourself into the pot of boiling oil. "You guys wouldn't dare jump, would you? Well, here goes!" and you jump. You're so angry that you'll dare to try out the hells, be they mountains of knives or pots of boiling oil. That's what happens when you give vent to hatred. I am telling all of my disciples: If you have a bad temper hurry up and change. If you don't have a bad temper, don't develop one. Don't let this pass through one ear and out the other. It is extremely important. Don't think, "It's no big thing. The Dharma Master is just talking. It's not for sure that if I have a bad temper I'll fall into hell." If you try it out and end up in hell, it will then be too late. You will think, 'My teacher told me all along that this would happen. Now, I know he was telling the truth." But then it's too late. Now, do you still dare to get angry?

I have set up the law that if one person gets angry all three have to kneel for twenty-four hours. I did this because I am afraid you'll all fall into hell. How can those who have left home get angry? There are now three shramaneras, and if one gets angry the other two have to kneel along with him for twenty-four hours. No ifs ands or buts about it, no politeness at all. You have been warned in advance and no clemency will be shown. The best way to deal with it is simply not to get angry. Then my method will be rendered totally useless. If you get angry, my law goes into effect.

Kneeling for twenty-four hours isn't really all that severe. On top of that, however, you will not be allowed to eat, drink or go to the bathroom. How about that for firmness? Really strict! I set up this law several days ago, and now when I ask each of the shramaneras,"Have you gotten angry?" they all say, "Nooooo!" I say, "Little shramanera, how is it that you have managed not to get angry?"

"Arrgh," he says between his teeth, "I don't know."

He doesn't know offhand why he hasn't gotten angry. Would you say this method was wonderful or not? Truly wonderful! Wonderful to the extreme. If you get angry you may fall into hell. Because I am afraid that you will fall into hell, I have established this severe law.

Stupidity: Do you like being stupid? Do you neglect your study of the Buddhadharma? If you don't like being stupid, then study the Buddhadharma. Studying the Buddhadharma augments your wisdom and helps you to develop wonderful Prajna. If you don't study the Buddhadharma, you will remain stupid and where will you go? Stupidity will take you off to the animal realm. Why are horses, cows, sheep, chickens, and pigs so unintelligent? Pigs, for example, are quite intelligent. When they've eaten their fill they sleep and when they have slept enough, they eat again. Other than those two activities, they don't have a third thing to do. Horses and cows do a little work, but they're also very stupid. Why are they stupid? Simply because they did not study the Buddhadharma. Not only did they fail to study, but when other people took an interest in it, they said, "Hey, don't study that stuff; that's the dumbest thing you could do." They say others are dumb, but they are the dumbest. In the future they turn into animals just because they didn't study the Buddhadharma.

You say, "I can't believe that. I'll not study it and we'll just see if I turn into a pig or a horse."

Sure, go ahead and try it out. Once you've tried it out, you can come back and study the Buddhadharma. There's no need for force. As long as you want to be an animal, the opportunity is there. You can do it anywhere, anytime.

The wheel of rebirth is heavy indeed. Depending on what cause you plant, you reap the fruit accordingly.

If you plant good causes,you reap good fruit. If you plant bad causes, you reap bad fruit. If you plant squash, you get squash. If you plant beans, you get beans. Let's see what causes you plant. If you plant the causes of becoming a Buddha, you will become a Buddha. If you plant the causes of hell, you will fall into hell. You pick your own path.

The living beings in the six destinies all appeared in the white hair-mark light of the Buddha.

The white hair-mark light of Shakyamuni Buddha represents the final principle of the Middle Way which does not veer off either to the side of existence or the side of emptiness. It is also the Perfect and Sudden Dharma-door of *The Dharma Flower Sutra*. It is the principle of the Middle Way and the Real Mark.

This passage of text begins the manifesting of the Six Portents in other Worlds. The portent is that of seeing the beings in the Six Destinies.

The Thus Come One's white hair-mark can be extended or contracted,far or near. It's like a flashlight or the headlights on a car. Turn them on and they shine across a great distance. When the Thus Come One shines the white hair-mark light, it shines not for just a mile or two, but into the eastern direction across eighteen thousand worlds.

"Does it only shine in the eastern direction?" you ask.

It's like the flashlight. You can point it wherever you wish. If you want to you can shine it to the east, south, north, west, up or down, heaven or earth--wherever you like. In previous Sutras, Shakyamuni Buddha didn't emit light from the white hair-mark. In *The Shurangama Sutra* Shakyamuni Buddha emits light from the flesh cowl, the "invisible summit" atop his head, as the text of that Sutra tells us:

"At that time, the World Honored One,
From the flesh curl atop his head,
Sent forth a hundred jeweled lights."

The light from the "invisible summit" is not the same as the light from the white hair-mark.

To say nothing of being able to listen to *The Dharma Flower Sutra* every day as we do, to hear even a single word, a sentence, or an evening's lecture, is to plant the causes of Buddhahood. Even if you never come back again to listen, the Buddha within you will not run off and you are certain to become a Buddha. But that's in the future, not the present. How long will it take? There's nothing fixed about it.

Those of you who now are hearing the Sutra all have

good roots. People with good roots should study the Buddhadharma. Don't slight yourself as worthless saying, "What has the Buddhadharma got to do with me?"

You should know that, outside of the Buddhadharma, nothing else has anything to do with you! Only the Buddhadharma has anything to do with you, and it relates to you in a most important way. It will lead you to your future realization of Buddhahood.

You say, "I don't believe it. How could I become a Buddha?"

It's just your disbelief that will enable you to become a Buddha. Since you don't believe you can become a Buddha--Ah!--in the future you will become one. That's just the wonderful Dharma. Despite your disbelief--much to your suprise--all of a sudden--it will have happened!! *The Wonderful Dharma Lotus Flower Sutra* is just that wonderful.

Sutra:

FURTHER WERE SEEN ALL THE PRESENT BUDDHAS IN THOSE LANDS.

Outline:

F2.portent of seeing the Buddhas

Commentary:

The second of the Six Portents is that of seeing the Buddhas.

Within the white hair-mark light emitted by Shakyamuni Buddha appeared the Buddhalands, and within the Buddhalands there were Buddhas teaching and transforming living beings. This passage of text is the portent of seeing the Buddhas. The white hair-mark light represents the Middle Way.

Why did the Buddha emit light? And why did he choose to emit light from the white hair-mark?

The Buddha emitted light in order to illumine those whose potentials had ripened; the living beings who should be taught, the living beings who should be taken across. Those ready to be taught are called "those with potential." They have the opportunity to be taught. The teaching is dispensed in response to the potential of living beings. Depending upon an individual's potential, a certain teaching is given.

Thus, the emitting of light represents the dispensing of the teaching in response to potentials.

There's another way to explain the white hair-mark. It represents the severing of delusions and casting out of doubts. The light which was emitted got rid of all the doubts of living beings. It broke through their deluded thoughts. That is why the light was emitted.

As to the white hair-mark: Amitabha Buddha also has a white hair-mark as we as other Buddhas. The verse in praise of Amitabha Buddha runs:

> Amitabha's body is the color of gold;
> The splendor of his hallmarks has no peer.
> The light of his brow shines 'round a
> hundred worlds;
> Wide as the seas are his eyes pure and clear.
>
> Shining in his brilliance by transformation,
> Are countless Bodhisattvas and infinite
> Buddhas.
> His forty-eight vows will be our liberation;
> In nine lotus stages we reach the further
> shore.

The brilliance of Amitabha Buddha's thirty-two marks and eighty minor characteristics is incomparable. The hair-mark, located between his eyebrows, winds around and around like a dragon, not in a straight course but winding and coiling. How big is it? As big as five Mount Sumerus. Within his light are many, many Buddhas. And the Bodhisattvas are also beyond all count. He has made forty-eight vows to save living beings; every vow contains the wish that living beings might realize Buddhahood.

There are nine grades of lotuses:

superior-superior;
superior-middle;
superior-inferior;
middle-superior
middle-middle;
middle-inferior;
inferior-superior;
inferior-middle;
inferior-inferior.

All living beings are led to the other shore--to Nirvana--to realize Buddhahood.

Shakyamuni Buddha's white hair-mark is also as big as five Mount Sumerus. According to *The Sutra of the Samadhi of Contemplating the Sea of Buddhas,* when the Buddha came into the world, his white hair-mark measured five feet. When he cultivated ascetic practices, it was fourteen feet. When he realized Buddhahood, it was fifteen feet.

The white hair-mark is empty in the center, like a glass tube. It represents the Four Virtues of Nirvana:

1. permanence;
2. joy;
3. (true) self;
4. purity.

The emptiness in the center represents the Middle Way and permanence. Its softness represents joy, its whiteness, purity. The ability to extend or contract it at will represents true self. Thus represented are the Four Virtues of Nirvana. The white hair-mark represents the Middle Way, the Real Mark's precious seal.

Within the light from the white hair-mark could be seen all the Buddhas in other lands. Also could be seen from the time of the Buddha's birth up to his Nirvana, all the bitter practices he cultivated in all their various aspects, and then, following his Nirvana, all his merit and virtue.

Sutra:

...AND ALL THE SUTRAS AND DHARMA SPOKEN BY THE BUDDHAS WAS HEARD.

Outline:

F3. the portent of hearing the Dharma

Commentary:

This is the third, the portent of hearing the Dharma. The Six Portents in the Other Worlds fall into three pairs. The first two portents, that of seeing the six destinies and seeing the Buddhas make of the pair of the common and sagely. Those in the six destinies are common people and the Buddhas are sages.

Sutra:

ALSO SEEN WERE THE BHIKSHUS, BHIKSHUNIS, UPASAKAS, UPASIKAS IN THOSE LANDS WHO CULTIVATED AND ATTAINED THE WAY.

Outline:

F4. the portent of seeing the four-fold multitude attain the Way

Commentary:

What were the Buddhas in their respective Buddhalands doing? They were speaking the Dharma, lecturing on the Sutras and expounding the Teaching.

What is the use of speaking the Buddhadharma?

It was so that the Bhikshus, Bhikshunis, Upasakas, and Upasikas--the four-fold assembly of disciples--could cultivate in accord with the Dharma and certify to the fruit, perhaps to the fruit of Arhatship, or perhaps become Bodhisattvas or Buddhas.

Within the Buddha's white hair-mark could be seen the Buddhas speaking the Dharma and the four assemblies who cultivated and attained the fruit. These two portents represent the pair of people and Dharma, the people being the four-fold assembly, and the Dharma being the Way which they certified to.

Sutra:

MOREOVER WERE SEEN THE BODHISATTVAS MAHASATTVAS, THE VARIOUS CAUSES AND CONDITIONS, THE VARIOUS BELIEFS AND UNDERSTANDINGS, AND THE VARIOUS APPEARANCES OF THEIR PRACTICE OF THE BODHISATTVA WAY.

Outline:

F5. the portent of seeing the cultivation of the Bodhisattva Way

Commentary:

MOREOVER WERE SEEN THE BODHISATTVAS MAHASATTVAS, THE VARIOUS CAUSES AND CONDITIONS by which they cultivated the Dharma-doors to teach and transform various kinds of living beings. THE VARIOUS BELIEFS AND UNDERSTANDINGS: Perhaps they cultivated through belief and understanding of the Four Holy Truths, or perhaps through belief and understanding of the Twelve

Causes and Conditions, or perhaps through belief and understanding of the Six Perfections and the Ten Thousand Conducts. THE VARIOUS APPEARANCES OF THEIR PRACTICE OF THE BODHISATTVA WAY: This does not refer to the physical appearances of the Bodhisattvas, but to the various practices and Dharmas they cultivated. They practiced the Bodhisattva Way.

What is the Bodhisattva Way?

It is to benefit oneself and benefit others, to enlighten oneself and enlighten others. The Thus Come One's white hair-mark shines from this land into other Buddhalands and this represents the Dharma-door of enlightening oneself and enlightening others, benefitting oneself and benefitting others. Walking the Bodhisattva Way, you must enlighten yourself and enlighten others, benefit yourself and benefit others. This is the fifth, the portent of seeing the practice of the Bodhisattva conduct.

Sutra:

FURTHER WERE SEEN THE PARINIRVANA OF THE BUDDHAS AND, AFTER THE PARNINIRVANA OF THE BUDDHAS, THE BUILDING OF STUPAS WITH THE SEVEN JEWELS TO HOLD THEIR SHARIRA.

Outline:

F6. portent of seeing the the Buddhas enter Nirvana

Commentary:

FURTHER WERE SEEN THE PARINIRVANA OF THE BUDDHAS... Within the white hair-mark light the Buddhas could be seen. Nirvana is a Sanskrit word which is interpreted as meaning "perfect stillness."[1] It is said that the merit is nowhere not perfect and the virtue nowhere not still. Nirvana is also interpreted as meaning "not produced or destroyed."[2] Birth and death have

---

[1] 圓寂 *-yüan chi.*

[2] 不生不滅 *-pu sheng pu mieh.*

been brought to an end.

AND, AFTER THE PARINIRVANA OF THE BUDDHAS, THE BUILDING OF STUPAS WITH THE SEVEN JEWELS TO HOLD THEIR SHARIRA. Stupas made of the seven jewels were built to honor the sharira of those Buddhas. Sharira is a Sanskrit word which means "efficacious bones."[1] Stupas are buildings used to house the sharira. After Shakyamuni Buddha entered Nirvana, his body was cremated and in the remains an uncountable number of sharira, bright, gem-like relics, were found. Jeweled stupas were built to contain them, so that people could worship and make offerings to them.

In the Thus Come One's white hair-mark light one could see how, in other lands, after the Buddhas entered Nirvana, their bodies were cremated and the sharira were obtained. Then stupas were built for them. Stupa, also a Sanskrit word, means "square grave;"[2] it also means a "high and manifest place,"[3] because they are tall structures which can easily be seen.

What are the stupas used for?

They are used to house the Buddhas' sharira so that people can make offerings to them. Wherever the Buddhas' sharira are present, the Buddhas' Dharma-body is also present. This is the sixth, the portent of seeing the Nirvana of the Buddhas.

The fifth and sixth portents make up the pair of the beginning and the end. The Bodhisattvas are at the beginning; they are cultivating the Way. The Buddhas have reached the end, the ultimate state of Buddhahood.

This ends the discussion of the Six Portents in Other Worlds.

I lecture to you coming and going and you pay no attention. You must pay close attention to the Buddhadharma in order to understand it fully. If it goes in one ear and out the other, it's of no use at all. You could listen for a hundred years; yet it would be just as if you never heard. Why? Because you don't remember it. You don't take note of it.

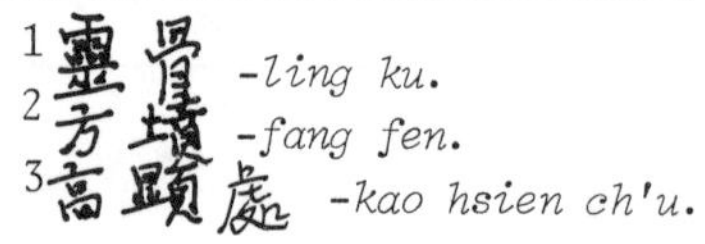

1 靈骨 -*ling ku.*
2 方墳 -*fang fen.*
3 高顯處 -*kao hsien ch'u.*

You are now listening to the Sutras and studying the Buddhadharma. If you were to go somewhere else and were invited to speak, you could speak in such a way that it gushed forth unceasingly. Your mouths would be like raging rivers; everyone would be very pleased. But then if someone said, "Just one moment, excuse me, but I have a question. How many kinds of Nirvana are there? Please tell me."

You would gape, "Ohhh? Ahhh...I forgot!"

"Well, who did you study under?"

"I studied with a Dharma Master for several years, but although I heard them, I've forgotten now."

Would you say that was losing face or not? You may not understand any of the profound aspects of the Dharma, but if you don't even know what the four kinds of Nirvana are, you'd really lose face, wouldn't you?

There's not much time left, so I'll just tell you the names. No doubt when I do, you will all recall them. If I didn't tell you, you wouldn't be able to remember them. Once I tell you, you'll pipe up and say, "I didn't forget. Oh, you mean *those* four kinds!" If you know ahead of time, that's okay. If you have to wait until after you've been told and then insist you knew it all along, it won't work. What are they?

1. The Nirvana of the purity of the self-nature.
2. The Nirvana with residue.
3. The Nirvana without residue.
4. The Nirvana of no dwelling place.

Sutra:

THEN THE BODHISATTVA MAITREYA HAD THIS THOUGHT: "NOW, THE WORLD HONORED ONE MANIFESTS SIGNS OF SPIRITUAL TRANSFORMATIONS. WHAT IS THE REASON FOR THESE PORTENTS? THE BUDDHA, THE WORLD HONORED ONE, HAS NOW ENTERED SAMADHI, YET THESE ARE INCONCEIVABLE AND RARE EVENTS. WHO SHOULD I ASK CONCERNING THEM? WHO COULD ANSWER?"

HE FURTHER THOUGHT: "THE DHARMA PRINCE, MANJUSHRI, HAS IN THE PAST DRAWN NEAR AND MADE OFFERINGS TO LIMIT-

LESS BUDDHAS. SURELY HE HAS SEEN SUCH RARE SIGNS. I SHALL NOW ASK HIM."

Outline:

D3. the doubtful thoughts
E1. doubts of Maitreya

Commentary:

In this passage of text, Maitreya Bodhisattva gives rise to doubts. What are his doubts? He doesn't understand what the Buddha is about to do. The Buddha has emitted light and the earth shook. Six portents were seen in this world and in other worlds as well. Maitreya Bodhisattva does not understand what the portents mean. For this reason he has some doubts. When Maitreya Bodhisattva gives rise to doubts, the rest of the assembly does so too.

THEN THE BODHISATTVA MAITREYA HAD THIS THOUGHT... Which Bodhisattva is he? He's the very fat one, the one who is always laughing. He is extremely compassionate. Whether you are a good or an evil person, he likes you all the same. He regards all living beings with equal compassion and doesn't make discriminations among them.

"NOW, THE WORLD HONORED ONE MANIFESTS SIGNS OF SPIRITUAL TRANSFORMATIONS...Now, the World Honored One has manifested states of spiritual penetrations transformations and changes. He emitted light from the white hair-mark, and there were the six types of earthquakes--all as a result of the Buddha's spiritual powers. The Bodhisattva had never seen them before and so he didn't know what they meant.

The Bodhisattva Maitreya is a "successor-Bodhisattva," a Buddha-to-be. He is waiting for Shakyamuni Buddha to retire and then he will realize Buddhahood in the Saha world. Although he is basically very wise, he still didn't know what the Buddha was going to do.

Why didn't he know?

Those at one level do not understand those on a higher level. The Bodhisattvas on the first ground do not know the state of those on the second. Those on the tenth ground do not know the realm of Equal Enlightenment, and the Equal Enlightenment Bodhisattvas do not understand the Wonderful Enlightenment of the Buddha.

It is said, "The common folk don't know the wise." Simple common people are incapable of understanding the state of the wise. Why? Because, being simple and common, their thoughts are stupid and dull. Either they don't go far enough or they go too far. People with scattered thoughts do not understand those with samadhi. People who are continually flustered, and always glancing nervously about the the north, east, south and west, do not know what the person sitting there in samadhi is experiencing.

Ordinary people do not understand the sage. Those who have not certified to the fruit can't know the state of the worthy sages. Sages of lesser wisdom cannot understand the wisdom of Shariputra, "Body-seed," who is the foremost of the Buddha's disciples in wisdom. Shariputra is known as the "greatly wise Shariputra" but even he cannot fathom the wisdom of the Bodhisattvas. He is just an Arhat and, compared to the Bodhisattvas, his wisdom is small. Bodhisattvas, that is, Bodhisattvas in general, cannot know the state of the successor-Bodhisattvas and the successor-Bodhisattvas do not understand the state of the Ultimately Venerable Ones, the Buddhas.

The Bodhisattva Maitreya is a successor-Bodhisattva, and he will become a Buddha in the future and succeed Shakyamuni Buddha. But when Shakyamuni Buddha manifested states of spiritual transformations, Maitreya did not understand them, and so he gave rise to false thinking. Yes, even the Bodhisattva Maitreya can have false thinking! He thought, "Shakyamuni Buddha is now revealing these appearances. Why? What is the reason? Why? Why the signs? Usually, Bodhisattvas do not indulge in false thinking, but he gave rise to three doubts:

1. First, he thought about the Buddha's spiritual transformations, wondering, "What is the reason for these portents? THE BUDDHA, THE WORLD HONORED ONE, HAS NOW ENTERED SAMADHI. THESE ARE INCONCEVIABLE AND RARE EVENTS, which cannot be thought of with the mind or expressed in words. No one knows what they mean. What am I going to do? Such things have simply never happened before."

2. Secondly, he wondered who he should ask. "WHO SHOULD I ASK CONCERNING THEM? Which Bodhisattva? WHO COULD ANSWER?"

3. His third thought was to ask Manjushri Bodhisattva about them. "Who should I ask? THE DHARMA PRINCE MANJUSHRI HAS IN THE PAST DRAWN NEAR AND MADE OFFERINGS TO LIMITLESS BUDDHAS. SURELY HE HAS SEEN SUCH RARE SIGNS. I SHALL NOW ASK HIM. Since he has surely had the experience already, I will now ask him." This third thought cancelled out the second thought, for he had found someone to ask.

Sutra:

THEREUPON THE BHIKSHUS, BHIKSHUNIS, UPASAKAS, AND UPASIKAS, AS WELL AS THE GODS, DRAGONS, GHOSTS, SPIRITS, AND OTHERS, ALL HAD THIS THOUGHT: WHO SHOULD NOW BE ASKED CONCERNING THE BUDDHA'S BRIGHT LIGHT AND SIGNS OF SPIRITUAL PENETRATIONS?"

Outline:

E2. the doubts of the assembly

Commentary:

This passage expresses the doubts of the assembly. Not only did the Bodhisattva Maitreya have doubts, but so did everyone in the Dharma assembly. They wondered what the Buddha was going to do. The gods and dragons and the ghosts and spirits also did not understand. "From the white hair-mark light, the Buddha now emits light and manifests spiritual penetrations. Who should we ask about them? These are the two doubts of the assembly:

1. They wondered about the six portents.
2. They wondered who to ask concerning them.

Now, was Maitreya Bodhisattva really perplexed by all of this? Did he really have doubts?

I don't believe so.

Why not?

Because in the past he had also drawn near to limitless Buddhas. By all rights, he should have had this experience himself. But he pretended that he didn't know so that he could request the Dharma for the sake of the assembly. The doubts of the assembly were real enough, however, and this passage expresses their confusion.

Sutra:

AT THAT TIME, THE BODHISATTVA MAITREYA, WISHING TO RESOLVE HIS OWN DOUBTS, AND FURTHER REGARDING THE THOUGHTS OF THE FOUR-FOLD ASSEMBLY OF BHIKSHUS,

BHIKSHUNIS, UPASAKAS, AND UPASIKAS, AS WELL AS THE THOUGHTS OF THE ASSEMBLED GODS, DRAGONS, GHOSTS, AND SPIRITS AND OTHERS, QUESTIONED MANJUSHRI AS FOLLOWS:

Outline:

D4. the questions
E1. the prose section
F1. narration

Commentary:

We have talked about "ghosts" many times, but what *are* ghosts?

"I know!" you say. "There are hungry ghosts and there are full ghosts!"

Well what are hungry ghosts and what are full ghosts?

In Chinese the word for ghost 鬼 is pronounced *kuei* which sounds the same as the word which means "to return," 歸 -*kuei*. This means that when people die and become ghosts, they return.

Where did they come from?

They came from the Buddha. Now they return to the hells or to the path of hungry ghosts.

Why must they return there?

Because they took the wrong road. They took for their own territory that which is not their own territory. They took the wrong road and so they must return as ghosts.

After this, when the word "ghost" comes up you should remember that they are ghosts because they took the wrong road. They still must come back, return. In Chinese ghosts are called *kuei* and in English they are ghosts. You could say, "Go! Go! Ghost!"

Go where?

They go off to hell--to hell--to hell! In English a ghost is one who goes. Although I can't speak English, I can explain this English word.

"Spirits" are called "natural minded."[1] They have spiritual penetrations and evoke spontaneous responses.

---

1 天心 -*t'ien hsin*.

Maitreya Bodhisattva asked Manjushri as follows:

Sutra:

"WHAT ARE THE REASONS FOR THESE PORTENTS, THESE SIGNS OF SPIRITUAL PENETRATIONS, FOR THE EMANATION OF GREAT LIGHT WHICH ILLUMINES EIGHTEEN THOUSAND LANDS TO THE EAST SO THAT THE ADORNMENTS IN ALL THOSE BUDDHA WORLDS ARE FULLY SEEN?"

Outline:

F2.the questions proper

Commentary:

"Great Bodhisattva! Son of the Dharma King! Please be compassionate and tell me, WHAT ARE THE REASONS FOR THESE PORTENTS? What is the principle involved? Why has the Buddha now emitted light which is so great that it ILLUMINES EIGHTEEN THOUSAND LANDS TO THE EAST? THESE SIGNS OF SPIRITUAL PENETRATIONS are truly rare. I have never seen the likes of them before. What is the reason FOR THE EMANATION OF GREAT LIGHT. It doesn't just shine nearby. It shines across eighteen thousand lands."

We think that going to the moon is so remarkable and a historical first. Shakyamuni Buddha put forth light which shone across eighteen thousand worlds. That's even farther than eighteen thousand moons or eighteen thousand stars.

SO THAT THE ADORNMENTS IN ALL THOSE BUDDHA WORLDS ARE FULLY SEEN. Not just a little bit was seen. They were seen in their entirety. How big the country was, how it was superbly adorned--all this appeared.

Sutra:

THEREUPON, MAITREYA BODHISATTVA, WISHING TO RESTATE HIS MEANING, SPOKE VERSES ASKING:

"MANJUSHRI, WHAT IS THE REASON
FOR THE GUIDING MASTER'S EMANATION
FROM THE WHITE HAIR BETWEEN HIS BROWS
OF A GREAT LIGHT WHICH SHINES EVERYWHERE,

AND FOR THE RAIN OF MANDARAVAS
AND OF MANJUSHAKA FLOWERS,
THE BREEZE OF FRAGRANT CHANDANA WHICH
DELIGHTS THE HEARTS OF THOSE ASSEMBLED?
THROUGH THESE CAUSES AND CONDITIONS
THE EARTH IS ALL ADORNED AND PURE,
AND WITHIN THIS WORLD THE EARTH
TREMBLES IN SIX DIFFERENT WAYS.
THEN THE FOUR-FOLD MULTITUDE
REJOICES ALTOGETHER;
IN BODY AND IN MIND ENRAPTURED,
THEY OBTAIN WHAT THEY HAD NEVER HAD.

Outline:

E2. Verse section
F1. restatement of former questions
G1. asking about six portents

Commentary:

The Bodhisattva Mairtreya wished to RESTATE HIS MEANING, to speak the doctrine one more time. Why did he want to go to the trouble of saying it all over again?

It was just because he feared that you and I, the living beings of today, would not understand. And you have the nerve to think of it as trouble? Don't have such thoughts!

He spoke verses ASKING:

MANJUSHRI, WHAT IS THE REASON/ FOR THE GUIDING MASTER'S EMANATION/ What is a Guiding Master? "Guide" means to lead forth, off of the road of darkness onto the road full of bright light. That is what is meant by "Guiding Master."

Who is the Guiding Master?

Shakyamuni Buddha is the Great Guiding Master.

He takes us outof the hells and back to our original home. Now, we should return to our genuine home, to the place where Shakyamuni Buddha lives, the Pure Land of Eternal, Still Light. That's our true home.

WHAT IS THE REASON FOR/ THE GUIDING MASTER'S EMANATION/ Why has the World Honored One emitted light FROM THE WHITE HAIR BETWEEN HIS BROWS? This GREAT LIGHT WHICH SHINES EVERYWHERE, illumining the entire universe.

Previously, in the prose text, the light was said to shine across eighteen thousand worlds to the east. Here it says, "Shining everywhere," and so I explained it saying that the light shines not only to the east, but to the south, north, and west, and the four points in between, and up and down as well. It shines in all possible directions.

AND FOR THE RAIN OF MANDARAVAS/ AND OF MANJUSHAKA FLOWERS/ It rains, not water, but Mandarava Flowers. They are as beautiful as you could possibly imagine. When you see them, your heart is overjoyed. "I have never seen such beautiful flowers before." They cause your heart to be extremely happy and so they are called the "flowers which go along with your wish."

Manjushaka flowers are red flowers. They are not only beautiful, but soft as well. They can't be crushed, however, and if you wish for big blossoms, they are big. If you wish for small blossoms, they are small. They are especially beautiful.

THE FRAGRANT BREEZE OF CHANDANA WHICH/ Chandana incense can be smelled at a distance of forty miles.

DELIGHTS THE HEARTS OF THOSE ASSEMBLED/ Seeing the flowers, their hearts rejoice. They are filled with joy. They've never been so happy before. Not just one of them was happy; the entire assembly was happy.

THROUGH THESE CAUSES AND CONDITIONS/ THE EARTH IS ALL ADORNED AND PURE? Because the flowers have cleansed, purified, and adorned the earth, no one needs to sweep it; it's sparkling clean.

AND, WITHIN THIS WORLD, THE EARTH/ that is, our world here,TREMBLES IN SIX DIFFERENT WAYS/ The six types of earthquakes have already been discussed. They represent the six sense organs. Those who don't work hard won't know about this, but those who do may sometimes find that their eyes blink very fast, like an electric fan. If you haven't had any experience, you may wonder, "Has a ghost come? Why are my eyes blinking like this?"

It's not a ghost! It's a result of your hard work. Sometimes you may hear birds warbling or the sounds of cows or horses. You needn't be afraid. It's just the occurrence of one of the six types of earthquakes:shaking, surging, rising, crashing, roaring, and banging.

"Shaking" refers to movement in one place. "Universal shaking" refers to shaking throughout the Four Continents, but you should not think this is a particularly big earthquake. It is not as big as the shaking of the entire three thousand great thousand worlds, which is called a "cosmic shaking."

Shaking, universal shaking, and cosmic shaking represent the eye organ, the object of the eye, and the eye-consciousness; the same also applies to the other five sense fields. The six sense organs, the six sense objects, and the six sense consciousnesses make up the eighteen realms of sense. Each of the six types of earthquakes has three divisions making eighteen which represent the eighteen fields of sense. The light illumining the eighteen thousand worlds to the east also represents the eighteen realms of sense.

Crashing occurs in one world. Universal crashing occurs in Four Continents. Cosmic crashing occurs throughout the entire three thousand great thousand worlds. Each of the six types of earthquakes has these three divisions corresponding to the eighteen realms of sense.

THEN, when the great earth shakes THE FOUR-FOLD MULTITUDE/ the Bhikshus, Bhikshunis, Upasakas, and Upasikas, REJOICES ALTOGETHER/ This is the portent of the rejoicing of the assembly. AND BODY AND IN MIND ENRAPTURED/ pleased to the extreme as THEY OBTAIN WHAT THEY HAD NEVER HAD/ In the past they had never been as delighted and happy. They obtain what they never had before.

Sutra:

THE BRIGHT LIGHT FROM BETWEEN THE BROWS

SHINES INTO THE EASTERN QUARTER,

CAUSING EIGHTEEN THOUSAND LANDS

ALL TO BECOME OF GOLDEN HUE.

AND FROM THE AVICHI HELL,

UPWARDS TO THE PEAK OF BEING,
WITHIN EACH OF THE WORLDS ARE SEEN
THE BEINGS WITHIN THE SIX PATHS,
THEIR DESTINIES IN BIRTH AND DEATH,
THEIR KARMIC CONDITIONS, GOOD OR EVIL,
THEIR RETRIBUTIONS, FAVORABLE OR ILL--
ALL OF THIS IS SEEN, HEREIN.

Outline:

G2. asking about portents in other worlds
H1. asking about living beings in the six destinies

Commentary:

THE BRIGHT LIGHT FROM BETWEEN THE BROWS/ the white hair-mark, located between the Buddhas eyebrows, emits a great light which SHINES INTO THE EASTERN QUARTER/ CAUSING EIGHTEEN THOUSAND LANDS/ ALL TO BECOME OF GOLDEN HUE/

AND FROM THE AVICHI HELL/ from the lowest point, UPWARDS TO THE PEAK OF BEING/ There are three realms of existence: the realm of desire, the realm of form, and the formless realm. The peak of being refers to the Heaven of Neither Perception nor non-Perception, which is the fourth station of emptiness. This is located in the form realm and can't be said to have any particular form. Nevertheless, the Buddha now emits light which shines all the way up to the top of the formless heavens. WITHIN EACH OF THE WORLDS ARE SEEN/ In all the worlds in the limitless Buddhalands THE BEINGS IN THE SIX PATHS/ the path of the gods, humans, asuras, and hell-beings, hungry ghosts, as well as the animals. THEIR DESTINIES IN BIRTH AND DEATH/ Within the six paths, living beings are

born and then they die; they
die and then are born:
birth, birth, death--
death, death, birth--
death, birth,
birth, death--

they spin around in the revolving wheel of the six paths of rebirth.

Although you are a human being in this world, don't think that you will always be so. If your actions are good, you may be assured of keeping a human body, but if you do evil deeds, you will lose it.

Then what will one become?

Haven't I already told you? You can go to hell, become a hungry ghost, or turn into an animal.

THEIR KARMIC CONDITIONS, GOOD OR EVIL/ Perhaps your deeds are good or perhaps they are evil. Goodness creates good karmic conditions and evil has evil karmic conditions, but the deeds are done and the conditions created by you alone. It is said,

> Good and evil are two diverging roads;
> You can cultivate the good, or commit crimes.

"Cultivate" means to practice the Way. "Commit" means to create offenses. There is a good road and a bad road. It's up to you to choose which one you will walk. If you walk down the good road, you'll create good karma. If you walk down the evil one, you will create evil karma.

THEIR RETRIBUTIONS, FAVORABLE OR ILL/ Good and evil refer to conditions on the causal ground. If you plant good causes, you will receive favorable retribution; if you plant evil causes you will receive bad retribution. A favorable retribution means that everything is as you wish it to be. An unfavorable retribution goes against your wishes. Favorable and ill refer to the effect of prior actions. If you plant good seeds you will reap a favorable fruit. If you plant evil seeds, you'll reap an ill fruit. ALL OF THIS IS SEEN HEREIN/ The turning wheel of the six paths, the interrelated process of creating karma and undergoing retribution is all seen in the Thus Come One's white hair-mark light.

Sutra:

> FURTHER SEEN ARE ALL THE BUDDHAS,
>
> THE LIONS, THE SAGELY MASTERS,
>
> EXPOUNDING ON THE SUTRA SCRIPTURES,
>
> OF FOREMOST SUBTLETY AND WONDER.
>
> CLEAR AND PURE IS THE SOUND
>
> OF THEIR SOFT, COMPLIANT VOICES,

TEACHING ALL THE BODHISATTVAS,
NUMBERING IN THE COUNTLESS MILLIONS.
THE BRAHMA SOUND, PROFOUND AND WONDROUS,
FILLS THOSE WHO HEAR WITH JOY
AS, WITHIN HIS WORLD, EACH ONE
PROCLAIMS THE PROPER DHARMA.
THROUGH VARIOUS CAUSES AND CONDITIONS,
AND LIMITLESS ANALOGIES,
THEY CLARIFY THE BUDDHADHARMA
TO ENLIGHTEN LIVING BEINGS.

Outline:

H2. asking about seeing the Buddhas & hearing the Dharma

Commentary:

FURTHER SEEN ARE ALL THE BUDDHAS/ The Buddhas are seen as well. THE LIONS, THE SAGELY MASTERS/ They are the masters among the sages EXPOUNDING ON THE SUTRA SCRIPTURES/ the Great Vehicle Sutras which are OF FOREMOST SUBTLETY AND WONDER This is truly rare, #1, wonderful Dharma.

CLEAR AND PURE ARE THE SOUNDS/ The Buddhas' sounds are extremely clear and resonant. OF THEIR SOFT, COMPLIANT VOICES/ Their voices are both resonant and soft, compliant, delicate, and beautiful sounds, which please the ear and delight the hearts of the entire assembly. According to whatever kind of sound each person likes to hear, the Buddha's voice takes on that quality. TEACHING ALL THE BODHISATTVAS/ The Buddhas teach and transform all the Bodhisattvas NUMBERING IN THE COUNTLESS MILLIONS/ Their number in the countless myriads of millions.

THE BRAHMA SOUND, PROFOUND AND WONDROUS/ The clear, pure sounds are extremely deep and fine. FILLS THOSE WHO HEAR WITH JOY/ The more people hear it, the more they enjoy hearing it. AS, WITHIN HIS WORLD, EACH ONE/

PROCLAIMS THE PROPER DHARMA/ All the Buddhas residing in their own worlds, expound upon the proper Dharma, the genuine Buddhadharma. THROUGH VARIOUS CAUSES AND CONDITIONS/ People are not the same. They have varying dispositions, and so when teaching the Dharma, the Buddha employs various types of causes and conditions to teach them and cure them of their differing bad habits and faults. AND LIMITLESS ANALOGIES/ Limitless means that they can't be counted. The Buddha uses numberous analogies to teach the Dharma, all for the sake of leading living beings to understand the genuine Buddhadharma and cultivate in accord with it.

So the text says TO CLARIFY THE BUDDHADHARMA/ How do they clarify it? They use wisdom to brightly illuminate it. They use the bright light of wisdom to bring about the understanding of all the Buddhadharmas.

TO ENLIGHTEN LIVING BEINGS/ They cause all living beings to gain increasing wisdom and Bodhi. It's like digging a mine. The mine may contain gold, but unless you find a way to dig it out, the gold will not appear. The Buddhanature is inherent within the self-nature of living beings, but unless you explain it to them clearly, they will not understand their inherent Buddhanature and they will be unable to cultivate it.

Sutra:

TO THOSE WHO'VE ENCOUNTERED SUFFERING,
WEARY OF SICKNESS, AGING, DEATH,
THEY SPEAK ABOUT NIRVANA,
WHICH BRINGS ALL SUFFERING TO AN END.
TO THOSE POSSESSED OF BLESSINGS WHO'VE
MADE OFFERINGS TO PAST BUDDHAS AND
RESOLVED TO SEEK THE SUPERIOR DHARMA
THEY SPEAK OF ENLIGHTENING TO CONDITIONS.
TO THOSE WHO ARE THE BUDDHA'S SONS,
WHO CULTIVATE VARIOUS PRACTICES,
SEEKING WISDOM UNSURPASSED,
THEY SPEAK OF THE WAY OF PURITY.

Outline:

H3. asking about the four-fold multitude

Commentary:

TO THOSE WHO'VE ENCOUNTERED SUFFERING/ Although common people suffer, the more they suffer the more they like it, and the more they suffer, the more suffering they encounter. Basically affliction is the cause of the suffering we undergo, but people don't want to put their afflictions aside. They want to keep the communication link between themselves and their afflictions. They can't leave them. They can't separate from the causes of their suffering. The more they suffer, the more they must suffer. When their suffering reaches its extreme point, they fall into the hells, where they suffer eternally, never obtaining happiness. That's the way it is with common people.

Those of other religions wish to end suffering, but they are unable to find a path which will lead them out. They cultivate and uphold methods of their religions, but they are unable to end suffering. They continue to undergo suffering, and although it is not as intense as that in the hells, they may still run off and become hungry ghosts if they are not careful. Those of outside ways cannot ultimately put an end to suffering.

There are also people who are intelligent and clever and have a bit of worldly wisdom. They have a thorough understanding of mundane dharmas, but they do not understand transcendental dharmas. When they run into the causes and conditions of suffering, they have no way to bring them to an end. Wishing to end suffering, they only succeed in running into more suffering. Do you know how they think? They think, "Perhaps I shall rob someone of his money and then I won't have to suffer." Because this kind of person has a small measure of intelligence, he knows how to cheat people. He catches someone off-guard and sneaks off with his wealth or takes it by force. In spite of the fact that he is "wise" other people also have wisdom. He may think he can get away with his clever tricks, but eventually he sets off a burglar alarm. The police get the call and take him to jail. If the crime is minor, his time may not be long; for a heavy offense, he may be in for a long time. He thus receives his retribution in the world of people.

What about the future? People like this cannot

end suffering. Where do they go? In the future they may become animals. There are various reasons for falling into the hells or becoming an animal or a hungry ghost. It's not just a matter of one kind of cause or condition. I'm simply mentioning some of them, but these are not the only ones. There are all manner of causes and conditions which can lead one to fall into the three evil paths and endure the suffering there.

AND GROWN WEARY OF SICKNESS, AGING, DEATH/ Fundamentally there are Three Sufferings, Eight Sufferings, and all the limitless sufferings.

The Three Sufferings are:

1. The suffering within suffering.
2. The suffering of decay.
3. The suffering of process.

The suffering within suffering refers to the suffering of poverty. The suffering of decay occurs when ones happiness starts to wear thin, and ones wealth eventually runs out. It is simply happiness gone bad. The suffering of process refers to the life process itself. One grows from youth to middle age and then to old age. The constant change in every thought is like the action of the waves on the sea. When the first wave disappears, the next one takes its place, and yet another follows it. No one can avoid the suffering of the life process.

The first of the Eight Sufferings is that of birth.

"But when I was born, I didn't even know what was happening!" you say. "How could that be considered suffering?"

You didn't know what was happening? It's just that you don't know that reveals the intensity of the suffering. It is a trauma you cannot even remember. Later on, just because of the suffering of birth, you will be forced to endure the suffering of old age.

What is the suffering of birth?

When children are born, they cry as if to say, "This world is truly full of suffering, suffering, suffering." Although they suffer, later they forget. They get caught up in the flow of life and forget to look back. They start thinking, "This world isn't so bad." In the beginning they knew it was suffering, but after they are three years old, they forget their suffering.

Forget what suffering?

When a child is still in its mother's womb, he feels like he's inside a volcano if she eats something hot. If she eats something cold, he feels like he's in the hells of ice. But there's no way he can speak up and object to these problems. As he is born, he feels like he's being squeezed between two mountains. What is more, while in the womb, the child was never exposed to the air, and the moment the air hits his body, he feels as if he is being slashed with knives. And so he screams and cries.

Having forgotten the suffering of birth, during his prime he doesn't feel particularly troubled, but once he gets old, his eyes refuse to help him, his ears refuse to work, and so do his teeth. He can't see or hear clearly, and having lost his teeth, he can't appreciate the taste of the food he eats. This is the second suffering, that of old age.

Getting old in itself is not all that bad, but once old, he can't walk anymore and has to lean on a cane to get around. When he walks, his legs don't listen to his orders. He may think to take a step, but his legs are lazy and refuse to move; it takes a great deal of energy to walk a single step. Would you say that this was suffering or not? Not many years before when he sent down an order, his six senses all obeyed promptly, but now they refuse to obey. But even that cannot be considered real suffering.If you have a bit of skill in being patient, you won't mind it so much.

The suffering of sickness, however, is definitely frightening. Sickness is most democratic. From an emperor, president, king, or a great official, to the lowest beggar, no matter who you are, if you get sick you will feel you have lost your freedom. Forced to stay in a hospital and follow the doctor's orders, you'll feel that sickness is terrible suffering. There are many kinds of diseases and many kinds of suffering to go along with them. But even these are not as extreme as the suffering of death. There is no suffering greater than that of death. Birth, old age, sickness, and death are all suffering, and birth and death are the extremes. Death and birth involve the same kind of suffering. Dharma Masters of the past have said that birth is like ripping the shell from a live tortoise and death is like skinning a live cow. Would you call this suffering or not?

Why do we study the Buddhadharma?

Because we wish to end birth and death and escape from the revolving wheel. So the text says, "Weary of sickness, aging, death/" The suffering of birth is included in these lines.

Not only do we face the sufferings of aging, sickness, and death, but there is also the suffering of being separated from what one loves.

"Ah!" you say, "I really love that person." Maybe you are a man who loves a woman or a woman who loves a man. You love each other and it makes you very happy, but when you have to part, you suffer.

"I can avoid that kind of suffering," you say. "We will simply never part! Wherever she goes, I will follow. If the one I love runs to the ends of the heavens, I will follow her there. If she runs to the moon, Ill go to the moon. If she runs off to the sun, I'll follow her there."

You will? When she dies, will you go along with her?

"Yes!" you say defiantly.

If you do, then you'll suffer. But if you don't, you'll suffer, too. Either way, you'll have to suffer. It just doesn't work out.

Then there is the suffering of being around what one hates. "I just basically can't stand that person," you say. Perhaps it's even your own spouse. You may really be dissatisfied, but she follows you wherever you go. Or perhaps you say, "I can't stand that friend of mine. I've got to get away from him." But when you move to another city you make another friend who turns out to be exactly like the first. This is called the suffering of being around what you hate." Those with whom you have no affinity you grow to detest. But, the way fate would have it, when you leave that person and go somewhere else, you run into someone exactly like him. The person you left behind was half a pound and this person turns out to be eight ounces--no more, no less--exactly the same.

There is also the suffering of not getting what one wants. You may want to get rich, but you're always poor. You may want to become an official, but you are always a clerk. You may want a good wife, but you can't find one. You may want a good husband, but you can't find one. You can't get what you want and you brood on it morning and night, causing yourself endless affliction. Why? Because you can't get what you seek. Because you can't get it, you suffer even more, to the point that insomnia strikes. You toss and turn; you roll over on one side, but you can't get to sleep; you roll over on the other side, and you still can't get to sleep. From dusk 'til dawn, you don't sleep a wink. The next morning your eyes hurt, your body is tired, and you feel listless. Would you say that was suffering or not?

"I don't suffer in that way," you say. "I am not greedy to get rich, to become an official or to find a good wife or husband. I don't want anything at all. I don't hate or love anyone. So I don't endure suffering, do I?"

Your body is still subject to the tricks played on it by the five skandhas, form, feeling, thought, activity, and consciousness. They rattle around in your body, hopping back and forth all day long, driving you to the point that you haven't even the time to take a breath. Form, feeling, thought, activity, and consciousness are the five skandhas and no one can avoid the suffering of the raging blaze of the five skandhas; it is the most suffering of all.

THEY SPEAK ABOUT NIRVANA/ Because of all this suffering, the Buddhas teach the Dharma of Nirvana.

What is Nirvana? "Nir" means not produced. "Vana" means "not destroyed." You must not be attached to the false shell of the body, the physical body. Don't be attached, but seek instead the supreme Way and attain the happiness of Nirvana where there is no birth or death. Without birth or death you will have ended the three sufferings, the eight sufferings, and all the limitless sufferings. You will have attained the Four Virtues of Nirvana: permanence, joy, true self, and purity.

WHICH BRINGS ALL SUFFERING TO AN END/ If you obtain Nirvana, you will have exhausted the limits of suffering.

TO THOSE POSSESSED OF BLESSINGS/ people who have cultivated the Way and MADE OFFERINGS TO PAST BUDDHAS AND/ who have in the past made offerings to the Triple Jewel. If you would like to avoid suffering, then make offerings to the Triple Jewel. In the presence of the Triple Jewel, perform acts of merit and virtue. However, when you do, don't say, "I gave money to the temple! What did they spend it on?" You shouldn't ask. You shouldn't pay attention to how the offering is used. You plant your own blessings and don't worry about what is done with your offering. If you make offerings to the Triple Jewel, do everything within your power to seek blessings and wisdom before the Triple Jewel.

How does one seek blessings? To foster merit and virtue is to cultivate blessings.

How does one seek wisdom?

Study the Buddhadharma, listen to the Sutra lectures, and read and recite Sutras. The text says, "To those possessed of blessings/" Why do they have blessings? Because, in the past, they made offerings to the Buddha, the Dharma, and the Sangha.

RESOLVED TO SEEK THE SUPERIOR DHARMA/ They are determined to go on, to make progress, to seek the superior Dharma. Superior means "special," a special kind of Buddhadharma.

THEY SPEAK OF ENLIGHTENING TO CONDITIONS/ The Buddhas teach them the Dharma of the Twelve Conditioned Causes:

1. ignorance which conditions
2. action, which conditions
3. consciousness, which conditions
4. name and form, which conditions
5. the six sense organs, which conditions
6. contact, which conditions
7. feeling, which conditions
8. craving, which conditions
9. grasping, which conditions
10. becoming, which conditions
11. birth, which conditions
12. old age and death.

Those of the Vehicle of Conditioned Enlightened Ones, one of the Two Vehicles, cultivate by means of the Twelve Conditioned Causes.

TO THOSE WHO ARE THE BUDDHA'S SONS/ WHO CULTIVATE VARIOUS PRACTICES/ SEEKING WISDOM UNSURPASSED/ THEY SPEAK THE WAY OF PURITY/ The Way of purity is the Six Paramitas.

Sutra:

MANJUSHRI, WHILE DWELLING HERE,

I SEE AND HEAR SUCH THINGS AS THESE,

REACHING TO A THOUSAND MILLION THINGS;

SUCH A MULTITUDE OF THEM

WHICH I SHALL NOW EXPLAIN IN BRIEF.

Outline:

H4. summation of preceding questions and beginning of next questions

Commentary:

MANJUSHRI, WHILE DWELLING HERE/ I SEE AND HEAR

SUCH THINGS AS THESE/ Like what? Like the things described above! REACHING TO A THOUSAND, MILLION THINGS/ SUCH A MULTITUDE OF THEM/ WHICH I SHALL NOW DESCRIBE IN BRIEF/ All the many things I've seen I'll now describe in general. I ask the Bodhisttva Manjushri to explain them to me in detail, but first I shall talk about them in general.

Sutra:

I SEE IN OTHER LANDS

BODHISATTVAS LIKE GANGE'S SANDS,

THROUGH VARIOUS CAUSES AND CONDITIONS

SEEKING THE BUDDHA WAY.

Outline:

H5. asking about the cultivation of Bodhisattva practices
I1. general questions

Commentary:

I SEE, IN OTHER LANDS/ Maitreya Bodhisattva says, "I can see in other words BODHISATTVAS LIKE GANGE'S SANDS/ as numberless as the grains of sand in the Gange's River THROUGH VARIOUS CAUSES AND CONDITIONS/ using all manner of causes and conditions SEEKING THE BUDDHA WAY/ In seeking the Buddha Way, we must foster merit and virtue. Don't think you can obtain the Buddha Way cheaply. See, Bodhisattvas in number as many as the grains of sand in the Gange's River use all kinds of causes and conditions...

What does that mean, "all kinds of causes and conditions?"

It means to foster all kinds of merit and virtue, to cultivate all kinds of blessings and wisdom, and to study all the various Buddhadharmas. It's not just one kind of cause and condition which is used in seeking for the Buddha Way.

Sutra:

PERHAPS THEY PRACTICE GIVING,

WITH GIFTS OF SILVER, GOLD, AND CORAL

OF TRUE PEARLS, AND OF MANI,
MOTHER-OF-PEARL, CARNEILIAN,
OF VAJRA AND OF OTHER GEMS,
OF SERVANTS AND OF CARRIAGES,
JEWELED HAND DRAWN CARTS AND PALANQUINS.
THESE THEY OFFER UP WITH JOY,
IN DEDICATION TO THE BUDDHA WAY,
VOWING TO OBTAIN THE VEHICLE
FOREMOST IN THE TRIPLE REALM,
THE ONE WHICH ALL THE BUDDHAS PRAISE.
THERE ARE BODHISATTVAS WHO
GIVE A JEWELED COACH -AND-FOUR,
WITH RAILS AND FLOWERED CANOPIES,
RICHLY ORNAMENTED CARRIAGES.
AGAIN ARE BODHISATTVAS SEEN
WHO GIVE THEIR FLESH, HANDS, AND FEET,
WHO EVEN GIVE THEIR WIVES AND CHILDREN,
SEEKING FOR THE UTMOST WAY.
AGAIN ARE BODHISATTVAS SEEN
WHOSE HEADS, EYES, AND BODIES WHOLE
ARE OFFERED UP MOST JOYFULLY,
SEEKING THE BUDDHA'S WISDOM.

Outline:

I2. questions about
the six pefections
J1. giving

Commentary:

PERHAPS THEY PRACTICE GIVING/ the first of the Six Perfections. What do they give? WITH GIFTS OF SILVER, GOLD, AND CORAL/ OF TRUE PEARLS AND OF MANI/ The Mani pearl is also called the As-You-Will Pearl. MOTHER-OF-PEARL, CARNEILIAN/ Mother-of-pearl is a precious substance, white in color. It appears to have tracks in it, but when you touch it, it's smooth. Carneilian is a red stone that looks as if it had blood in it.

OF VAJRA AND OF OTHER GEMS/ Vajra refers to diamonds. OF SERVANTS AND OF CARRIAGES/ Perhaps they give their slaves or servants, or their JEWELED HAND DRAWN CARTS AND PALANQUINS/ Carts refers to hand-drawn carts, such as the Imperial Chariot which the ancient emperors used to ride in. Palanquins are sedan chairs which are carried on the shoulders.

THESE THEY OFFER UP WITH JOY/ They give with joy and delight. They aren't like us. We give five, ten, or twenty dollars, and think it's a big thing. The Bodhisattvas gave away the seven jewels--such priceless things--and they did so happily. IN DEDICATION TO THE BUDDHA WAY/ They dedicated their gifts to attaining the Buddha Way. Why did they wish to offer up such valuable things? "I give away these expensive things, those things which are the hardest for me to give. I give them happily in exchange for the realization of Buddhahood, in dedication to seeking the Buddha Way, the road to Buddhahood." VOWING TO ATTAIN THE VEHICLE/ I wish to attain the Buddha Vehicle because it is FOREMOST IN THE TRIPLE REALM/ in the desire realm, the form realm, and in the formless realm. THE ONE WHICH ALL THE BUDDHAS PRAISE/ After realizing Buddhahood, all the Buddhas of the ten directions praise it in exultation.

Maitreya Bodhisattva addresses Manjushri Bodhisattva saying, "Within the white hair-mark emitted by the Buddha, the World Honored One, I see that THERE ARE BODHISATTVAS WHO/ GIVE A JEWELED COACH-AND-FOUR/ They have exquisitely beautiful carriages pulled by four horses. The carriages are adorned with gems, WITH RAILS AND FLOWERED CANOPIES/ In the Land of Ultimate Bliss there are seven tiers of railings, too. The carriage-tops are made of flowers. RICHLY ORNAMENTED CARRIAGES/ adorned with beautiful things.

AGAIN ARE BODHISATTVAS SEEN/ WHO GIVE THEIR FLESH, HANDS, AND FEETS/ WHO EVEN GIVE THEIR WIVES AND CHILDREN/

Not only do these Bodhisattvas give valuable objects, but they can even give their bodies, their own flesh, their hands or feet, or their wives and children to others. Would you say that such giving was practicing that which is hard to practice? We give a little money or a small gift and feel extremely self-satisfied, even arrogant, and think that we have earned a great deal of merit. And yet here we see Bodhisattvas who can, if someone else needs them, give away their bodies, their flesh and blood, their hands and feet.

"But," you say, "what use is there in giving away my body? If you give someone a body, they can't eat it. Why give it?"

When Bodhisattvas practice the Bodhisattva Way, they may encounter someone who has a particular illness and needs, perhaps, a heart transplant such as those present day doctors perform. Or perhaps they need a liver, spleen, lungs, or kidneys. The doctors remove the sick organ and replace it with a healthy one. The Bodhisattva, seeing such living beings, will supply the needed organs. The Bodhisattva will sacrifice his very life for another living being. Perhaps there is a living being who has injured his hand. Seeing this, the Bodhisattva will give his own hand to him. The same goes for the feet. Maybe someone was hurt in an auto accident, his bones smashed and his legs crippled. Seeing this, the Bodhisattva will give his own feet to him. This is done in order to teach and transform living beings.

The Bodhisattvas will even give their wives and children. We are not talking about Bodhisattvas who have already attained spiritual penetrations; they are simply those who have brought forth the Bodhisattva resolve. They simply have hearts full of giving.

What do they give?

They give that which is most difficult for people to give, their spouses. To say nothing of giving up one's wife or husband, most people find it extremely painful even to be separated from them for a short period of time. They find this extremely painful. However, these Bodhisattvas, seeing that others need wives, will give their own wives away. There are many causes and conditions surrounding such giving.

In my book, *Record of the Water and Mirror Turning Back Heaven,* I wrote about the Abbot of the monastery where I cultivated, the Venerable High Elder Master Ch'ang-jen. When he was cultivating the Way, he gave away his wife. How did that happen?

He had a wife, but when his father and mother died,

he resolved to observe the practice of filial piety by sitting beside their graves for a period of three years. While he sat, his wife was at home observing "widowhood" and she didn't like it one bit. She was a living widow. Her husband hadn't died, but had gone off to observe filial piety. He did not return home. The living widow finally couldn't stand it, and she went to the gravesite and insisted that her husband return home with her. She went once, twice, three, four and even five times, but he wouldn't return home. His heart was sincere; he cultivated the Way with a sincere heart.

Now, those who have sincere hearts are bound to encounter demons. It is said,

> When the Way grows a foot,
> the demon grows taller by ten;
> When the Way grows ten feet,
> the demon sits right on your head!

Because he was sincere and refused to return home, his wife thought of an ingenious plan. "So you won't return home? I'll just find some other man to spend my days with," she threatened.

"Take up with some other man if you like," he said. "I'm through with household affairs. I have renounced everything. I have put *everything* down! I pay no attention to such matters whatsoever."

If he hadn't truly been intent on cultivating the Way, when his wife threatened to find another man, how could he have endured it? But he said, "All right. Fine. If you find a man you like, someone you think you love, then go with him."

"Go with him?" she said. "Okay, I'm going to go looking," and she went back and found herself a man. Then she brough him with her to the gravesite and spoke to her husband, saying, "If you do not return home with me now, I'm going to marry this man!"

What do you think? Someone without genuine samadhi power and a true mind of the Way would have gone home, don't you think? But he didn't go. "I'm going with him," she said, and off she went. He gave his wife away and didn't ask for so much as a cent in return. This is truly an example of Bodhisattvas giving their wives away SEEKING FOR THE UTMOST WAY.

Why do they do this? Because they seek the utmost Way. Bodhisattvas who seek the utmost way must be able to renounce that which is difficult to renounce. The harder it is for you to give it up, the more meaningful your act of renunciation becomes. It then truly counts as:

Seeing through it,
Breaking it open,
Giving it up and
Winning your freedom.

You can't say, "I'm going to hold onto those things I can't part with. Even if I could become a Buddha by giving them up, I still won't let go of the things I love, or the people I love." If you think like this, it's because you don't place importance on the Buddha Way. If you saw the Buddha Way as truly important, you would be able to put down absolutely everything. If the Buddhadharma was of primary importance to you, you wouldn't become influenced by improper external circumstances.

AGAIN ARE BODHISATTVAS SEEN/ WHOSE HEADS, EYES, AND BODIES WHOLE/ These are other Bodhisattvas who give their heads, eyes, and bodies. The Bodhisattvas mentioned above gave outer wealth and inner wealth. The outer wealth refers to wives and children; the inner wealth is their bodily flesh, their hands and feet. But they did not give their entire bodies. They only gave their flesh, or their hands or feet. Now these Bodhisattvas give their very heads and eyes, their entire bodies. ARE OFFERED UP MOST JOYFULLY/ If any living being at all is in need of a head, they will give up their heads; if they need eyes, they will give their eyes. In fact, they'll give their whole bodies, or any part of them.

Someone thinks, "That's idiotic! How can you give your own body to others?"

You think the Bodhisattvas are stupid, but they think that you are stupid. Why? In being able to give, seeking the utmost Way, they are able to end birth and death. In not giving you may feel that you are intelligent, but you'll never be able to end birth and death. If you wish to end birth and death, you must imitate the great, fearless spirit of these Bodhisattvas who give up their bodies, hearts, and lives to others, to the world.

They give cheerfully. They don't give angrily. They don't say, "So you're giving? Let's have a little contest. If you give ten thousand dollars, I'll give twenty thousand. If you give twenty thousand, I'll give thirty thousand." They are not competitive in their giving. On the contrary, they give happily and cheerfully.

Why do they give? They are SEEKING THE BUDDHA'S WISDOM.

Sutra:

MANJUSHRI,
I SEE ROYAL MONARCHS WHO
VISITING THOSE BUDDHAS' COURTS
ASK ABOUT THE UTMOST WAY,
AND THEN FORSAKE THEIR PLEASANT LANDS,
PALACES, MINISTERS, CONCUBINES,
AND, CUTTING OFF THEIR BEARDS AND HAIR,
CLOTHE THEMSELVES IN DHARMA ROBES.

Outline:

J2. **mora**lity

Commentary:

MANJUSHRI! Wonderful Virtue Bodhisattva! I SEE ROYAL MONARCHS/ I also see kings, not just one king, but many of them, VISITING THOSE BUDDHAS' COURTS/ What are they doing? They are going off to visit the Buddhas. TO ASK ABOUT THE UTMOST WAY/ They ask about the supreme Buddha Way. After they ask about it, the Buddha instructs them in the doctrines of suffering, emptiness, impermanence, and non-self. He says, "Everything in this world is bound up in suffering.

Wealth and honor
are like a dream before dawn.
Power and fame are like a floating cloud.
The bones and flesh of the present
Also are unreal.
Devotion turns to hatred...

Wealth and honor are as insubstantial as a dream just before the sun comes up. Power and fame are like floating clouds in space. They do not last. The bones and flesh of the present moment, the relationships of father and son, husband and wife, elder and younger brothers, are also unreal. You may love someone and be very close to them, but in the future, as time goes by, love will turn into contempt and hatred."

When the kings hear this instruction from the

Buddhas, they immediately, without further thought, FORSAKE THEIR PLEASANT LANDS/ their happy pleasure grounds. They give them away. PALACES, MINISTERS, CONCUBINES/ their palaces made of jewels, their halls and pavilions made of aloeswood and sandalwood, their ministers and their concubines. Why do they give them away?

AND, CUTTING OFF THEIR BEARDS AND HAIR/ they become novices, and they CLOTHE THEMSELVES IN DHARMA ROBES/ They put on the clothing worn by those who have left home, the kshaya or five-piece sash worn by novice monks.

The kings leave the home-life seeking the Dharma of the precepts, and so this section deals with morality.

Sutra:

SEEN ARE BODHISATTVAS WHO
BECOMING BHIKSHUS, DWELL ALONE
WITHIN THE WILDS, IN QUIETUDE,
RECITING SUTRA TEXTS WITH JOY.

Outline:

J3. patience

Commentary:

SEEN ARE BODHISATTVAS WHO/ leave the home-life to become Bhikshus. BECOMING BHIKSHUS, DWELL ALONE/ This section deals with the perfection of patience. Perhaps Bodhisattvas are seen who dwell deep in the forests or in mountain caves. Evil people may come upon them. When such people strike or rebuke them they must patiently endure it. When evil beasts bite them, them also must be patient and not become frightened or alarmed. So these four lines discuss patience. They like to read and recite Sutras.

Sutra:

AGAIN ARE BODHISATTVAS SEEN,
STRIVING WITH HEROIC VIGOR,

ENTERING THE MOUNTAINS DEEP,

TO PONDER ON THE BUDDHA WAY.

Outline:

J4. vigor

Commentary:

AGAIN ARE BODHISATTVAS SEEN/STRIVING WITH HEROIC VIGOR/ How are they vigorous? They go without eating to study the Buddhadharma. They go without sleeping to study the Buddhadharma. They aren't like some people who go without eating but make up for it by sleeping more, saying, "I haven't eaten so I can't cultivate. I'll sleep a little more instead." When others are not sleeping they are asleep. That is not heroic vigor. Those with heroic vigor will go without eating because they forget about food altogether. They don't deliberately refrain from eating in order to put on that they are cultivating. They just forget about eating and sleeping; they forget about everything. What do they think of? They think only to cultivate and to study the Buddhadharma. ENTERING THE MOUNTAINS DEEP/ They go deep into the mountain valleys TO PONDER ON THE BUDDHA WAY/ Ponder means that they cultivate the Buddhadharma; they cultivate in accord with the Dharma.

Sutra:

SEEN, TOO, ARE THOSE WHO'VE LEFT DESIRE,

WHO DWELL IN CONSTANT SOLITUDE,

DEEPLY CULTIVATING DHYANA SAMADHI

AND ATTAINING FIVE SPIRITUAL PENETRATIONS.

AGAIN ARE BODHISATTVAS SEEN

IN THE PEACE OF DHYANA, WITH PALMS JOINED,

WHO, WITH A THOUSAND TEN THOUSAND LINES,

SING PRAISES OF THE DHARMA KINGS.

Outline:

J5. samadhi

Commentary:

Maitreya Bodhisattva contines, saying, "I also see Arhats and Bodhisattvas who have LEFT DESIRE." To leave desire means to separate oneself from lust. If you separate from lust you can cultivate the Way. Those who cultivate the Way should not have thoughts of greed. They should not be greedy for wealth. They should not be greedy for sex. They should not be greedy for material possessions. Once rid of all thoughts of greed one may be said to have "left desire." WHO DWELL IN CONSTANT SOLITUDE/ They like to live in the wilds, where few people go. DEEPLY CULTIVATING DHYANA SAMADHI/ All day they sit in Dhyana. If you wish to develop your wisdom, it is essential that you cultivate samadhi. Without samadhi you will have no wisdom. So this passage of verse deals with Dhyana samadhi. You should deeply cultivate Dhyana samadhi. This is not to say that you cultivate it today and fail to cultivate it tomorrow. You can't cultivate for one day and rest on the next, or rest for a day and then cultivate for half a day, or cultivate one day and rest for ten days. You should cultivate every day without resting, not the other way around. If you rest every day and do not cultivate, you'll not attain Dhyana samadhi. If you wish to obtain deep Dhyana samadhi, truly to take the joy of Dhyana as your food, and come to know the true flavor of Dhyana, then you must work hard at your cultivation every single day.

When the time comes to sit in Dhyana, you must go ahead and do so, regardless of how busy you are. You must find time in the midst of all your myriad activities to sit in Dhyana, without missing a single day. Then you can obtain the realm of skill in Dhyana samadhi.

AND ATTAINING FIVE SPIRITUAL PENETRATIONS/ Through deep Dhyana samadhi they attain five kinds of spiritual penetrations.

And what are they? The Penetration of the Heavenly Eye, the Penetration of the Heavenly Ear, the Penetration of Others' Thoughts, the Penetration of the Knowledge of Past Lives, Penetration of the Complete Spirit. They have not obtained the Penetration of the Extinction of Outflows because this Penetration is only attained at the level of Equal Enlightenment and Wonderful Enlightenment. Because these are Bodhisattvas who have just brought forth the resolve to cultivate, they obtain only five of the Six Spiritual Penetrations.

Where do the Five Spiritual Penetrations come from? They come from the cultivation of Dhyana samadhi, from the recitation of Sutras, and from holding mantras. If you can sit in Dhyana meditation every day with singleminded concentration, you can obtain them.

You can obtain them from reciting Sutras. For example, the Great Master Chih-che recited *The Dharma Flower Sutra* all day long until he became enlightened. When he came to the "Chapter of the Events of Medicine King Bodhisattva" where it says, "This is true vigor; this is called a true Dharma offering," as he recited the words he entered the Dharma Flower Samadhi and obtained a most lofty state. He saw the Dharma assembly at Vulture Peak still in progress; it had not dispersed. He saw that Shakyamuni Buddha was still there speaking the Dharma. So, one can also become enlightened by reciting the Sutras. But you must recite with a sincere heart. You can't recite on the one hand and strike up false thinking on the other. Don't recite on the one hand and climb on conditions on the other, thinking, "So and so has a lot of money. I've got to think of a way to get some money out of him for my own use." You can't open enlightenment reciting Sutras that way because you're not reciting Sutras, you're reciting "money."

You must recite mantras and Sutras singlemindedly in order to become enlightened.

AGAIN ARE BODHISATTVAS SEEN/ IN THE PEACE OF DHYANA, WITH PALMS JOINED/ They are sitting in Dhyana with their hands placed together, WHO WITH A THOUSAND TEN THOUSAND LINES /They make up verse after verse, to SING PRAISES OF THE DHARMA KINGS/ They praise the Buddhas of the ten directions. They do not simply praise Shakyamuni Buddha, but all the Buddhas of the ten directions, because they have been revealed in the light of Shakyamuni Buddha's white hair-mark. But praising the Buddhas of the ten directions is just to praise Shakyamuni Buddha. Why? Because Shakyamuni Buddha himself is one of the Buddhas of the ten directions!

Sutra:

AGAIN ARE BODHISATTVAS SEEN,

OF PROFOUND WISDOM AND SOLID WILL,

ABLE TO QUESTION THE BUDDHAS AND

ACCEPT AND HOLD ALL THEY HAVE HEARD.
FURTHER SEEN ARE BUDDHA'S DISCIPLES,
WITH WISDOM AND SAMADHI PERFECT,
WHO, WITH LIMITLESS ANALOGIES,
PREACH DHARMA TO THE MULTITUDES.
JOYFULLY THEY PREACH THE DHARMA,
TRANSFORMING ALL THE BODHISATTVAS,
DEFEATING THUS THE TROOPS OF MARA,
AND BEATING ON THE DHARMA DRUM.

Outline:

J6. Prajna

Commentary:

Maitreya Bodhisattva says to Manjushri Bodhisattva, AGAIN ARE BODHISATTVAS SEEN/ I also see Bodhisattvas OF PROFOUND WISDOM AND SOLID WILL/ Their wisdom is extremely profound, and their determination is extremely firm and solid. ABLE TO QUESTION THE BUDDHAS AND/ ACCEPT AND HOLD ALL THEY HAVE HEARD/ They are well able to question the Buddhas concerning their doubts. They ask about the Dharma, and having received their answers, they can put what they have heard into actual practice in accord with Dharma--that is, they accept, uphold, and cultivate in accord with Dharma.

FURTHER SEEN ARE BUDDHA'S DISCIPLES/ Also seen are sons of the Dharma King. WITH WISDOM AND SAMADHI PERFECT/ Their samadhi power and their wisdom power are perfected. WHO, WITH LIMITLESS ANALOGIES/ They use an uncountable number of parables, analogies, and doctrines in order to PREACH DHARMA TO THE MULTITUDES/ They expound the Buddhadharma for the sake of living beings. JOYFULLY THEY SPEAK THE DHARMA/ The more they speak, the more they like to speak. This is known as "unobstructed eloquence." The Dharma which they speak is extremely profound, subtle, and wonderful. TRANSFORMING ALL THE BODHISATTVAS/ They teach and convert all the Bodhisattvas. DEFEATING THUS THE TROOPS OF MARA/ They smash through the demonic hosts.AND BEATING ON THE DHARMA DRUM/ They loudly beat the great drum of the Law. Their Dharma preaching sounds like the beating of the Dharma drum.

Sutra:

SEEN TOO ARE BODHISATTVAS
IN SILENCE AND TRANQUILITY;
THOUGH WORSHIPPED BY THE GODS AND DRAGONS,
THEY DO NOT FIND IT CAUSE FOR JOY.
ALSO SEEN ARE BODHISATTVAS
DWELLING IN FORESTS, EMITTING LIGHT,
RELIEVING THOSE SUFFERING IN THE HELLS,
AND LEADING THEM TO THE BUDDHA WAY.

Outline:

I3. miscellaneous questions concerning the Six Perfections
J1. Dhyana samadhi

Commentary:

SEEN TOO ARE BODHISATTVAS/ IN SILENCE AND TRANQUILITY/ They are silent; they do not speak. They sit in full lotus, meditating. As they meditate, because they have skill in Dhyana samadhi, various beings come to worship them. THOUGH WORSHIPPED BY THE GODS AND DRAGONS/ THEY DO NOT FIND IT CAUSE FOR JOY/ They don't think that it's of any consequence. Why not? Because they have ability, profound skill, in Dhyana samadhi. Their thoughts do not stir. In cultivation it is most important to be without thought. Do not have thought. Do not have what thought? Do not have false thought.

If you can be without false thought, just that is non-production. If you have no false thought, just that is no extinction. If you have no false thought, just that is no impurity. If you have no false thought, just that is no increase. If you have no false thought, just that is no decrease. If you have no false thought, there will be no "right." If you have no false thought, there will be no "wrong." If you have no thought, there will be no good, no evil. Why? Because, if you have no thoughts at all, that is purity, the purity of the self-nature, the wonderful nature, True Suchness. However, being without thought isn't just a matter of saying, "I don't have any thought." If you hold onto the "not having of thought," that means you still have thought! If you can have no thought, just that is subduing your mind. If you can be without thought, you have defeated the troops of Mara. The absence of thought is most wonderful.

Why do they take no delight when the gods and dragons worship them? Because they have no thought. It is also because they have patience. They have "patience with production." If you have no thought, then when people make offerings to you and revere you, you will not become arrogant and think, "I'm really an accomplished cultivator. Look at all the people who are making offerings to me." If you have no thought, then if people rebuke you, beat you, defame you or try to ruin you, you will be able to endure it. This is no thought. No thought is something which everyone who studies the Buddhadharma should learn. If you are without thought, then you have no affliction. With no affliction, that is Bodhi. Bodhi is just affliction; affliction is just Bodhi. Still, if you can use it, it's Bodhi; if you can't use it, it's affliction.

Before Patriarch Bodhidharma went to China,he sent ahead two of his disciples, Fo-t'o and Ye-she. The two Indian disciple went to China where they taught the Dharma-door of the Dhyana School. Their teachings are not based on language. It is a direct pointing to the mind, to see the nature and realize Buddhahood.

At that time in China there was another Indian monk named Bodhiruchi. The two monks taught the Dhyana School, and Bodhiruchi taught the Madhyamika School. Bodhiruchi persuaded the Chinese Dharma Masters to run Bodhi-dharma's two disciples right out of the country. They were driven to Lu Mountain. At Lu Mountain, the Venerable Master Yüan, seeing them, asked, "Why did they expel you? Ultimately, what Dharma-door do you transmit?"

Fo-t'o and Ye-she said, "We teach the doctrine of the Dhyana School. The Chinese Dharma Masters and Bodhiruchi,on one hand are jealous of us, and on the other hand they do not understand the Buddhadharma. Because we were outnumbered, they succeeded in driving us out. The Dharma-door we teach we will now illustrate with an analogy:

Then, sticking their hands up in the air, they opened and closed their fists several times."Was that fast or not?" they asked.

"Very fast," replied the Venerable Yüan.

"Bodhi and affliction," they replied, "are just that fast. With one turn, affliction becomes Bodhi. Change again and Bodhi becomes affliction. It's as fast as opening and closing your hand. Opening the hand is like Bodhi. The fist is like affliction. The fist and the palm are both the same hand undergoing changes. The Dhyana School teaches that the mind itself is the Buddha. Understand the mind and see the nature. It is not the case that Bodhi is to be found apart from affliction,nor is there any affliction apart from Bodhi. Affliction is just Bodhi; Bodhi is just affliction. Birth and death is just Nirvana; Nirvana is just birth and death. If you have no thought, that is Nirvana. If youhave thought, that is birth and death. So, the Dharma-door of no thought is the foremost, the most wonderful. If you can not produce a single thought, then the entire substance manifests. If you are without a single thought, that is no thought. Without thought, your inherent Buddha nature manifests. If you have not arrived at the level of no thought, then you have not ended birth and death. If you arrive at the state of no thought, then the ghosts and spirits have no way to disturb you. So the text says, "though gods and dragons worship them/ they do not find it cause for joy." Why don't they rejoice? Because they have entered deep Dhyana samadhi and arrived at the state of no thought. At the state of no thought, they have returned to the root and gone back to the source. They have returned to their original face, to the wind and light of their native land. Everything belongs to them; it's all theirs,and so when the gods and dragons pay them reverence, it's just the way things are. It's no cause to rejoice. The Bodhisattvas employ the skill of Dhyana samadhi.

ALSO SEEN ARE BODHISATTVAS/ DWELLING IN FORESTS, EMITTING LIGHT/ They cultivate self-benefit and they benefit others as well. They dwell in the forests where they cultivate Dhyana meditation. After awhile they put forth great light. Why do they do this? They are RELIEVING THOSE SUFFERING IN THE HELLS/ They use their light to illumine the dark recesses of the hells, and cause the denizens of hell and the hungry ghosts to leave suffering and attain bliss. The Bodhisattvas meditate, benefitting themselves, and then they emit light to benefit others. AND LEADING THEM TO THE BUDDHA WAY/ They give the hell-beings and the hungry ghosts the chance to seek the Buddha Way.

Sutra:

ALSO SEEN ARE BUDDHA'S DISCIPLES
WHO HAVE NOT SLEPT, BUT WALK AT EASE,
WITHIN THE FOREST GROVES; THEY SEEK
WITH DILIGENCE THE BUDDHA WAY.

Outline:

J2. vigor

Commentary:

ALSO SEEN ARE BUDDHA'S DISCIPLES/ WHO HAVE NOT SLEPT, BUT WALK AT EASE/ They don't ever sleep. If they do sleep, they just sit there and doze off for perhaps a second. What are they doing? They are cultivating the Pratyutpanna Samadhi, the Standing Buddha Samadhi. To cultivate this Dharma, a person stays in a single room and walks continually without sitting or reclining for ninety days. For ninety days they do not sleep. They are allowed to eat and go to the toilet, but not to sleep. They battle exclusively with the demon of sleep for three months.

WITHIN THE FOREST GROVES; THEY SEEK/ WITH DILIGENCE THE BUDDHA WAY/ They want to find the road to the accomplishment of Buddhahood.

Sutra:

SEEN TOO ARE THOSE WITH PERFECT PRECEPTS
INTACT, WITH AWE-INSPIRING MANNER,
THEIR PURITY LIKE PRECIOUS PEARLS,
WITH WHICH THEY SEEK THE BUDDHA WAY.

Outline:

J3. morality

Commentary:

SEEN TOO ARE THOSE WITH PERFECT PRECEPTS/ Also seen are those Bodhisattvas who observe the moral precepts, guarding them as they would hold a precious pearl. This section of text refers to the Ten Types of Precepts:

1. Intact precepts. The Bodhisattva who has intact precepts has not violated the heavy-grade of the ten evils and five rebellious acts. If these offenses are committed it is as if one had lost one's life raft. Without the raft, you cannot get across the sea. This means that you will not be able to cross from this shore of birth and death, over the heavy current of afflictions, to the other shore which is Nirvana. So it is most important to have intact precepts, meaning that offenses have not been committed on the heavy-grade.

2. Unbroken precepts. The Bodhisattva who has unbroken precepts has not committed offenses of the ten evils and five rebellious acts on the middle-grade. If these offense have been committed, it is as if one has torn a hole in the life raft; it is ruined and cannot be used. If you do not observe the precepts, then, carrying such offenses,you will not be able to become a Buddha.

3. Unpunctured precepts. If the precepts are punctured, this is like a life raft which is not ripped, but has a leak the size of a pin-point. It soon becomes useless. Unpunctured morality means that one does not violate the lesser-grade of the ten evils and five rebellious acts. To commit offenses of the lesser-grade is not so serious,and so it is said to be like a hole. With a hole, the raft won't float. If you do not hold the precepts purely, you won't be able to become a Buddha.

4. Unscattered precepts. Scattered means that an evil awareness causes one to give rise to evil thoughts. Although pure in body and mouth, the mind is plagued with afflictions. In cultivation, one must practice precepts which are unscattered. These are also called the samadhi precepts, for with samadhi, precepts can be held on this level.

5. Following the Way precepts. When those who have certified to the first fruit of Sagehood walk or plant the fields, the bugs of themselves stay four inches away from their feet. In this way, the Sage avoids harming them. This is a precept power which follows upon your cultivation of the Way.

6. Unattached precepts. This refers to Arhats who have eternally severed their greed and attachment to

the six objective sense objects in the Triple Realm. Numbers five and six are also called Way precepts, or the Precepts of the Absolute Truth.

7. Precepts praised by the wise. The person who holds the precepts at this level is well able to "emerge from the false and blend with the common." Although he does not practice the Middle Way, he is able to use the provisional dharmas within both the common and false truths as an expedient device. Although he does not cultivate the doctrines of the Middle Way, he uses the common truth and the false truth to benefit living beings. Therefore, because he can use provisional dharmas to benefit living beings, he is lauded by those who have wisdom.

8. Precepts of self-mastery. This is the self-mastery of the Bodhisattva Who Contemplates Self-mastery (Avalokiteshvara). They can use their spiritual penetrations to freely roam at play among human beings, and manifest both in opposition and in accord. Although they may appear to do evil deeds, they break neither the precept-nature nor the precept-covering. To keep the precept-nature means that one doesn't even bring forth the thought to break the precepts. To have the thought to break a precept is to violate the nature of the precept; this has no outward appearance. The precept-covering has a visible form. When one breaks the precept-covering that means one has committed an outward act of precept violation. At this level, neither the precept-nature nor the precept-covering is violated. It may appear that they are broken, but they are not.

The Shurangama Sutra mentions the smashing of demons' heads to bits. Someone asked me if this wasn't a case of violating the precepts. I said it was not. That's a case of non-violation in a state of opposition.

Another example is Dhyana Master Pao-chih of the Liang Dynasty, about the time when Bodhidharma went to China. He was a meat-eater, not a vegetarian. Everyday, he ate two pigeons. In fact, he ate two pigeons at every meal. The cook gave him two pigeons and he ate every last bit--bones and all! The cook thought, "They're probably pretty tasty," and one day he snuck one of the wings to take a taste, thinking it wouldn't matter, that Dhyana Master Chih-kung would never know. But the moment Dhyana Master Chih-kung saw them he said, "Why did you steal a taste of my pigeons?"

"I didn't eat them!" the cook said.

"Really?" said Master Chih-kung. "Very well, watch this!" and he ate both of the pigeons. Then, he opened his mouth and the two pigeons flew out again. One of them flew away, but the other was missing a wing. "Well, where's that pigeon's wing," he said, "if you didn't eat it?"

"I cleaned and cooked the two birds myself," said the cook. "How could he spit them back up alive and well?" From this, he knew that Master Chih-kung was no ordinary person; he truly dwelt in the state of a great Bodhisattva. This was a manifestation of a state in opposition to the precepts. Basically, eating meat is wrong, but he could swallow pigeons and spit them out again whole. A while ago someone asked me if one could eat meat and still become enlightened. I said, "If you can swallow a cow in one gulp and then spit it out again alive and well, then you could. If not, you'll surely fall into the hells; youll be obliged to pay your debts. If you eat their meat, in the future they will eat yours. There's not the slightest bit of courtesy involved."

So, the eighth is the Precepts of self-mastery. This means that whatever you want to do, you can do it and it's all right.

You say, "I'd like to try it out."

If you have spiritual penetrations, you can give it a try. If you don't, then you won't be able to pull it off.

Numbers seven and eight are also called Common Truth Precepts.

9. Precepts in accord with samadhi. Whenever you do something, it is as if you were in samadhi. At all times and in all places it is just like being in samadhi.

10. Perfect precepts. In what respect are they perfect? With regard to the perfection of morality, everything one does is in accord with it. One maintains the precepts in all one's actions. Although it may look to you as if such people had violated a precept, they exist in the realm of the Bodhisattvas and so they cannot be judged as one would judge ordinary people. That is the perfection of precepts.

Numbers nine and ten are also called the Precepts of the Absolute Truth of the Middle Way.

INTACT, WITH AWE-INSPIRING MANNER/ Their precepts are not the slightest bit deficient. THEIR PURITY LIKE PRECIOUS PEARLS/ Their clear and lofty purity is as priceless as a jewel. WITH WHICH THEY SEEK THE BUDDHA WAY.

Sutra:

ALSO SEEN ARE THE BUDDHA'S DISCIPLES
ABIDING IN THE STRENGTH OF PATIENCE;
THOUGH BY THOSE OF OVERWEENING PRIDE
MALICIOUSLY REBUKED AND BEATEN,
THEY ARE ABLE TO ENDURE IT ALL,
SEEKING FOR THE BUDDHA WAY.

Outline:

J4. patience

Commentary:

This section of the verse deals with the cultivation of the perfection of patience. Maitreya Bodhisattva again says to Manjushri Bodhisattva ALSO SEEN ARE THE BUDDHA'S DISCIPLES/ true disciples of the Buddha, ABIDING IN THE STRENGTH OF PATIENCE/ They cultivate the perfection of patience. Patience requires no thought. Arriving at the level of no thought is just patience with production, patience with dharmas, and also the patience with the non-production of dharmas. These Bodhisattvas exclusively cultivate the practice of patience.

THOUGH BY THOSE OF OVERWEENING PRIDE/ What does patience cure? It counteracts hatred. If, in any situation you encounter, you are able to endure it without getting angry, that's patience.

Cultivation is something you must do yourself. It is not a matter of instructing others to cultivate. Someone asked me, "If someone is cultivating patience, is it all right if I test him? Can I try his patience?" You shouldn't. Don't test other people; test yourself. "No matter what happens, can I bear it? Can I remain unmoved? Do my thoughts remain unmoved? Whether in accord or in opposition, do I remain at peace, just as if nothing had happened? Can I refrain from getting the least bit perturbed?"

Take care not to test other people. Cultivators of the Way should test themselves, not others. If you test others, you'll get way off the track. For example, if you wanted to go to New York, and went directly, you could get there by train, bus, or in a car in just a few days. If you didn't go directly, but first took off to the south or north, took a lot of different roads, you'd waste a lot of time. The meaning here is if you don't test others but cultivate directly, you can realize Buddhahood very quickly. But if you test others you'll neglect and waste your own skill. You may have been destined for Buddhahood, say, in three great asankheya kalpas, but if you start testing people, it might take you nine! You forget your own skill in testing others.

When can you test others? When you have reached the level where you have spiritual penetrations and can actually manifest the eighteen transformations in empty space, putting forth water from the top of your body and fire from the lower part or emitting fire from the top of your body and water from the lower part. When fire and water do not obstruct each other, when you have arrived at that state, then you may test others. Until then, I would recommend that you refrain.

So the text says, "though by those of overweening pride"/ What are such people like? They are arrogant. They look down on everyone they see. They feel that they themselves are Number One. "I am number one in intelligence and number one in wisdom and in learning. I am number one in everything!" They don't mention that they are number one in stupidity. They don't *feel* that they are number one in stupidity, when in fact they are. People of overweening pride are arrogant, you see, and only stupid people are arrogant. Unless one was stupid, one would not be arrogant and look down on others.

Why? Take a look at Shakyamuni Buddha. Is he stupid or wise? Obviously, he is wise. He is the Greatly Enlightened One. He sees that all living beings can become Buddhas. He sees all living beings as his parents from former lives and as the Buddhas of the future. Therefore, he does not dare to slight living beings. Now, Shakyamuni Buddha is the Greatly Wise, Greatly Enlightened One, and he is not arrogant. We petty little common people--what do we have to be arrogant about? What do we have to be self-satisfied about? Arrogant people of overweening pride are really number one in stupidity, because they are arrogant towards everyone.

MALICIOUSLY REBUKED AND BEATEN/ In cultivating patience, if someone scolds you, you must bear it. If someone beats you, you must bear it. Why? THEY ARE ABLE TO ENDURE IT ALL/ How can they endure the abuse of others? How can they bear the beatings? SEEKING FOR THE BUDDHA WAY/ It is because they seek the Buddha Way. If you wish to seek the Buddha Way, you can't have a temper, you can't get angry. You must cultivate patience.

Sutra:

AGAIN ARE BODHISATTVAS SEEN,
APART FROM ALL FRIVOLITY,
AND FROM STUPID FOLLOWERS,
DRAWING NEAR TO THOSE WITH WISDOM.
SINGLEMINDEDLY CASTING OUT CONFUSION,
COLLECTING THEIR THOUGHTS IN THE
MOUNTAIN FORESTS,
FOR TENS OF THOUSANDS OF MILLIONS OF YEARS
IN QUEST OF THE WAY OF THE BUDDHA.

Outline:

J5. Dhyana samadhi

Commentary:

AGAIN ARE BODHISATTVAS SEEN/ APART FROM ALL FRIVOLITY/ I've explained the word "all" many times. You can explain it as meaning "a lot," that is, removing oneself from all, every bit of, frivolity. You can also explain it as "one," that is, from every single type of frivolity. Frivolity means playing around and laughing. Bodhisattvas who cultivate the Way must not laugh all the time. They also should not play all the time. In everything they do they must be upright and proper. This is not to say that you may never laugh. But laugh when it is appropriate. When it is not, don't laugh.

To be apart from all frivolity is to have removed one of the Five Coverings. The Five Coverings cover the self-nature. To separate from all frivolity is to remove the covering of inconstancy. When an inconstant person undertakes something, he does it in a haphazard manner, with nothing definite about it. He thinks of doing it one way, and then does it another way. Then he changes his mind back again. He can't make a firm decision and he keeps changing his mind back and forth.

Cultivators of the Way can't do as they please and laugh when they feel like it. When it's time to laugh, laugh. At other times,don't. You can't just "Ha, ha,ha!" all day long.

AND FROM STUPID FOLLOWERS/ Who are the stupidest people? They are those who don't study the Buddhadharma. Because they do not study it, they get stupider every day. When their stupidity reaches the extreme, they run off to become animals. Therefore, you should leave stupid followers. This sentence of verse implies the removing of the covering of anger. Anger means hatred. Hatred covers your self-nature. If you have no real wisdom, you are covered by inconstancy, as mentioned above . When you separate from stupid followers, you get rid of the covering of anger.

Why do people get angry? Where does anger come from? It comes from ignorance. What is ignorance? Ignorance is just stupidity. So you don't understand? If that's not stupidity, what is it? By separating from stupid followers one removes the covering of rage. Why do you hate? Why do you lose your temper? It's because you are just plain stupid. So remember this. No matter how intelligent people are, once they get angry, their intelligence vanishes, covered by their anger. They can't do anything. Nothing works out; everything goes wrong. Separating from stupid followers removes the covering of anger.

DRAWING NEAR TO THOSE WITH WISDOM/ Having left stupid followers, they draw near to those who have wisdom. This removes the covering of stupidity. If you draw near to those who have wisdom, you will gradually lose your stupidity. Why?

Those who get near the rouge turn red; those who get near the ink turn black. Those with wisdom like to draw near to those with wisdom. Those without wisdom, if they draw near to the wise, will come to have wisdom. So,you should draw near to those with wisdom, those with learning, those with Way virtue, those with intelligence. If you draw near those with wisdom, you won't do stupid things. Take a look at those who are wise. They don't get angry all day long.If you get near them, you may wish to lose your temper, but you won't find any occasion to lose it. You may be just on the verge of getting angry, but then you think, "That person doesn't get angry. I won't either." There's a common saying:

The good flock together;
The evil run in packs.
People seek out their own kind.

Now, in the Buddhist Lecture Hall, everyone wishes to study the Buddhadharma. This is drawing near to those with wisdom. In America there are very few places where the genuine Buddhadharma is lectured. Take a look. What other Buddhist organization has lectures on the Dharma every single day? Only the Buddhist Lecture Hall. Attending the daily lectures on Buddhadharma is just drawing near to those with wisdom.

Not just anyone can come to the Buddhist Lecture Hall. Some people come, sit for just a minute, and then run off. They can't sit comfortably, and they can't stand comfortably. The moment they get here, their hearts start racing, and they get nervous. Why? Because their karmic obstacles are too heavy.

To draw near to those with wisdom is to remove the covering of stupidity.

SINGLEMINDEDLY CASTING OUT CONFUSION/ This removes the covering of greed. Why? If you have no greed, your mind will not become confused. If you have thoughts of greed, your mind will become confused, unclear. When your mind is unclear, you will do muddled things.

Greed: Greed for what?

First of all, there is greed for wealth. At this point, we should each return the light and reverse the illumination. What is meant by "return the light and reverse the illumination?" Each of you ask yourselves: "Do I have thoughts of greed? Am I covered with greed? Am I greedy for other people's money? Because of greed for money, would I lie? Would I kill? Would I steal? Would I do things I clearly know are wrong simply out of greed? Am I greedy for money even in my dreams? "So and so has a lot of money. How can I get my hands on it?" Obsessed! You recite the Buddha's name sincerely, but your greed for money is even more sincere. You recite the Buddha's name in the morning a few times, and then forget all about it. "I've done quite enough recitation. Nobody's as good as me. No one can compare to me. Nobody recites the Buddha's name as much as I do." But what about your avarice? You never forget it, never. "No matter what, I'm going to get my hands on that person's money." You exert all your influence, and exhaust your shrewd intellect to cheat other people out of their money.

As you scheme for money, your heart grows confused. Your brains reel with scrambled thoughts, "What, oh, what method can I use...Will that one work? No? Well, then, what about this one? That one? I've got to have a plan. They'll never know what happened." All their schemes and plans confuse them.

To cast out confusion is to cast off the covering of greed. Greed covers your basic wisdom, your self-nature's bright light. If you can get rid of your greed, remove the covering of greed, your self-nature's bright light will manifest.

COLLECTING THEIR THOUGHTS IN THE MOUNTAIN FORESTS/ "Thoughts" refers to the thoughts present in our minds. People have great spiritual penetrations when it comes to thought. In one thought they can run as far as eighteen thousand miles. Shakyamuni Buddha emitted the white hair-mark light which shone across eighteen thousand worlds to the east. In a single thought we can think ourselves eighteen thousand worlds to the east.

However, there's a great deal of difference between our thoughts and the Buddha's light. The Buddha can emit light that reaches that far, but we can only day-dream; we can't send forth light. But our thoughts do have that much strength.

In one thought, we're in heaven.
In one thought, we're in hell.
In one thought, we are among the human beings.

It all happens in a thought. The heavens and the hells are created in a thought. Even the realization of Buddhahood is accomplished in a single thought. If you become a Bodhisattva, it's also in a thought. If you become an Arhat, it's also in a thought. When the thought matures, you can actualize your siritual penetrations and transformations.

Now, the thoughts are collected. They are not allowed to roam. They are all gathered back to the original self-nature. It's like using a magnet on your thoughts, so that they can't run off.

This method is one of using poison to fight poison. When people take poison, another kind of poison may be used to counteract the poison they have taken. Your "collecting of thoughts" is also a kind of poison. The very best thing would be, as I said earlier, to have no thought at all. If you have no thought, you have no production, no extinction. No thought is the most wonderful of states. If you can be without thought as you dwell there in the mountains and forests, your inherent, greatly enlightened Buddha nature will naturally be perfected and will naturally manifest. But now, one is unable to be without thought, and so the thoughts are gathered together. This collecting together also removes the covering of sleep.

Keeping away from frivolity removes the covering of inconstancy. Separating from stupid followers removes the covering of anger. Drawing near to those with wisdom removes the covering of stupidity. Singlemindedly casting out confusion removes the covering of greed. Collecting one's thoughts in the mountain forests removes the covering of the sleep demon.

When you cultivate, the sleep demon can be very fierce. If you tend to be lazy, the sleep demon loves to encourage you. He says, "It's all right. Rest a bit. Sleep some more," and he tells you to sleep. And you think, "Sleep is not bad. Sleep is really fine. There's nothing better than sleep! Why, it's the most comfortable state there is because you don't know anything at all, so you don't have false thinking, either!"

But when you sleep, you sometimes dream. You may dream a very common dream which causes you not to cultivate. What dream is that? Hah! Very strange. When men who cultivate the Way sleep, they very often dream about women. When women who cultivate the Way sleep, they very often dream about men. Why? Because, although you say, "I keep the precepts. I cultivate. I don't want to break the precepts," the demon king wants you to break them. When you sleep he comes and transforms into all kinds of forms to disturb your samadhi power. When you are awake, you may have samadhi power, but when you are asleep, it fails you. You are moved by the state. You have no precept power, and your samadhi power runs off. You have no idea at all where your wisdom power went. You can't find any of them. The three powers of precepts, samadhi and wisdom are non-existent. Your support topples over, and you are turned by the demonic state. This is the covering of sleep. So, sleep can also cover the self-nature's light.

If you cultivate, you can remove the five coverings gradually. Collecting one's thoughts in the mountains and forests FOR TENS OF THOUSANDS OF MILLIONS OF YEARS/ Life after life, Bodhisattvas like to stay in the mountains to cultivate. "If in this life I don't become enlightened," they resolve, "then in my next life I will continue to dwell here on the mountain and cultivate here for trillions of years." IN QUEST OF THE WAY OF THE BUDDHA/ "Why do I wish to dwell in the mountains? Why do I wish to be pure? Because I seek the Buddha Way."

Sutra:

BODHISATTVAS THERE ARE SEEN,
WHO, WITH FINE FOOD AND DRINK AND WITH
A HUNDRED KINDS OF BROTHS AND HERBS
MAKE OFFERINGS TO THE BUDDHA AND THE SANGHA.
WHO, WITH FINE ROBES AND SUPERIOR GARMENTS,
OF VALUE IN THE MILLIONS,
OR WITH IN VALUABLE ROBES
MAKE OFFERINGS TO THE BUDDHA AND THE SANGHA.
WHO, WITH A MILLION DIFFERENT KINDS
OF DWELLINGS OF PRECIOUS SANDALWOOD
AND WITH MUCH FINE BEDDING
MAKE OFFERINGS TO THE BUDDHA AND THE SANGHA.
WHO, WITH GARDENS AND GROVES, CLEAR AND PURE,
WITH FLOWERS AND FRUITS IN ABUNDANCE
WITH FLOWING SPRINGS AND BATHING PONDS,
MAKE OFFERINGS TO THE BUDDHA AND THE SANGHA.
OFFERINGS SUCH AS THESE,
OF MANY KINDS, EXTREMELY FINE,
DO THEY GIVE WITH JOY UNTIRING,
SEEKING FOR THE UTMOST WAY.

Outline:

J6. giving

Commentary:

BODHISATTVAS THERE ARE SEEN/ WHO, WITH FINE FOOD

AND DRINK AND WITH/ with fine vegetarian delicacies.A HUNDRED KINDS OF BROTHS AND HERBS/ MAKE OFFERINGS TO THE BUDDHA AND THE SANGHA./ The fine food and drink and the broths and herbs make up two of the offerings to the Triple Jewel, those of food and drink. You may make offerings to the Triple Jewel of food and drink or of broths and herbs, making some fine medicines so that when those who have left home get sick, they can use them to cure their illness. There are four kinds of offerings: food and drink, clothing, bedding, and medicine. The clothing given here is no ordinary clothing. They are FINE ROBES AND SUPERIOR GARMENTS/ very expensive clothing OF VALUE IN THE MILIONS/ OR WITH INVALUABLE ROBES/ These clothes are absolutely priceless. MAKE OFFERINGS TO THE BUDDHA AND THE SANGHA/ they are given to the Buddha and the Sangha.

AND WITH A MILLION DIFFERENT KINDS/ OF DWELLINGS OF PRECIOUS SANDALWOOD/ AND WITH MUCH FINE BEDDING/ MAKE OFFERINGS TO THE BUDDHA AND THE SANGHA/

WITH GARDENS AND GROVES, CLEAR AND PURE/ WITH FLOWERS AND FRUITS IN ABUNDANCE/ WITH FLOWING SPRINGS AND BATHING PONDS/ MAKE OFFERINGS TO THE BUDDHA AND THE SANGHA/ All these offerings, of many different kinds, are given to the Triple Jewel SEEKING FOR THE UTMOST WAY/ the Buddha Way.

Sutra:

THERE ARE BODHISATTVAS WHO
SPEAK OF STILL EXTINCTION'S DHARMA
WITH VARIOUS INSTRUCTIONS TEACHING
LIVING BEINGS WITHOUT NUMBER.
SEEN ARE BODHISATTVAS WHO
CONTEMPLATE ALL DHARMAS' NATURE
AS LACKING THE MARK OF DUALITY,
LIKE EMPTY SPACE.
ALSO SEEN ARE BUDDHA'S DISCIPLES
WHOSE MINDS HAVE NO ATTACHMENTS AND
WHO USE THIS WONDROUS WISDOM,

SEEKING FOR THE UTMOST WAY.

Outline:

J7. Prajna

Commentary:

THERE ARE BODHISATTVAS WHO/ Maitreya Bodhisattva continues speaking to Manjushri Bodhisattva. SPFAK OF STILL EXTINCTION'S DHARMA/ The dharma they teach is that of still extinction.

What is the dharma of still extinction?

It is "all dharmas are empty appearances." It means "the mark of still extinction of all dharmas cannot be expressed in words." The dharma of still extinction cannot be spoken. It has no appearance and it has no color. It is not green, yellow, red, white, or black. It isn't long or short, square or round. It is the dharma of still extinction. WITH VARIOUS INSTRUCTIONS TEACHING/ They use all manner of devices and teaching methods to:

1. cause living beings to turn their backs on the dust and unite with enlightenment.
2. lead living beings to clear understanding and awakening.
3. help beings awaken to the fact that all involvement with the dust of worldly affairs is a form of suffering.

SEEN ARE BODHISATTVAS WHO/ CONTEMPLATE ALL DHARMAS' NATURE/ they look at the nature of all dharmas as LACKING THE MARK OF DUALITY/ Not only are they not marked by duality, they don't even have one mark. It's not to say that they lack two marks and so they have one mark. They don't even have one mark. If they don't have even one mark, ultimately what are they like? LIKE EMPTY SPACE/ Take a look at empty space. What is contained in it? There's nothing in it at all, no forms and no appearances. But all the forms and appearances are not separate from empty space. All the forms and appearances are enclosed within empty space.

Would you say there is empty space in the earth? Dig a foot of earth out of the ground and you'll have one foot of empty space. If you dig out ten feet, you'll have ten feet of empty space. Before you dug the whole, was the space not there? The space was there all the time. So, although forms and shapes are found in space, they cannot envelop empty space; empty space envelops them. Even when there are material forms, empty space is still there. Empty space is also present in places where there are no material shapes. Well, if it's present, then grab some and take a look at it! Oh? There's nothing there. You can't see it! If you try to taste empty space, it has no flavor. What color would you say empty space was? Empty space has no color. The Realm Mark of all dharmas is also that way. It is just like space. So, if you understand the principle of empty space, you will understand the principle of the self-nature. Therefore, it is said,

> The self-nature is like empty space.
> It contains both the true and the false.
> Awaken, fathom the basic substance.
> In one understanding, understand all.

The self-nature is just like empty space. It contains both the true and the false. Within the self-nature both True Emptiness and Wonderful Existence are found. True Emptiness is just Wonderful Existence and Wonderful Existence is just True Emptiness. It is most certainly not the case that Wonderful Existence is to be found apart from True Emptiness. Nor is it the case that True Emptiness is to be found apart from Wonderful Existence. The very True Emptiness itself is Wonderful Existence, and Wonderful Existence itself is True Emptiness.

> When the truth is not postulated,
> The false is basically empty.
> When existence and non-existence are both
> cast out,
> What is not empty has been made empty.

The Truth is also non-existent. What is the Truth? To speak about the Truth is just to cheat people. What *is* the Truth?

What is the false?

The false is also non-existent. If you talk about the false, you are also cheating people. It's merely the case that within their hearts, living beings, as common worldly creatures, hold to a true and a false. When you arrive at the self-nature, however, it is like empty space.

Empty space would never say, "I am empty space." It has no ego, no self. If it said, "I am empty space," then it wouldn't be empty space. It would turn into an existing entity, so how could it remain empty space?" Emptiness has no "self" at all. Our own self-natures are also like that.

"Oh?" you say, "Is there nothing at all? That's really a shame. Nothing whatever?"

Don't be afraid. When you have nothing at all

then you truly "have." All the mountains, rivers, and the great earth, the forests and trees and the myriad objects within the world system of three thousand great thousand world--none of them are not yours! They are all yours. But you must truly have nothing at all. If you have even a hairsbreadth of obstruction, then none of it counts as yours.

Because you have that one little bit of obstruction, you cannot enjoy the possession of all those things. You have attachments and impediments. If you had no attachments or impediments, then you would truly have wealth and honor to the extreme, so that all of empty space and the entire Dharma Realm would be included in your self-nature. Enlightened, you understand the basic substance of your self-nature; then, in one understanding, you understand all. When you are clear about one thing, then you are clear about everything. There is nothing you do not comprehend, nothing you do not understand. You penetrate the Three Bodies, the Four Wisdoms, the Five Eyes, and the Six Spiritual Penetrations. You don't have to look for them outside. They are the jewels within your own household. Hearing this, if you don't become greatly enlightened, you should at least have a minor enlightenment. Don't waste your time. Though I might speak for half a day, it's as if I hadn't spoken. If you don't listen, that's even more wonderful. I haven't spoken and you haven't heard. That's the genuine, miraculous Prajna wisdom!

ALSO SEEN ARE BUDDHAS' DISCIPLES/ WHOSE MINDS HAVE NO ATTACHMENTS/ How's that? Everything's quite all right; everything's okay. This kind of non-attachment, however, is not easy to achieve. You must truly understand the Way, obtaining the birght light of the self-nature in order to be unattached. But how does one obtain wisdom? It's just by being unattached. The non-attachment itself is wisdom.If you've a single bit of attachment you won't have that wisdom. What wisdom? Doesn't it say right here in the text: WHO USE THIS WONDROUS WISDOM, THEN/ SEEKING FOR THE UTMOST WAY/ This wondrous wisdom comes simply from your non-attachment. If you have attachments, you will not be able to have this subtle, wondrous wisdom. This wisdom arises from your non-attachment. So, you're attached? Attached, you're stupid. Unattached, you are wise. You should have no attachment. You should not think, "I can't put this down and I can't give that up..." If you can't put it down, then you won't have this wondrous wisdom. If you can put it down, your wondrous wisdom and intelligence will manifest.

One of my disciples has said to me a number of times,

"Uh, no one's making offerings to the Triple Jewel. So many people and only one of them has made offerings. No one else has given."

When I heard that, I wanted to cry. Why did I want to cry? Because I was afraid that my three disciples were going to starve to death. What would we do then? So, I wanted to cry. Just as I was about to burst into tears, it occurred to me, "That's an attachment!" and I didn't cry. I laughed! Why did I laugh? I thought, "Why, that's the very best thing that could possibly happen! If no one makes offerings it will reveal whether or not you really want to cultivate the Way. It will draw out and harden your spiritual skill."

If you have spiritual powers and real samadhi power, then you can meditate and cultivate. When you can sit for ten days straight do you think there will be no offerings? No doubt they'd come from all over the country to make offerings to you. Why?

"Among Westerners, there are sages!" people would cry. "They can sit for ten days, 'thus, thus, unmoving!'" Would you still fear that no one would make offerings to the Triple Jewel? There would be nothing to fear.

On the other hand, you could also say that starving to death was the ultimate, the most glorious sacrifice. "I left home for the sake of the Buddha's teaching. I do not take advantage of circumstances. I am going to sit here and, if no one makes offerings, I'm not going to go out and try to finagle them. If I starve to death, I will certainly get enlightened. It will be just like the Bhikshu who held the precept against killing so purely that he refused to drink water which had bugs in it and consequently died of thirst. Because he was so sincere, the Buddha used his spiritual power to bring him to where the Buddha was and he met the Buddha even before his travelling companion, who drank the water, did. Although the Buddha has already entered Nirvana, you can still hear him speak the Dharma to you. Don't be nervous. So today it is publically announced that the Shramaneras are not to have money; they may not have money in their hands.

"But," you say, "what about doing my laundry and buying soap and things? I need money for that, don't I?"

A small amount, three or five dollars, is all right. But don't carry more than that. More just leads to trouble. If you take care of money, you won't be able to cultivate. You'll have to keep books. If you don't keep books, the donors will think, "I gave them money, but they have no record of it. What are they doing with it, anyway?" and they will distrust you.

In all the years I have left home, I will tell you, I have never told anyone to make offerings to me so that I could eat. I'll tell you something else: This Master to whom you bow, is one without ability. What ability does he lack? He is unable to get money from people. I talk to people, and if they give, they give. If they don't I do not pressure them. Besides, you should all know:

A single grain of the donor's rice
Is as heavy as Mount Sumeru;
If you eat it and fail to cultivate,
You'll end up wearing a fur coat and horns.

If you eat and drink the offerings of the faithful but do not cultivate the Way, if you do nothing but chatter all day long, senselessly, with never a time when your mouth is shut, do you think you can cultivate that way? I'm telling you to talk less and work harder. That is the fundamental duty of one who has left home.

When the laypeople look at those who have left home, they think, "They are just like us. We eat, they eat. We talk, they talk. We sleep, they sleep. They are no different from us, are they? Why should we make offerings to them?" I'm included in this myself. That's why I don't speak about useless matters. Anyway, I can't speak English. I don't like to talk a lot, so I don't. Besides, I don't have the time.

If you eat and fail to cultivate the Way, in the future it will be disastrous. Why should people go out and work and then give offerings to you? Only because you cultivate the Way. If you do not cultivate the Way, if you do not work hard, if you do not sit in Dhyana, you are not entitled to receive people's offerings. This concerns me greatly.

I'll tell you about something that happened to me. The first year I was in Hong Kong I had no money and I did not beg for any. Later, a layperson took me to Fu-jung Mountain to life in Kuan-yin Cave. The cave was extremely damp. In the cave, to say nothing of tea cups, there was nothing at all—no tables, no chairs, nothing at all; it was totally empty. I sat on a flat rock which jutted out from the wall. I sat there for several days and what do you think happened? My legs refused to move. They were numb and had no feeling in them at all. At that point I had a false thought. It was, "I don't want to sit here; I think I'll leave." But then I thought, "Someone took me here to cultivate; if I just stay for three days and leave, how could I possibly face anyone? How could I explain my actions? I'd have no way to do so. I don't care if I die here, I'm not going to leave the cave." I sat and sat for over half a month until my legs regained their feeling and I could use them once more. They no longer refused to cooperate. Then, everyday I went down the mountain, carrying a bowl, to beg for food and brought it back to eat. But my obstacles loomed large. After a year, because of the dampness inside the cave, I built a tiny hut right outside it. As soon as it was built, the obstacle arose. The neighboring Dharma Master grew jealous of me and told the people at the nearby monastery, "Don't make offerings to him. He's got money. If he's got the money to build a hut, how could he not have money for food? Don't make offerings to him."

The Supervisor of the monastery believed him and refused to give me food. At that time I was without offerings altogether. No one made offerings, but I thought, "I have a few scraps of food here. I'll eat them and then meditate." I did not tell anyone that I had no food to eat. I did not go out and no one came to see me. I thought, "If I starve to death, I starve to death, so what! To starve to death is even better, even more glorious. To sacrifice one's life for the Buddhadharma--there could be no greater glory, nothing more wonderful!"

I sat for several days. There was a layperson in his fifities who had been bitten in the leg by a dog. Two or three months had gone by and the wound still hadn't healed. He had gone to both Chinese and Western doctors, but none had been able to cure him. One night he had a dream. In his dream, Wei-t'ou Bodhisattva appeared and told him, "If you want your leg to heal, you should go make offerings to the Dharma Master in Kuan-yin Cave on the far side of Fu-jung Mountain."And then Wei-t'ou Bodhisattva said my name."Go make offerings to him and the dog bite on your leg will heal; it will be no problem." He had that dream several times in one night. Wei T'ou Bodhisattva also told him what the Dharma Master looked like and he saw how I looked. When he awoke from his dream he believed it and took over seventy Hong Kong dollars as well as thirty catties of rice, which he carried on his back, up to Kuan-yin Cave.

When the neighborning Dharma Master saw a food donor, a Dharma protector coming up the path, he ran right out to welcome him and see what he was carrying. The donor asked, "Does a Dharma Master live here?" he asked.

"I am in charge here," came the reply. "Whatever you wish to give, you may give to me. Don't go looking for any other Dharma Masters."

"But I saw a certain Dharma Master in my dream," the layperson continued. He didn't look anything like you. Wei T'ou Bodhisattva told me to give the offerings to him and he wasn't like you at all. I want to give these things to him!"

"Hah!" the Dharma Master's temper blazed. "What are you talking about! What kind of talk is that? I am the supervisor here. He most certainly is not. Any offerings you wish to give you should give to me," and he started to wrangle with the layperson.

I was in the cave and could hear them. When my name came up in the conversation, I went out to take a look at what was going on. When the layperson saw me, he exclaimed, "That's him! That's the person I saw in my dream. I have come to make offerings to this Dharma Master!"

The Dharma Master was furious. I asked the layperson what had happened and he told me about his dream. I said, "Good, make your offerings. Making offerings to other people is just the same as making offerings to me. You wish to make offerings to me, and this Dharma Master is my neighbor. Although we eat separately, we divide up everything. You should give half the rice and money to him. The Dharma Master was sputtering with rage and he wanted to argue, but he couldn't think of anything to say. The offerings were divided in half and he said to the layperson, "After this, if you want to give offerings, you must first give them to me."

At any rate, I didn't starve to death. The layperson got the name "Dharma Master Homegrown" because he liked to speak the Dharma and he was "homegrown," that is, not an imported, Dharma Master. He wasn't really a Dharma Master, of course, he was a layperson. People kidded him by using that nickname and everywhere he went he said, "Oh, it's really strange. In Kuan-yin Cave there is a Dharma Master. In a dream, Wei-t'ou Bodhisattva told me I should go make offerings to him and my leg would heal. I did, and sure enough, as soon as I got back, my leg healed all by itself without the aid of a doctor." He though it was very strange. After that incident, which was really nothing in itself, I did not starve to death. Although no one had made offerings to me, the laypeople in Hong Kong started coming from long distances, and they all made offerings. No matter who gave offerings, I divided them all in half between myself and the Dharma Master next door. Although they were given to me, I gave him half. Later, he used all kinds of methods to try to ruin me. Finally, I had to leave. I couldn't live there. I went to build the

Western Bliss Gardens. When I was staying at Kuan-yin Cave, there were two pools of water from the mountain in front of the cave. They came from the mountain and provided enough water for the daily use of ten or twenty people. What do you think happened after I moved out? The water stopped flowing down the mountain. There was no water. When I built the Western Bliss Gardens, there was no water there. But then the water came. All the monks said I took the water with me. I didn't starve to death after all, although I came close to it.

If you are not afraid of starving to death, then don't worry. There will certainly be offerings. If you are afraid of starving to death, no one will make offerings. If you are not afraid of starving to death, everything will work out fine. You need only have no fear and then spontaneously your Way karma will increase. So don't worry that you'll get no offerings. Besides, when it gets right down to the point of having no offerings at all, they will appear of themselves; if you have cultivation you will evoke that response.

Those who have left home should worry about whether or not they have accomplished their Way karma. They should not worry about whether or not there are offerings. If you receive offerings but do not become enlightened or realize your Way karma, then you are still just a common person. If you have accomplished your Way karma, you are still a sage, even if you get no offerings. Those of you who have left home, do you think about the fact that, as the days go by, you have not accomplished your Way karma? Do you consider it a problem? Or do you worry that, as you cultivate and recite Sutras, you are not yet perfect in your recitations? In the West, this is a beginning, and we all must be pioneering patriarchs. Just what gives you the right to be patriarchs? What merit and virtue, what accomplishment, do you have? Which Sutra do you really understand, can you truly explain? As far as your spiritual skill goes, can you sit for one, two, three, four five hours and so forth until we come to one day, two days, one month, two months without moving your legs? If you have that kind of samadhi, then why are you so worried about not receiving offerings? If you have no samadhi power, you may look for offerings, but the more you look for them, the farther they will recede. Why? People will see you and think, "Oh, there's that monk who climbs on conditions. He goes around everywhere telling people to make offerings and exploiting them, but he doesn't cultivate. He just takes advantage of other people in order to get offerings." This is an extremely grave mistake. You should now return the light and reverse the illumination.

Ask not whether people have made
offerings to you;
Ask what you have done to deserve offerings.

If you were busy cultivating the Way, how would you have time to notice whether or not people have made offerings. If you really cultivate the Way, you won't know whether they have or not. Why? Because your heart will not be caught up in food and drink. It is said,

Superior people yearn for the Way;
They do not yearn for food.

If someone makes offerings to them, that's the way they are; if no one makes offerings to them, they are still that way. "I would rather die cultivating the Way than get away with loafing and ask for pity in order to live." Your determination should be so strong that you stand with the top of your head in the sky and your feet firmly on the ground. "My head can burst its way right up to the highest heaven; it can poke right through the Heaven of Neither Perception nor Non-Perception. Such is my resolve!"

It shouldn't be that you go for a day or two without eating and think, "I can't stand it." Don't be like that; that's being entirely too spineless, and I don't want any spineless disciples. So, you should stand firm on your resolve. People in the world all like money. You should not want money; you should pay no attention to money. Cultivate the Way with a true heart and everything will be okay. If you cultivate the Way without a true heart, it will be all muddled, and you will create even more offense karma.

So today I have taken the lecture period to explain a bit of genuine principle. After this, if one has virtue, even if people want to give one money, one shouldn't want it. They must kneel, make obeisance very respectfully, and then I will accept it. But if they are not respectful, I will not accept it. I will not accept their offering."

I have something further to say. Those who are at home should protect the Dharma of those who have left home. If you let the left-home people starve to death, then when you want to do acts of merit and virtue, you'll have nowhere to go to do it. Why? The Triple Jewel will have starved to death! Even if you wanted to foster merit and virtue, you wouldn't be able to do it.

Those who have left home should know what they are

supposed to do and those who are at home should also know what they are supposed to do. Don't wait until the Triple Jewel has starved to death. If you try to make offerings to them then, you won't be able to, because there won't be any Triple Jewel to make offerings to! Everyone should do his job and carry out his responsibilities. Those who have left home must cultivate the Way and those who are at home have the responsibility to make offerings. If those who have left home do not cultivate, then those at home will not make offerings. If those at home do not make offerings, then those who have left home will not be able to cultivate. Those who have left home should cultivate and those at home make offerings. That's called "working together."

Sutra:

MANJUSHRI,
AGAIN ARE BODHISATTVAS WHO,
AFTER THE BUDDHAS CROSS INTO EXTINCTION,
MAKE OFFERINGS TO THE SHARIRA.
AGAIN ARE SEEN BUDDHA'S DISCIPLES,
BUILDING STUPAS, BUILDING TEMPLES,
COUNTLESS AS THE GANGES SANDS,
TO ADORN THOSE REALMS AND LANDS.
THE JEWELED STUPAS, TALL AND FINE,
ARE FIVE THOUSAND YOJANAS IN HEIGHT,
TWO THOUSAND YOJANAS IN BREADTH.
EACH STUPA AND TEMPLE IS ADORNED
WITH A THOUSAND CURTAINS AND BANNERS
CIRCLING AROUND AND WROUGHT WITH GEMS,
AND JEWELED BELLS WHICH HARMONIOUSLY CHIME.

ALL THE GODS, DRAGONS, AND SPIRITS,
HUMANS AND NON-HUMANS,
WITH INCENSE, FLOWERS, AND INSTRUMENTAL MUSIC,
CONSTANTLY MAKE OFFERINGS.
MANJUSHRI,
ALL THE BUDDHAS' DISCIPLES,
ADORN THE STUPAS AND THE SHRINES
MAKING OFFERINGS TO THE SHARIRAS;
SPONTANEOUSLY, THE REALMS AND LANDS
ARE SUPERBLY FINE AND EXQUISITE,
LIKE THE KING OF HEAVENLY TREES
WHEN ITS FLOWERS BLOOM.

Outline:

H6. asking about offerings to the sharira

Commentary:

In this passage of text, Maitreya Bodhisattva continues his questioning of Manjushri Bodhisattva concerning the various states which the Buddha caused to manifest within the white hair-mark light. The Buddha had revealed six portents, but Maitreya Bodhisattva did not know the causes and conditions which underlay them. Actually it is certainly the case Maitreya Bodhisattva was not unaware of them. He deliberately requested the Dharma for the sake of living beings. This is called "manifesting a great provisional device."[1] He said, MANJUSHRI/ AGAIN ARE BODHISATTVAS, WHO,/ AFTER THE BUDDHAS CROSS INTO EX-

---

1 大權示現 -*ta ch'üan shih hsien.*

TINCTION/ After all the Buddhas have completed the stillness, have entered Nirvana, the Bodhisattvas MAKE OFFERINGS TO THE SHARIRA/ The word sharira means "efficacious bones." and they represent the true body of the Buddha because they remain after the Buddha's cremation. When people make offerings to the Buddha's sharira it is the same as making offerings to the Buddha. Making offerings to the Dharma Jewel is also the same as making offerings to the Buddha and making offerings to the Sangha Jewel is the same as making offerings to the Buddha. All you have to do is bring forth the resolve and be true to the extreme, without the slightest bit of defiled thought. What is meant by "defiled thought?" It is to make offerings to the Triple Jewel in the hope of obtaining something in return. That's not making offerings with a true heart. When you make offerings to the Triple Jewel, you should feel, "Making offerings is my responsibility. Why? I have food to eat. The kindness the Buddhas shows towards living beings is limitless and boundless. The Dharma's kindness to living beings is limitless and boundless and so is the Sangha's kindness. If the Triple Jewel did not dwell in the world, this world would be completely destroyed. Why? Because if the Triple Jewel was not present, the demon kings would come into the world and destroy it. So, in making offerings to the Triple Jewel, we should think, "I eat everyday. If no one makes offerings to the Triple Jewel, how could I possibly swallow my food? As one of the Buddha's disciples I should protect and uphold the Triple Jewel and cause it to be free from all difficulties. Therefore, making offerings to the shariras is just one way of making offerings to the Triple Jewel.

AGAIN ARE SEEN BUDDHA'S DISICPLES/ BUILDING STUPAS, BUILDING TEMPLES/ Stupas are places where people may come and make offerings to the Buddha's sharira which are housed inside them. Temples are used for making offerings to Buddha images. For example, T'ien Hou Temple here (the Buddhist Lecture Hall) is a place where many spirits are worshiped and so it is called a temple. In this case,we are making offerings to many Buddhas. AS COUNTLESS AS THE GANGE'S SANDS/ They do not build one stupas or temple and leave it at that, but they build limitless, countless numbers of them, as many as the Gange's sands TO ADORN THOSE REALMS AND LANDS/ so that they are extremely beautiful.

THE JEWELED STUPAS, TALL AND FINE/ FIVE THOUSAND YOJANAS IN HEIGHT/ How tall is that? One small yojana is forty miles; a middle-sized yojana is sixty miles; a big yojana is eighty miles. So, how tall would five thousand yojanas be?

Long ago, when the Buddha was in the world, the following incident took place: There was, at that time, a freak. He was wider than he was tall. He was five feet across and only two and a half, not quite three feet, tall. Do you think he was attractive or not? He was probably about two feet nine or so. He looked like a frying pan, but the sound of his voice was extremely resonant and clear. It sounded like a bell. People did not understand what causes and effects were at work with him, and so they asked the Buddha. The Buddha smiled and said, "In the past, limitless kalpas ago, he was also a Buddhist disciple. At that time someone brought forth the resolve to build a jeweled stupa which was to be extremely tall. The man said, "Why build such a tall stupa? People won't even be able to see the top of it, for cryin' out loud. What use is such a tall one? If you build a stupa, build one, and have done with it. Such a big one is really, in my opinion, utterly useless. Well, I'll contribute a little something, not a whole lot. I'll contribute the bell to put at the top of the stupa," and that's just what he did. Because he said that one sentence, "Why build such a high jeweled stupa? Don't make it so tall," in every life he was born as a dwarf, never over three feet tall. Because he had contributed the bell, his voice was extremely clear and resonant and sounded like the chiming of a copper bell.

From this we can see that people cannot just talk casually. If someone wants to build a big temple and you go there and say, "Why build such a big temple? If you make it smaller, it will still be a temple," in the future you may be very small. People with small bodies should bring forth a big resolve. "I am going to build a big temple!" and in the future you will get a big body. That's the record for your consideration. Don't just say whatever you please. If people are building a temple or a jeweled stupa, take care not to go there and criticize it saying it is too tall or too short, too big or too small.

EACH STUPA AND TEMPLE IS ADORNED/ WITH A THOUSAND CURTAINS AND BANNERS/ CIRCLING AROUND AND WROUGHT WITH GEMS/ AND JEWELED BELLS WHICH HARMONIOUSLY CHIME/

Circulate curtains are streamers of netting which are cylindrical in shape and hang from the ceiling. They may be embroidered with flowers or they may have interstices in them. Banners are streamers made of cloth and hung before the Buddhas as an adornment. When the wind blows, the little bells ring, and ALL THE GODS, DRAGONS, AND SPIRITS/ HUMANS AND NON-HUMANS/ WITH INCENSE, FLOWERS, AND INSTRUMENTAL MUSIC/ CONTANTLY MAKE OFFERINGS/ Incense refers to various types of incense. They use these things to make offerings to the Triple Jewel.

MANJUSHRI/ Bodhisattva! ALL THE BUDDHAS' DISCIPLES/ ADORN THE STUPAS AND THE SHRINES/ MAKING OFFERINGS TO THE SHARIRA/ SPONTANEOUSLY THE REALMS AND LANDS/ ARE SUPERBLY FINE AND EXQUISITE/ LIKE THE KING OF HEAVENLY TREES/ WHEN ITS FLOWERS BLOOM/ When the flowers on the heavenly king of trees bloom, they are extremely beautiful and wonderful.

Sutra:

THE BUDDHA SENDS FORTH THIS SINGLE RAY,
AND I AND THOSE ASSEMBLED HERE
VIEW WITHIN THOSE REALMS AND LANDS,
THE VARIOUS SPECIAL WONDERS.
THE SPIRITUAL MIGHT OF THE BUDDHAS
AND THEIR WISDOM IS MOST RARE,
EMITTING A SINGLE, PURE LIGHT,
THEY CAN ILLUMINE LIMITLESS LANDS.
SEEING THIS, WE HAVE ALL
OBTAINED WHAT WE HAVE NEVER HAD.
DISCIPLE OF THE BUDDHA, MANJU,
PRAY RESOLVE THE ASSEMBLY'S DOUBTS.

Outline:

F2. requesting an answer
G1. statement of matters which are not understood and asking for an answer

Commentary:

THE BUDDHA SENDS FORTH THIS SINGLE RAY/ the white hair-mark light AND I AND THOSE ASSEMBLED HERE/ I, and the great assembly, VIEW WITHIN THOSE REALMS AND LANDS/ see the territories which contain THE VARIOUS SPECIAL WONDERS/ an ineffable number of them.

THE SPIRITUAL MIGHT OF THE BUDDHAS/ AND THEIR WISDOM IS MOST RARE/ The spritual power of the Buddhas, the strength of their spiritual penetrations and their wisdom is rare; there's nothing in the world that compares with them.

EMITTING A SINGLE, PURE LIGHT/ THEY CAN ILLUMINE LIMITLESS LANDS/ They illumine limitless lands. SEEING THIS, WE HAVE ALL/ I myself, and all present in the assembly OBTAIN WHAT WE HAVE NEVER HAD/ None of us has ever seen anything like them.

DISCIPLE OF THE BUDDHA, MANJU/ Disciples of the Dharma King, PRAY RESOLVE THE ASSEMBLY'S DOUBTS/ I hope that you will resolve everyone's questions on these matters, so that we may be free of doubts.

Sutra:

THE FOUR-FOLD MULTITUDE WITH JOY
LOOKS UP TO YOU, HUMANE ONE, AND TO ME.
WHY HAS THE WORLD HONORED ONE
EMITTED SUCH A BRILLIANT LIGHT?
DISCIPLE OF THE BUDDHA, ANSWER NOW;
RESOLVE OUR DOUBTS, SO WE MAY REJOICE.
WHAT BENEFIT IS TO BE GAINED
BY PUTTING FORTH THIS BRILLIANT LIGHT?
THAT WONDROUS DHARMA THE BUDDHA GAINED
AS HE SAT IN THE FIELD OF THE WAY--
DOES HE WISH, NOW, TO PREACH IT?
OR IS HE GOING TO GIVE PREDICTIONS?
THE MANIFESTING OF THE BUDDHA-LANDS,

ADORNED WITH MANY JEWELS, AND PURE,
AS WELL AS THE VISION OF THE BUDDHAS
DOES NOT BETOKEN SMALL CONDITIONS.
MANJU, IT SHOULD BE KNOWN,
THE FOUR ASSEMBLIES, DRAGONS AND SPIRITS,
LOOK TO YOU, HUMANE ONE, HOPEFULLY;
WHAT IS IT THAT IS TO BE SAID?

Outline:

G2. statement & avoidance of question

Commentary:

Manjushri is evading the question. But the Bodhisattva Maitreya continues to ask. With each question, Manjushri remains silent, however.

THE FOUR-FOLD MULTITUDE WITH JOY/ At this time the Bhikshusangha, the Bhikshunis, the Upasakas and Upasikas, the four-fold assembly LOOKS UP TO YOU, HUMANE ONE, AND TO ME/ They are all happy and waiting for your explanation. They look up at you, Humane One, and they look at me, because they want us to answer their questions and resolve their doubts.

WHY HAS THE WORLD HONORED ONE/ EMITTED SUCH A BRILLIANT LIGHT/ DISCIPLE OF THE BUDDHA, ANSWER NOW/ RESOLVE OUR DOUBTS SO WE MAY REJOICE/ Enable us to cast out our doubts and become happy. Why are there doubts? Because no one understands or recognizes these states. When everyone understands them they will certainly be happy.

WHAT BENEFIT IS TO BE GAINED/ What is it that the Buddha is planning to do in the way of benefitting living beings? BY PUTTING FORTH THIS BRILLIANT LIGHT/ He sends out bright light to shine across eighteen thousand worlds to the east, thus making use of the wonderful functioning of his spiritual penetrations.

THAT WONDROUS DHARMA THE BUDDHA OBTAINED/ AS HE SAT IN THE FIELD OF THE WAY/ The Buddha sat in the Bodhimanda and obtained the wonderful Dharma. DOES HE WISH, NOW, TO PREACH IT/ Does he want to speak the wonderful Dharma the Buddha certified to and obtained?

Does he wish to speak about it to everyone? OR IS HE GOING TO GIVE PREDICTIONS/ Or does he want to confer predictions upon everyone? Of the two alternatives, probably the Buddha has one in mind.

THE MANIFESTING OF THE BUDDHALANDS/ ADORNED WITH MANY JEWELS AND PURE/ Every Buddhaland is adorned with many precious ornaments. AS WELL AS THE VISION OF THE BUDDHAS/ DOES NOT BETOKEN SMALL CONDITIONS/ The causes and conditions, I believe, are most certainly not trivial ones. They are certainly great, but I do not *understand* them! MANJU, IT SHOULD BE KNOWN/ THE FOUR ASSEMBLIES, DRAGONS AND SPIRITS/ the four assemblies, and the eight-fold division of ghosts and spirits and so forth LOOK TO YOU, HUMANE ONE, HOPEFULLY/ They stand at attention with their gaze fixed upon you. O Humane One, WHAT IS TO BE SAID/ What Dharma is the Buddha going to speak? Which of the Dharmas is he going to speak? Please, Manjushri, be compassionate and instruct us in this matter.

Sutra:

AT THAT TIME, MANJUSHRI ADDRESSED THE BODHISATTVA MAHASATTVA MAITREYA AND ALL THE GREAT LORDS, SAYING, "GOOD MEN, IN MY ESTIMATION, THE BUDDHA, THE WORLD HONORED ONE, NOW WISHES TO SPEAK THE GREAT DHARMA, TO LET FALL THE GREAT DHARMA RAIN, TO BLOW THE GREAT DHARMA CONCH, TO BEAT THE GREAT DHARMA DRUM, AND TO PROCLAIM THE GREAT DHARMA DOCTRINE."

Outline:

D5. the answers
E1. the prose section
F1. answers according to his considered opinion

Commentary:

AT THAT TIME, right then, when the Bodhisattva Manjushri had heard the Bodhisattva Maitreya request that he explain away the doubts, he ADDRESSED THE BODHISATTVA MAHASATTVA MAITREYA AND ALL THE GREAT LORDS, all the great Bodhisattvas present in the assembly. He said, "GOOD MEN, you who cultivate, IN MY ESTIMATION according to my calculations, the causes and conditions taking place here seem to indicate that THE BUDDHA, THE WORLD HONORED ONE NOW WISHES TO SPEAK THE GREAT DHARMA which has never been spoken before!

TO LET FALL THE GREAT DHARMA RAIN, just like rain from the sky which moistens all the living beings with potential, i.e. all living beings. TO BLOW THE GREAT DHARMA CONCH to alert all living beings; TO BEAT THE GREAT DHARMA DRUM, to cause them all to awaken from their dreams; TO PROCLAIM THE GREAT DHARMA DOCTRINE, to expound the greatest Dharma principle."

Sutra:

"GOOD MEN, I HAVE, IN THE PAST, IN THE PRESENCE OF OTHER BUDDHAS, SEEN SUCH PORTENTS. HAVING EMITTED THIS LIGHT, THEY IMMEDIATELY SPOKE THE GREAT DHARMA. THEREFORE, IT SHOULD BE KNOWN THAT THE MANIFESTATION OF LIGHT BY THE PRESENT BUDDHA IS ALSO THUS. BECAUSE HE WISHES TO LEAD ALL LIVING BEINGS TO HEAR AND UNDERSTAND THIS DHARMA WHICH IN THE WHOLE WORLD IS HARD TO BELIEVE, HE THEREFORE MANIFESTS THESE PORTENTS."

Outline:

F2. answers referring generally to what he saw in the past

Commentary:

"GOOD MEN, all of you good men, I HAVE, IN THE PAST, IN THE PRESENCE OF OTHER BUDDHAS, during the time of other Buddhas in the past, SEEN SUCH PORTENTS. HAVING EMITTED THIS LIGHT, THEY IMMEDIATELY SPOKE THE GREAT DHARMA."Previously there was a discussion of making offerings to the Triple Jewel, but I have not yet finished and have something more to add.

"Why should people make offerings to the Triple Jewel," you may wonder. "Why shouldn't the Triple Jewel make offerings to me?"

The Triple Jewel does not make offerings to you

because you are not one of the Triple Jewel, and so you are not entitled to receive offerings.

Why should one make offerings to the Triple Jewel? It is because the Triple Jewel provides a place for one to plant blessings. If you would like to seek blessings, you must perform acts of merit and virute before the Triple Jewel. If you do not make offerings to the Triple Jewel, in the future, when you become a Buddha, no one will make offerings to you. To say nothing of becoming a Buddha, if you don't make offerings to the Triple Jewel now, even when you leave home to become a monk, no one will make offerings to you. Why not? Because when you were at home, you did not make offerings to the Triple Jewel.

I often think, "Why doesn't anyone make offerings to me? Ah, it's because before I left home, I didn't make offerings to the Triple Jewel. That is why now that I have left home, very few people make offerings to me. I constantly bring forth a heart full of repentance. I am extremely ashamed. So, now, I wish to explain this principle to you, so that you won't have to be like me and have no one make offerings to you.

By making offerings to the Triple Jewel, one cultivates blessings and cultivates wisdom. To cultivate wisdom, one must print Sutras and propagate the Buddhadharma, or do other types of work to spread the Dharma. Didn't I mention this before? An example is our present preparation forpublishing a magazine, which is all part of cultivating wisdom, If you want to cultivate wisdom, you must support the work of propagating the Dharma. If you want to cultivate blessings, you should make offerings to the Triple Jewel. If you don't make offerings to the Triple Jewel, then in the future, when you are one of the Three Jewels, no one will make offerings to you, as I just said. So, now, before you are part of the Triple Jewel, you must support it and take care of it. Cultivating both blessings and wisdom, If you cultivate blessings, but do not cultivate wisdom, you are like an elephant wearing a necklace of beads. If you cultivate wisdom but not blessings,you are like an Arhat with an empty begging bowl.

What does that mean? If you merely concentrate on cultivating wisdom and do not cultivate blessings, in the future, when you certify to the fruit and realize Arhatship, no one will make offerings to you.

"But yesterday you said that if someone sat for ten days people would certainly make offerings to them," you think. "How could it be that a certified

Arhat would receive no offerings? I find this terrifying. The Buddhadharma is too dangerous! It would probably be better not to study it at all."

That may be the case, but if you don't cultivate the Buddhadharma, you won't ever become a Buddha. If you want to slide down, do as you please. If you want to become a Buddha, if you think, "I understand the Buddhadharma quite clearly and I shall certainly be diligent and seek progress in my study of it, then you should break through all the various difficulties and go forward in your cultivation. Cultivate blessings and wisdom. If you don't cultivate blessings, no one will make offerings to you. If you don't cultivate wisdom, you will be stupid. The Buddha is complete in both blessings and wisdom. His blessings are perfect and his wisdom is perfect , and so he is known as the Doubly-Complete Honored One." In our cultivation, too, we should cultivate blessings and wisdom. In all circumstances we should cultivate wisdom. Don't be like the Arhat with the empty bowl who cultivated wisdom, but not blessings. No one makes offerings to him. If you only cultivate blessings, but not wisdom, then you are like an elephant with a necklace. It may look very beautiful,but it is still very stupid. Those of you who study the Buddhadharma should cultivate both wisdom and blessings. You must do so actually and in fact, and not just talk about so doing. It you speak it, it's the Dharma; if you do it, it's the Way. This is a point which everyone should know.

THEREFORE means "because of this reason," that is, because Manjushri Bodhisattva said that he had in the past seen limitless Buddhas manifest such portents, how, IT SHOULD BE KNOWN THAT THE MANIFESTATION OF LIGHT BY THE PRESENT BUDDHA, Shakyamuni Buddha, IS ALSO THUS. You should know that Shakyamuni Buddha now manifests the white hair-mark light, and it is also just as when the limitless Buddhas of the past were about to speak the great Dharma, to rain the great Dharma rain, to blow the great Dharma conch, to beat the great Dharma drum, and to proclaim the great Dharma doctrine; the principle is the same.

BECAUSE HE WISHES TO LEAD ALL LIVING BEINGS TO HEAR AND UNDERSTAND...Shakyamuni Buddha wants to cause all living beings to hear the Dharma and to understand it--THIS DHARMA WHICH IN THE WHOLE WORLD IS HARD TO BELIEVE. This kind of Dharma is hard to believe. It is difficult for living beings to have faith in it. Why didn't the Buddha speak *The Dharma Flower Sutra* before? Why did he first speak the teachings of the Three Storehouses, and expound the Small Vehicle Sutras? It was just because the Great Vehicle Dharma-door is a Dharma which is hard to believe. That is why , as it states later in the text, as soon as the Buddha began to speak the Sutra, five thousand people got up and walked out.

Why is it hard to believe? Because it is too wonderful and too profound. It is hard for people with their ordinary wisdom, to understand it. It is so wonderful, that it is hard for people with their ordinary thoughts, to understand it. They think about it, and they don't understand it; they ponder it, but they don't know what it means. So, the Buddha didn't speak this profound and wonderful Dharma right away.

HE THEREFORE MANIFESTS THESE PORTENTS. He displays these auspicious signs.

Sutra

"GOOD MEN, IT IS JUST AS IN THE PAST, LIMITLESS, BOUNDLESS, INCONCEIVABLE ASANKHYEYA AEONS AGO..."

Outline:

F3. answers referring extensivly to what was seen in the past.
G1. showing Shakyamuni Buddha's similarity with a single Buddha
H1. the time

Commentary:

GOOD MEN, all of you good men, IT IS JUST AS IN THE PAST, LIMITLESS,BOUNDLESS, INCONCEIVABLE ASANKHYEYA AEONS AGO...I remember, it is just like it was in the past, when limitless, uncountable, boundless, inconceivable, that is, they cannot be thought of with the mind or expressed in words, asankhyeya, a Sanskrit word meaning "uncountable"[1], aeons ago...

1 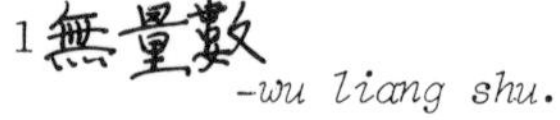
-*wu liang shu.*

Sutra:

"...THERE WAS AT THAT TIME A BUDDHA NAMED BRIGHTNESS OF SUN-MOON-LAMP THUS COME ONE, ONE WORTHY OF OFFERINGS, ONE OF PROPER AND UNIVERSAL KNOWLEDGE, ONE OF PERFECT CLARITY AND CONDUCT, WELL-GONE ONE, AN UNSURPASSED KNIGHT WHO UNDERSTANDS THE WORLD, A HERO WHO SUBDUES AND TAMES, A TEACHER OF GODS AND PEOPLE, THE BUDDHA, THE WORLD HONORED ONE..."

Outline:

H2. the name

Commentary:

"...THERE WAS AT THAT TIME A BUDDHA NAMED BRIGHTNESS OF SUN-MOON-LAMP[1] who appeared in the world.

How did he get that name?

The name of that Buddha has three meanings. The sun represents the Buddhas wisdom, which is like the sun. The sun dispels all darkness and gives light. The moon represents the Buddha's samadhi power. The Buddha's samadhi power is like the moon in space. The lamp represents the Buddha's precept power. Every Buddha has completely perfected precepts, samadhi, and wisdom.

THUS COME ONE[1] is one of the Buddha's ten titles. Every single Buddha has his own particular name. Like the Sutras, the Buddhas have specific and common names. This Buddha' specific name is Brightness of Sun-Moon-Lamp; it is a name which only this Buddha has. The common name is common to all Buddhas. The ten titles which follow are common to all Buddhas all Buddhas are known by these ten titles.

In the beginning, every Buddha had one hundred million names. Why did they have so many names? What

---

[1] *Skt., Chandrasuryapradipa, Chin.,* 日月燈明 *jih yüeh teng ming.*
[2] *Skt., Tathagata, Chin.,* 如來 *-ju lai.*

is the use of that? It was because each of the one hundred million names represented their adornment of the ten thousand virtues, their virtuous practices. Later, because living beings couldn't remember so many names clearly, they were decreased to one hundred thousand names. But that was also quite a few and so they were again reduced to ten thousand. Ten thousand names were still too many, and so they were reduced to one thousand names. Every Buddha had one thousand names, but that was still too many, and so they were reduced to one hundred. One hundred proved to be too many; it took too long just to say a Buddha's name, and so they were reduced to ten and all Buddhas had those ten titles, ten common names.

Some people who don't understand the Buddhadharma say, "Thus Come One Buddha." In fact, the Thus Come One is the Buddha and the Buddha is just the Thus Come One. They say, "Thus Come One Buddha," thinking that only one Buddha has the name "Thus Come One," and that the other Buddhas are not called Thus Come Ones." Actually, every single Buddha is called "Buddha" and "Thus Come One." Those who don't understand the Buddhadharma sometimes say very strange things.

What is meant by "Thus Come One?" *The Vajra Sutra* says, "Because he comes from nowhere and goes nowhere, he is called the Thus Come One." He neither comes nor goes, and so he is called the Thus Come One. You may also explain this title by saying, "Thus" means that, using the Way which is Thus, they come to realize the right enlightenment.

Further, "Thus" means unchanging and "Come" means to accord with conditions. "Thus" is stillness; "Come" is movement. Movement and stillness are one "thusness." movement is stillness, and stillness is movement. Movement does not obstruct stillness, and stillness does not obstruct movement. The meaning of the title Thus Come One could be greatly expanded upon, but we shall now proceed to the second of the ten titles:

One Worthy of Offerings:[1] This means that the Buddha should rightly receive the offerings of people and gods. People in the world should make offerings to the Buddha, and people in the heavens should also make offerings to him. He is one worthy of receiving their offerings.

One of proper and Universal Knowledge:[2] Proper and universal knowledge means that one understands that

---

1 *Skt., Arhat, Chin.,* 應供 *-ying kung.*

2 *Skt., Samyak-sambuddha* 正徧知 *-cheng pien chih.*

the ten thousand dharmas are produced from the mind and are not apart from the current thought in our minds. Understanding that the one current thought in our minds can produce the ten thousand dharmas is said to be Proper Knowledge. To know that the ten thousand dharmas are only the mind, that all dharmas do not go beyond one current thought of the mind is said to be Universal Knowledge. Proper and Universal Knowledge vertically exhausts the three limits: the past, present, and future, and horizontally pervades the ten directions.

One of Perfect Clarity and Conduct:[1] Clarity refers to wisdom. Conduct refers to blessings and virtues. He is complete with blessings and virtue and with wisdom.

Well-gone One:[2] He has gone to a good place, to the very best place.

Unsurpassed Knight Who Understands the World:[3] The Buddha understands all doctrines, both mundane and transcendental, and so he is the one who understands the world. The Buddha is an Unsurpassed Knight. The Bodhisattvas at the level of Equal Enlightenment still have one small, minute particle of production-mark ignorance which they have not yet destroyed. Because they haven't broken through that one particle of ignorance, one particle of the Dharmabody remains as yet unmanifested. Therefore, although they are Equal Enlightenment Bodhisattvas, they are called Surpassed Knights, because above them there is still the Buddha. The Buddha has reached the level of Wonderful Enlightenment and so he is called the Unsurpassed Knight.

A Hero Who Subdues and Tames:[4] To subdue means to use compassion to teach and transform living beings. Depending upon the kind of Dharma-door a living being likes, the Buddha uses just that Dharma-door to cross him over. To tame means that the Buddhas uses awesome virtue and dignity to control living being, to receive all living beings. Living beings who see the Buddha are respectful and stand in awe of him. They revere the Buddha's awesome virtue and are awed by his majesty. The Hero is a great hero, one who subdues and tames all the living beings in the world and so he is known as the Hero Who Subdues and Tames.

---

1 *Skt., Vidyacharana-sampanna, Chin.,* 明行足*-ming heng tsu.*

2 *Skt., Sugata, Chin.,* 善逝*-shan shih.*

3 *Skt., Lokavid/ Anuttara, Chin.,* 世間解 無上師 *-shih chien chieh, wu shang shih.*

4 *Skt., Purusha-damya-sarathi, Chin.,* 調御丈夫 *-t'iao yü chang fu.*

Teacher of Gods and People:[1] The Buddha is the master of the gods in the heavens and the people in the world.

The Buddha:[2] The word Buddha means "the enlightened one." There are three kinds of enlightenment: self-enlightenment, the enlightenment of others, and the perfection of enlightenment and practice. What is self enlightenment? How does it differ from other kinds?

Those with self-enlightenment are different from common people. Common people are all unenlightened. They have not awakened. They don't know that there is no peace in the three realms; they are just like a burning house. They don't know that this world is just like a raging fire and that it is very easy to be burnt to a crisp in it. There is not a single place in the three realms that is peaceful. It is just as dangerous as being in a flaming building. So the common people are not enlightened. Those with self-enlightenment have awakened themselves. They have certified to the attainment of the fruit of Arhatship.

How do those who enlighten others differ from the self-enlightened? Self-enlightenment if the realm of the Arhat. The enlightenment of others is the realm of the Bodhsiattva. The Bodhisattva himself is enlightened, and he thinks that enlightenment is not bad at all; it's extremely wonderful in fact, and he is very happy. Since he has obtained the subtle and wonderful happiness himself, as well as an understanding of the doctrines of the world, he also causes everyone to obtain this wonder and joy, these advantages. He takes that which he has experienced in his path of cultivation and teaches it to others. He speaks it for them all to hear.

For example, a certain layperson now wishes to be one of self-enlightenment who enlightens others. He is going to the university to lecture on the Buddhadharma. Although he has not claimed to have certified to any particular fruit, he has chosed to bring forth the Bodhisattva resolve: "I know as much as I know, and I am not afraid that people will say I lectured well or poorly. I'm just going to go ahead and lecture." That is the Bodhisattva heart which, self-enlightened, enlightens others. Besides, I have great faith in what

---

1 *Skt., Shasta devamanushyanam, Chin.,* 天人師 *t'ien jen shih.*

2 *Skt., Buddha, Chin.,* 佛 *-fo.*

this layperson says. He is very eloquent and takes the principles from Chinese and puts them into English in an inconceivable way. This is just the enlightenment of others. If one can constantly bring forth the Bodhisattva heart and not work for fame or profit and not think, "I'm going to lecture and when I'm done, I'll be famous," or, "When I'm done lecturing, I'll get so much money," this is self-enlightenment and the enlightenment of others.

Don't take this matter lightly! Any one of you can become self-enlightened and then enlighten others. I am lecturing the Sutras to you, and although it's not 100% fine, still, you can expand on what I say. For example, if I lecture one doctrine, you can obtain ten from it and then lecture ten. If I speak about the Thus Come One and say just a little bit, you can investigate the term in the Sutras and find a lot of different ways to explain it, and compare and collate them. I hope that all of you will self-enlighten and enlighten others. Regardless of whether you are male or female--don't be afraid! Don't say, "If I speak, will they laugh?" So what if they laugh! Laughter is just laughter after all. Pay no attention to them! "Let them laugh, but I am going to lecture!" You should bring forth this kind of Bodhisattva heart; this is self-enlightenment and the enlightenment of others. Although it is the resolve of the Bodhisattva, it is still not the same as the third type of enlightenment, the perfection of enlightenment and practice. The Buddha is one who has perfected his own self-enlightenment and his enlightenment of others. He has perfectly finished both of these jobs and so he is called a Buddha.

The World Honored One.[1] What is meant by the World Honored One? "Honored" means the most lofty, the most venerable, the most highly esteemed. There is no one higher than the one who is honored. "World" means his world. Is the Buddha merely honored by those in the world? No. He is honored by those in and those beyond the world. The people in the world all pay respect to the Buddha, and the people beyond the world also must respect the Buddha. Because he is honored by those in and beyond the world, he is called the World Honored One. If spoken in detail, the title World Honored One could be explained for several years without finish-

---

[1] *Skt., Bhagavan, Chin.* 世尊 *-shih tsun.*

ing. Now, I have explained the meanings of the Buddha's ten titles in a very general way. If you wish to look into them more deeply, you can do so on your own.

Sutra:

"...WHO EXPOUNDED THE PROPER DHARMA, GOOD AT ITS BEGINNING, GOOD IN ITS MIDDLE, AND GOOD AT ITS END, ITS MEANING PROFOUND AND FAR-REACHING, ITS WORDS CLEVER AND SUBTLE, PURE AND UNADULTERATED, COMPLETE WITH THE MARKS OF PURE, WHITE BRAHMAN CONDUCT.

"TO THOSE WHO SOUGHT TO BE SOUND-HEARERS, HE RESPONDED WITH THE DHARMA OF THE FOUR TRUTHS, BY WHICH ONE CROSSES OVER BIRTH, AGING, SICKNESS, AND DEATH TO THE ULTIMATE NIRVANA; TO THOSE WHO SOUGHT TO BE PRATYEKA BUDDHAS, HE RESPONDED WITH THE DHARMA OF THE TWELVE CONDITIONED CAUSES; FOR THE SAKE OF THE BODHISATTVAS, HE RESPONDED WITH THE SIX PARAMITAS, CAUSING THEM TO ATTAIN ANUTTARASAMYAKSAMBODHI AND REALIZE THE WISDOM OF ALL MODES."

Outline:

H3. speaking Dharma

Commentary:

What is meant by EXPOUNDED? It means to speak in an unfixed manner. When expounding, one must have spirit, and express the spirit of the doctrine, the essential points of the Dharma. There is nothing fixed about the way it is done. You should expound the Dharma in accord with the person you are speaking to. To those of an elevated nature, you should speak of the principle of the nature, that is, talk about the principle of the self-nature, saying, "The self-nature is present within everyone, but people are unable to understand the self-nature." To those who are intelligent, speak about the principle of the self-nature.

To average people you should speak logically, speak of worldly dharmas, even science and philosophy. To the most stupid people, you should speak about cause and effect, as this is most appropriate for those without much wisdom. Therefore, in expounding the PROPER DHARMA there is nothing fixed.

There are four methods to be applied in the art of expounding the Dharma. The first is called "opening," that is, introducing a certain doctrine to people. The second is called "closing," This means that you must bring to a conclusion the topic you have introduced. If you just open it and don't close it, then you have a beginning but not an end. If you just close it but don't open it, then you have an end but not a beginning. But just opening and closing it is still not enough. You must "turn" it; keep on talking, talking until everyone is rapt with attention, and then you turn off into another direction. Perhaps people are not paying close attention. They find your speech flat and dull and they are dozing off, so you use a clever method, perhaps tell a story or something interesting, to get their attention. Finally, you"intercept," that is, you again return to the main point. So when you lecture you should have an opening, closing, turning, and intercepting.

The voice should have four qualities. The first is to speak in a low voice. For example, one disciple speaks with this technique, very softly. If you didn't pay close attention, you wouldn't even hear him. So you pay attention. But if one pays attention like that for too long, one gets tired. The mind will wander and the sentences will drift off, and after a while one will just quit listening. At that time you should raise your voice and speak louder. When people hear that you have raised your voice, they figure there is an argument taking place and so they don't want to listen. Then, you should stop suddenly. You quit speaking, and when they hear nothing, they will pay attention again. When you have regained their attention you can continue speaking.

If you really know how to use your voice, then, even if people don't want to listen to you, they will have no choice. These principles are involved in expounding the Dharma.

Now, the Buddhas EXPOUND THE PROPER DHARMA, GOOD AT ITS BEGINNING, GOOD IN ITS MIDDLE,AND GOOD AT ITS

END...What is meant by "good at its beginning?" From the time Shakyamuni Buddha first produced the Bodhi heart up until the time he left home is called the beginning, "good at its beginning." After he left home, he cultivated all manner of bitter practices, and this is "good in its middle." After becoming a Buddha, he spoke the Dharma for forty-nine years in over three hundred Dharma assemblies until the time came when he entered Nirvana, and this is called "good at its end."

You could also say that "good at its beginning" refers to the time when Shakyamuni Buddha was a common person, just like you and me and all living beings. He brought forth the Bodhi heart, sought the Way to the realization of Buddhahood, left the home-life, cultivated and practiced the Buddhadharma. This is called "good in its middle." After studying and practicing the Buddhadharma, he walked the path of a Bodhisattva, benefitting living beings, giving up his own body, heart and life, his head, eyes, brains, and marrow, his kingdom, cities, wives, and children in order to benefit living beings. The three great asankheya aeons during which he practiced the Bodhisattva Way could be considered as "good in its middle." When, in this present life, he became enlightened and realized Buddhahood, that is "good at its end."

You could also say that the first asankheya aeon of cultivation of merit and virtue is "good at its beginning." The second asankheya aeon of cultivation of merit and virtue is "good in its middle." The third asankheya aeon of cultivation of merit and virtue is "good at its end." So "good at its beginning, good in its middle, and good at its end,"--no matter how you explain it, it's okay.

ITS MEANING PROFOUND AND FAR-REACHING...In expounding the Proper Dharma, good at its beginning, good in its middle, and good at its end, all that took place can be related to the roots" and the "traces." What is meant by "root?" The "root-door" refers to the Buddha as he first put forth the resolve. What is meant by "traces?" The traces are the various modes of practice which he appeared to undertake, the Dharma-doors which he cultivated. His experience was extremely profound and far-reaching. The Buddha, as he expounded the Proper Dharma speaking of the past, present, and future, used words which were CLEVER AND SUBTLE. When the Buddha spoke the Dharma, his expression was ingenious. "Clever" means that the Dharma he spoke was exactly appropriate for those who were being taught. "Subtle" means that it expressed a subtle, wonderful, inconceivable state.

PURE AND UNADULTERATED. The Dharma he spoke was pure, singular. No other Dharma-doors were mixed in with it. What Dharma was it? I will tell you: It was the sudden Dharma, the perfect-sudden dharma. COMPLETE WITH THE MARKS OF PURE, WHITE BRAHMAN CONDUCT. "Complete" means that there is neither too little nor too much. "Pure" means clear and pure."White" refers to bright light.

What are SOUND-HEARERS? You've been listening to Sutras for so long. Do you know what they are?

They are one of the Two Vehicles: the Sound-Hearers and the Pratyeka Buddhas. The Sound Hearers become enlightened through the cultivation of the Four Truths. They hear the Buddha's sound and awaken to the Way, and so they are called Sound Hearers. They are of the Small Vehicle. The Small Vehicle is the beginning level of study of the Buddhadharma, also called the Storehouse Teaching. From the Storehouse Teaching, studying more deeply, one gradually progresses through the Vaipulya and the Prajna Teachings, returning from the smalls towards the great, entering the Great Vehicle Dharma-door. The Sound-Hearers cultivate the Dharma of the Four Truths: suffering, origination, extinction, and the Way. The Four Truths was the first dharma which the Buddha taught. He taught it to the five Bhikshus who, upon hearing this Dharma-door, became enlightened. That is why they are called "Sound Hearers." They heard the sound of the Buddha's voice and awakened to the Way.

...TO CROSS OVER BIRTH, AGING, SICKNESS, AND DEATH...They have been delivered from the sufferings of birth, old age, sickness, and death; they have separated from birth and death, ended birth and cast off death.

...TO ULTIMATE NIRVANA...They obtain the ultimate Nirvana without residue. It is said,

> They've done what they had to do.
> Their Brahman conduct has been established
> They undergo no further becoming.

They've already done the work they were supposed to do and succeeded in their cultivation of pure Brahman conduct. They don't have to undergo birth and death again. That's the Sound Hearers.

The Twelve Conditioned Causes, also known as the Twelve Links of Causation, are:

1. Ignorance, which conditions
2. actions, which conditions
3. consciousness, which conditions
4. name and form, which conditions

5. the six sense organs, which condition
6. contact, which conditions
7. feeling, which conditions
8. craving, which conditions
9. grasping, which conditions
10. becoming, which conditions
11. birth, which conditions
12. old age and death.

Ignorance and activity are "the limbs which are able to lead forth,"[1] because they draw out the following conditions.

Consciousness, name and form, the six sense organs, contact, and feeling are "the limbs which are led forth."[2] Craving, grasping, and becoming are "the limbs which are able to produce."[3] Birth, old age, and death, are "the limbs which are produced."[4]

The Twelve Conditioned Causes can be put together with the Four Truths as follows: The first seven of the Twelve Limbs, "the limbs which are able to lead forth and the limbs which are led forth," belong to the Truth of Suffering. The following five limbs, "the limbs which are able to produce and the limbs which are produced," belong to the Truth of Origination.

The extinction of ignorance and so forth up to the extinction of old age and death belongs to the Truth of Extinction. In the contemplation of the Twelve Conditioned Causes, one uses a kind of wisdom and this wisdom belongs to the Truth of the Way.

For the sake of all the BODHISATTVAS he rightly taught the Dharma for the SIX PARAMITAS. The Six Paramitas are cultivated by Bodhisattvas and the Twelve Conditioned Causes are cultivated by those Enlightened to Conditions, the Pratyeka Buddhas. Pratyeka Buddha is a term which may be interpreted as "Enlightened to Conditions," or as "Solitarily Enlightened." When they are born in a period when a Buddha is in the world, they cultivate the Twelve Conditioned Causes and become enlightened, and certify to the fruit. In that case they are known as "those Enlightened to Conditions." If they cultivate at a time when there is no Buddha in the world they cultivate the Twelve Conditioned Causes

---

1 能引支 -*neng yin chih.*
2 所引支 -*suo yin chih.*
3 能生支 -*neng sheng chih.*
4 所生支 -*suo sheng chih.*

and,

In stillness,
Contemplating the myriad things
--they attain them all.

In the deep mountain valleys, in the caves and on the cliffs, in the Spring they see the ten thousand things begin to grow. The brooks babble as they flow. The ten thousand things are flourishing. Another year has gone by and they realize that their lifespans have decreased another year. If they don't hurry and realize the Way, how meaningless it will all have been.

So it is that, in the mountains, they put forth intense effort and apply themselves to their cultivation. When they first begin meditating, I'll tell you, their legs hurt too. But they bear the pain; they bear what others cannot bear and sit all day without moving. They sit in Dhyana all day, investigating:

"What is ignorance, anyway? Where does ignorance come from?"They investigate the Twelve Conditioned Causes. From ignorance, karmic activity arose and karma was created. After karmic activity came consciousness, and then name and form. After name and form came the six sense organs. After the six sense organs came contact and then feeling. Craving followed feeling and grasping followed craving. Becoming followed grasping, and brith followed becoming and old age followed birth. They investigate it coming and going, back and forth, and--all of a sudden--they become enlightened! They know that originally their nostrils are pointing down! Although it appeared that they were facing downwards, they didn't know, for sure, whether or not they faced up or down. Now they know!

Ultimately, do your nostrils face up or down? *That* is the question. You can ask yourself about your own nostrils.

So they become enlightened and they know that hair grows on the tops of their heads. How strange! They also know that the body is constantly oozing filth from nine orifices and that it will eventually decay and become extinct. At that time they completely understand and enlightened to the continual cycle of production and extinction of all dharmas. They certify to the fruit and are called Solitarily Enlightened Ones. "Solitary" refers to their being born at a time when there is no Buddha in the world.

Bodhisattvas practice the Bodhisattva Way. They benefit themselves and benefit others. They renounce themselves for the sake of other people.

The hells are a place of great suffering and

everyone knows that it is no fun to fall into the hells. The Bodhisattvas see the living beings suffering in the hells, and they run off to the hells to suffer along with them.

"What's the use of suffering along with living beings in the hells?" you might wonder. "What benefit is to be gained from doing that?"

It is of no benefit to the Bodhisattvas themselves, but when they get there they speak the Dharma to the living beings and cause them to bring forth the Bodhi heart. Once they have done so, they will be able to leave suffering and attain bliss. So the Bodhisattvas are not afraid of undergoing any form of bitterness as they teach and transform living beings.

Don't think that Bodhisattvas are very comfortable. Many of them are very *uncomfortable*. They are incredibly busy all day long travelling to the north, east, south, and west, to the four pointsin between, and up and down, to rescue living beings. Why? Because they wish to practice the Six Paramitas and the Ten Thousand Conducts. They want to establish merit and virtue. To rescue a single person is the same as rescuing one living being within their own self-nature. If they do not cross that person over, then a living being in their self-nature remains to be saved. So the Bodhisattvas practice giving, morality, patience, vigor, Dhyana samadhi, and Prajna.

The Bodhisattvas who are missing even one of the Six Paramitas are not yet perfect. They must practice all six. Sometimes they may try to give things away, but people won't take them. They may even try to give some money only to hear, "You've got too much money. You're trying to give it to me, but I don't want it either." This happens all the time. It's not easy to practice the Bodhisattva Way! The Bodhisattvas cultivate the Six Paramitas, the six methods of making it to the other shore.

...CAUSING THEM TO ATTAIN ANUTTARASAMYAKSAMBODHI AND REALIZE THE WISDOM OF ALL MODES. They cause them to attain the utmost proper, equal, and right enlightenment, to realize the Buddha-fruit, and to accomplish the Wisdom of all Modes. There are three types of wisdom:

1. all wisdom, which belongs to the truth of emptiness.

2. wisdom in the Way, which belong to the truth of the false.

These first two fall into the two extremes of emptiness and existence.

3. the wisdom of all modes, which belongs to the

truth of the Middle Way. The first two wisdoms are one-sided, the third is the final meaning of the Middle Way which does not fall into the extreme of emptiness or into the extreme of existence.

"Realization" means that they certify to the attainment of this wisdom. They certify to the fruit of Buddhahood. The three truths and the three wisdoms interpenetrate. Now, in speaking of the wisdom of all modes, the other two wisdoms are also included.

Sutra:

"THEN, THERE WAS ANOTHER BUDDHA, ALSO NAMED BRIGHTNESS OF SUN-MOON-LAMP, AND THEN ANOTHER BUDDHA, ALSO NAMED BRIGHTNESS OF SUN-MOON-LAMP, AND SO FORTH FOR TWENTY-THOUSAND BUDDHAS ALL OF THE SAME NAME, BRIGHTNESS OF SUN-MOON-LAMP, AND ALSO OF THE SAME SURNAME, BHARADVAJA.

"MAITREYA, IT SHOULD BE KNOWN THAT ALL OF THOSE BUDDHAS, FROM THE FIRST TO THE LAST, HAD THE SAME NAME, BRIGHTNESS OF SUN-MOON-LAMP, AND WERE COMPLETE WITH THE TEN TITLES, AND THAT THE DHARMA THEY SPOKE WAS GOOD AT ITS BEGINNING, MIDDLE, AND END."

Outline:

G2. showing Shakyamuni Buddha's similarity with twenty thousand Buddhas

Commentary:

Previously, in explaining the passage, "Good at its beginning, good in its middle, and good at its end," I spoke of Shakyamuni Buddha. Actually, the analogy applies not only to Shakyamuni Buddha, but to all the Buddhas in the ten directions, throughout the three periods of time. The Sutra text itself speaks about Buddhas by the name of Sun-Moon-Lamp Brightness, who spoke the Dharma, good at its beginning, middle, and end.

THEN, THERE WAS ANOTHER BUDDHA, that is, after the previously mentioned Buddha named Brightness of Sun-Moon-Lamp, there was yet another Budddha ALSO NAMED BRIGHTNESS OF SUN-MOON-LAMP, AND THEN, after that, ANOTHER BUDDHA, ALSO NAMED BRIGHTNESS OF SUN-MOON-LAMP, AND THEN ANOTHER BUDDHA, ALSO NAMED BRIGHTNESS OF SUN-MOON-LAMP...Later, after the second Buddha by the name of Brightness of Sun-Moon-Lamp, yet another Buddha appeared and he didn't take a different name; he was also of the same name.

Why did he take that name? Because it has brightness and also wisdom, and also samadhi power and morality. The name carries the meaning of morality, samadhi, and wisdom--all of the Three Non-outflow Studies. If you have morality you will not "flow-out" and that's a non-outflow. If you have wisdom, you will not "flow-out" and that's also a non-outflow. If you have samdhi you will flow out even less. You will obtain the state of non-outflow, the perfection of the Three Non-outflow Studies.

The Buddhas liked this name and so the first, second, and third Buddhas all have the same name. And not only the third, but AND SO FORTH FOR TWENTY-THOUSAND BUDDHAS every one of them had the same name. The name sounded very fin , and so twenty thousand Buddhas like it.

AND ALSO OF THE SAME SURNAME. Not only did they have the same first names, their last names were the same, too. What were they? They were BHARADVAJA, a Sanskrit word which means "rapid,"[1] because they became Buddhas very quickly. If you had that name, you probably would realize Buddhahood very quickly, too. Pity you don't, and so you're very slow.

The word Bharadvaja may also be interpreted as "sharp-rooted"[2] because they were extremely intelligent and wise. Where did their wisdom and intelligence come from? It came from the cultivation of all manner of Dharma-doors. They studied the Sutras; they read and recited the Great Vehicle writings, and so their name

---

1 捷疾 -*chieh chi*.

2 利根 -*li ken*.

means "sharp-rooted." It may also be said to mean "full speech."[1] Their speech was perfect; they expressed the doctrines in their entirety; what they said was all in accord with the Buddhadharma. Those are the three meanings of Bharadvaja.

MAITREYA! IT SHOULD BE KNOWN...Manjushri Bodhisattva says, "Maitreya Bodhisattva, Bodhisattva Invincible, you ought to know THAT ALL OF THOSE BUDDHAS, FROM THE FIRST TO THE LAST, HAD THE SAME NAME, BRIGHTNESS OF SUN-MOON-LAMP, AND WERE COMPLETE WITH THE TEN TITLES. The name Brightness of Sun-Moon-Lamp is a specific name. The ten titles are common to all the Buddhas of the ten directions.

AND THAT THE DHARMA WHICH THEY SPOKE WAS GOOD AT ITS BEGINNING, MIDDLE, AND END. Right up to the last of the Buddhas, they all spoke Dharma which was good at its beginning, good at its middle, and good at its end. When they first brought forth the Bodhi-heart and began to cultivate, it was good; in the middle, while they were cultivating, it was good; and at the very end, when they became Buddhas, it was also good.

Sutra:

"BEFORE THE LAST BUDDHA LEFT THE HOME-LIFE, HE HAD EIGHT ROYAL SONS. THE FIRST WAS NAMED INTENTION, THE SECOND, GOOD INTENTION, THE THIRD, LIMITLESS INTENTION, THE FOURTH JEWELED INTENTION, THE FIFTH, INCREASING INTENTION; THE SIXTH, INTENTION RID OF DOUBT, THE SEVENTH, RESOUNDING INTENTION, AND THE EIGHTH, DHARMA INTENTION. THE EIGHT PRINCES WERE OF AWESOME VIRTUE AND SELF-MASTERY AND EACH RULED OVER FOUR CONTINENTS.

"WHEN THE PRINCES HEARD THAT THEIR FATHER HAD LEFT THE HOME-LIFE AND ATTAINED ANUTTARASAMYAKSAMBODHI, THEY ALL RENOUNCED THEIR ROYAL POSITIONS AND LEFT HOME AS WELL. THEY BROUGHT FORTH THE RESOLVE FOR THE GREAT

---

[1] 滿語 -*man yü*.

VEHICLE AND CONSTANTLY CULTIVATED BRAHMAN CONDUCT. ALL BECAME DHARMA MASTERS, HAVING ALREADY, IN THE PRESENCE OF TEN MILLION BUDDHAS, PLANTED THE ROOTS OF GOODNESS."

Outline:

G3. showing Shakyamuni Buddha's similarity with the last of the twenty thousand Buddhas.

H1. similarity of what was seen in the past with what has happened in the present.

Commentary:

BEFORE THE LAST BUDDHA HAD LEFT THE HOME-LIFE, before the last of the twenty thousand Buddhas had left the home-life, HE HAD EIGHT ROYAL SONS. Shakyamuni Buddha had one son, Rahula. The last of this series of Buddhas, Brightness of Sun-Moon-Lamp, had eight sons and each had his own name: THE FIRST WAS NAMED INTENTION, he had a great heart for the Way, and he had brought forth the intention, the thought, of one with the heart of the Great Vehicle. THE SECOND, GOOD INTENTION, he had no bad intentions. He had well brought forth the Bodhi-heart, well brought forth the great heart for the Way, so he was called Good Intention. THE THIRD, LIMITLESS INTENTION; he had brought forth an unlimited, great Bodhi-heart for the Way; this was his intention. THE FOURTH, JEWELED INTENTION; his intention was to bring forth the Bodhi-heart; his most cherished, most treasured intention was to seek for Buddhahood. THE FIFTH, INCREASING INTENTION. What intention was increased? The intention to bring forth the Bodhi-heart. THE SIXTH, RID OF DOUBT. In cultivation, only fear that you will have doubts. If you have doubts you may take the wrong path. So it is said,

The cultivator's heart
must be free of doubts.
Once doubt arises,
it's easy to go wrong.

When doubting thoughts begin to plague you, in your confusion, you may lose the right road and enter a dangerous path. THE SEVENTH, RESOUNDING INTENTION. His cultivation of the Great Vehicle Dharma was like an echo in a mountain valley. When you bring forth the Bodhi-heart, the Way heart, it works like an echo. You bring forth the heart, and the Buddha knows. THE EIGHTH, DHARMA INTENTION.

THE EIGHT PRINCES WERE OF AWESOME VIRTUE AND SELF-MASTERY. Each of them was very solemn, dignified, and accomplished in virtuous conduct, AND EACH RULED OVER FOUR CONTINENTS. The term "four continents" refers to a system of one sun, one moon, and one Mount Sumeru, and one set of four continents.

WHEN THE PRINCES HEARD THAT THEIR FATHER HAD LEFT THE HOME-LIFE...When they heard that their father had already left home and become a monk, and, on top of that, had become a Buddha, AND ATTAINED ANUTTARSAMYAKSAMBODHI, the utmostequal and proper enlightenment, all eight of them ALL RENOUNCED THEIR ROYAL POSITIONS. They didn't become emperors. They gave up their beautiful consorts and concubines. They didn't want them. They gave up their kingdoms, cities, wives, and children. They renounced their kingdoms, gave away their cities, gave away their wives and children, AND LEFT HOME AS WELL. They followed the last of the Brightness of Sun-Moon-Lamp Buddhas and left home.

THEY BROUGHT FORTH THE RESOLVE FOR THE GREAT VEHICLE AND CONSTANTLY CULTIVATED BRAHMAN CONDUCT. They always cultivated pure conduct and did so without resting; they were always vigorous. ALL BECAME DHARMA MASTERS and went about everywhere explaining the Sutras and teaching the Dharma, HAVING ALREADY, IN THE PRESENCE OF TEN MILLION BUDDHAS, PLANTED THE ROOTS OF GOODNESS, doing all kinds of good deeds: making offerings to the Triple Jewel, paying reverence to the Triple Jewel. The eight royal sons cultivated the giving of offerings and practiced the Bodhisattva conduct, cultivating the Buddha Way. They brought forth great Bodhi hearts.

Sutra:

AT THAT TIME, THE BUDDHA SUN-MOON-LAMP BRIGHTNESS SPOKE A GREAT VEHICLE SUTRA NAMED THE LIMITLESS PRINCIPLES, A DHARMA FOR INSTRUCTING BODHISATTVAS OF WHICH THE BUDDHAS ARE PROTECTIVE AND MINDFUL. WHEN HE HAD FINISHED SPEAKING THAT SUTRA, HE THEN, IN THE MIDST OF THE ASSEMBLY, SAT IN FULL LOTUS AND ENTERED THE SAMADHI OF THE STATION OF LIMITLESS PRINCIPLES; HIS BODY AND MIND WERE UNMOVING. THEN FROM THE HEAVENS THERE FELL A RAIN

OF MANDARAVA FLOWERS, MAHAMANDARAVA FLOWERS, MANJUSHAKA FLOWERS, AND MAHAMANJUSHAKA FLOWERS, WHICH WERE SCATTERED UPON THE BUDDHA AND THE ENTIRE GREAT ASSEMBLY. ALL THE BUDDHA UNIVERSES QUAKED IN SIX WAYS. AT THAT TIME THE ENTIRE GREAT ASSEMBLY OF BHIKSHUS, BHIKSHUNIS, UPASAKAS, UPASIKAS, GODS, DRAGONS, YAKSHAS, GANDHARVAS, ASURAS, GARUDAS, KINNARAS, MAHORAGAS, BEINGS HUMAN AND NON-HUMAN AS WELL AS THE MINOR KINGS AND THE WHEEL-TURNING SAGE KINGS AND SO FORTH, ALL ATTAINED WHAT THEY HAD NEVER HAD BEFORE. THEY REJOICED AND JOINED THEIR PALMS AND, WITH ONE HEART, GAZED UPON THE BUDDHA. THEN THE THUS COME ONE EMITTED FROM BETWEEN HIS BROWS A WHITE HAIR-MARK LIGHT WHICH ILLUMINED EIGHTEEN THOUSAND BUDDHA-WORLDS TO THE EAST, OMITTING NONE OF THEM.

Outline:

H2. similarity of what was seen in the past with what is occurring in the present.
 I1. similarity of the portents
  J1. six portents in this world

Commentary:

AT THAT TIME, right then, when the eight princes left home, the last of the Buddhas named Sun-Moon-Lamp Brightness SPOKE A GREAT VEHICLE SUTRA, NAMED THE LIMITLESS PRINCIPLES. This Sutra is a DHARMA-door FOR INSTRUCTING all the BODHISATTVA OF WHICH THE BUDDHA IS PROTECTIVE AND MINDFUL. All the Buddhas are protective and mindful of this Sutra.

WHEN HE HAD FINISHED SPEAKING THAT SUTRA, HE THEN, IN THE MIDST OF THE GREAT ASSEMBLY, he was right in the assembly of Bhikshus, Bhikshunis, Upasakas, Upasikas, Bodhisattvas, and Arhats, SAT IN FULL LOTUS, drew up his legs into the full lotus position AND ENTERED THE SAMADHI, the concentration, OF THE STATION OF LIMITLESS PRINCIPLES; HIS BODY AND MIND WERE UNMOVING. This passage has already been explained in detail, and we can merely read through it here without discussing it further.

When the Buddha entered the Samadhi of the Station of Limitless Principles, his body did not move and his mind did not move. His unmoving state of body and mind is an indication that he had attained concentration.

THEN FROM THE HEAVENS THERE FELL A RAIN...It looked like rain, but it wasn't water. What was it? It was a rain OF MANDARAVA FLOWERS, little white flowers, AND MAHAMANDARAVA FLOWERS, big white flowers. The white flowers, large and small, fell together in profusion, filling the air with a delectable fragrance. The ground was completely carpeted with flowers! It also rained MANJUSHAKA FLOWERS, small red flowers, AND MAHAMANJUSHAKA FLOWERS, big red flowers. These four kinds of flowers represent the four sets of positions: The Ten Dwellings, the Ten Practices, the Ten Dedications, and the Ten Grounds. WHICH WERE SCATTERED UPON THE BUDDHA AND THE ENTIRE GREAT ASSEMBLY of Dharma.

ALL THE BUDDHA UNIVERSES as many great trichiliocosms as the grains of sand in the Ganges, QUAKED IN SIX WAYS. I'm not going to test you now so you don't have to peek at your old notes!

THE ENTIRE GREAT ASSEMBLY OF BHIKSHUS, BHIKSHUNIS, UPASAKAS, UPASIKAS, the four-fold assembly of disciples, GODS, DRAGONS, YAKSHAS, that is, ghosts, GANDHARVAS, the music spirits in the court of the Jade Emperor. ASURAS, those who are "ugly," and "without wine." GARUDAS are the great golden-winged P'eng birds. KINNARAS are also music spirits in the court of the Jade Emperor. MAHORAGAS are big snakes. AS WELL AS THE MINOR KINGS, kings of small countries, AND THE WHEEL TURNING SAGE KINGS AND SO FORTH ...There are a lot more than the above-mentioned names, but not all of them have been listed separately. Everyone present ATTAINED WHAT THEY HAD NEVER HAD BEFORE. They had never seen or heard anything like it before. They saw that they had never seen and heard what they had never heard. Now, seeing and hearing, THEY REJOICED AND JOINED THEIR PALMS...Seeing the Buddha Sun-Moon-Lamp Brightness display such spiritual penetrations, everyone was happy. They put their palms together AND, WITH ONE HEART, GAZED UPON THE BUDDHA. They were singleminded as they looked at the Buddha.

THEN THE THUS COME ONE, the Buddha Sun-Moon-Lamp Brightness, also EMITTED FROM BETWEEN HIS BROWS A WHITE HAIR-MARK LIGHT WHICH ILLUMINED EIGHTEEN THOUSAND BUDDHA

WORLDS TO THE EAST, from that Buddha-world across Buddha-worlds eighteen thousand in number. The Buddha worlds here represent the eighteen realms. The six quakings mentioned earlier represent the six sense organs quaking. The six sense organs plus the six sense objects, plus the six consciousnesses make eighteen realms. So, the Buddha emitted light shining across eighteen thousand Buddha-worlds which represents the eighteen realms. OMITTING NONE OF THEM. There was no place in which there was a Buddha where the light did not reach; it reached them all.

Sutra:

...JUST LIKE ALL THE BUDDHA-LANDS NOW SEEN.

Outline:

J2. six portents in other worlds

Sutra:

MAITREYA, IT SHOULD BE KNOWN THAT THERE WERE AT THAT TIME IN THE ASSEMBLY TWENTY MILLION BODHISATTVAS WHO TOOK DELIGHT IN LISTENING TO THE DHARMA. UPON SEEING THIS BRIGHT LIGHT ILLUMINE ALL THE BUDDHA LANDS, ALL THE BODHISATTVAS OBTAINED WHAT THEY HAD NEVER HAD AND WISHED TO KNOW THE CAUSES AND CONDITIONS FOR THIS LIGHT.

Outline:

I2. similarity of the doubts

Commentary:

Once again, Manjushri Bodhisattva speaks to Maitreya Bodhisattva saying MAITREYA, Humane One, IT SHOULD BE KNOWN, you should know, THAT THERE WERE AT THAT TIME IN THE ASSEMBLY, in the Dharma assembly TWENTY MILLION BODHISATTVAS WHO TOOK DELIGHT IN LISTENING TO THE DHARMA. They all liked to hear the Buddha speak the Dharma. UPON SEEING THIS BRIGHT LIGHT emitted by the Buddha Brightness of Sun-Moon-Lamp, illumine all the

Buddha lands, ALL THE BODHISATTVAS gave rise to doubts; they didn't understand. Seeing the Buddha emit the white hair-mark light from between his brows which illumined eighteen thousand Buddhalands to the east, they also OBTAINED WHAT THEY HAD NEVER HAD. They had never seen anything like it before. AND WISHED TO KNOW THE CAUSES AND CONDITIONS FOR THIS LIGHT. The twenty million Bodhisattvas also wanted to know the reason for the light. Why did the Buddha emit the light? What was the reason?

Sutra:

THERE WAS AT THAT TIME A BODHISATTVA BY THE NAME OF WONDROUS LIGHT WHO HAD EIGHT HUNDRED DISCIPLES. THE BUDDHA BRIGHTNESS OF SUN-MOON-LAMP THEN AROSE FROM SAMADHI AND, FOR THE SAKE OF THE BODHISATTVA WONDROUS LIGHT, SPOKE A GREAT VEHICLE SUTRA CALLED THE WONDERFUL DHARMA LOTUS FLOWER, A DHARMA FOR INSTRUCTING BODHISATTVAS OF WHICH THE BUDDHA IS PROTECTIVE AND MINDFUL.

Outline:

H3. similarity of what was seen in the past with what is about to happen

I1. similarity of persons for whom the Dharma was spoken

Commentary:

THERE WAS AT THAT TIME A BODHISATTVA, in the Dharma assembly BY THE NAME OF WONDROUS LIGHT WHO HAD EIGHT HUNDRED DISCIPLES. THE BUDDHA BRIGHTNESS OF SUN-MOON-LAMP THEN AROSE FROM SAMADHI, he came out of concentration, the samadhi of the station of limitless principles, AND, FOR THE SAKE OF THE BODHISATTVA WONDROUS LIGHT, SPOKE A GREAT VEHICLE SUTRA. It was CALLED THE WONDERFUL DHARMA LOTUS FLOWER Sutra. It was a DHARMA-door FOR INSTRUCTING BODHISATTVAS OF WHICH THE BUDDHA IS PROTECTIVE AND MINDFUL.

Sutra:

FOR SIXTY SMALL AEONS HE DID NOT RISE FROM HIS SEAT. THOSE ASSEMBLED LISTENING ALSO SAT IN ONE PLACE FOR SIXTY SMALL AEONS WITH BODIES AND MINDS UNMOVING, LISTENING TO WHAT THE BUDDHA SAID AS IF IT WERE BUT THE SPACE OF A MEAL. AT THAT TIME, IN THE ASSEMBLY, THERE WAS NOT A SINGLE PERSON WHO GREW WEARY, EITHER PHYSICALLY OR MENTALLY.

Outline:

I2. similarity of the time

Commentary:

When the Buddha Brightness of Sun-Moon-Lamp spoke the Sutra, how long did it take him? SIXTY SMALL AEONS. If you're talking about a long time, sixty small aeons isn't really too long; if you're talking about a short period of time, it isn't exactly short. One aeons is 139,600 years. One thousand of those aeons makes one small aeon. So count it up: How long would sixty small aeons be?

However, one thought is ten thousand years, and ten thousand years is but a single thought. You could also say that one thought is ten thousand aeons, and ten thousand aeons is but a single thought. In the Heaven of the Four Kings a single day and night is equivalent to fifty years here in the world of human beings. In the Heaven of the Thirty-three, a day and night is one hundred years among humans. One day and one night seems like a very short space of time to them.

When people sit in meditation, if they don't strike up false thinking, they can sit for an entire day and feel as if it were a single second. If you strike up false thinking, it can seem as if a single second lasted, oh, who knows how many years? You sit there, and you can't sit still. You want to quit sitting and so:

> One thought is ten thousand aeons;
> Ten thousand aeons is but a thought.

When the Buddha Sun-Moon-Lamp Brightness was speaking the Dharma FOR SIXTY SMALL AEONS HE DID NOT RISE

FROM HIS SEAT. He spoke *The Dharma Flower Sutra* for sixty small aeons. Why did it take so long? It was because everyone had entered the "delight in listening samadhi." Although the Buddha spoke the Dharma, he did it from within samadhi and didn't rise for sixty small aeons. THOSE ASSEMBLED LISTENING ALSO SAT IN ONE PLACE FOR SIXTY SMALL AEONS, WITH BODIES AND MINDS UNMOVING. The Dharma assembly of twenty million Bodhisattvas, gods, dragons, ghosts, and spirits and all the Arhats, Bhikshus, Bhikshunis, Upasakas, Upasikas, and so forth, and so on, sat there listening to the Dharma for sixty small aeons.

For example, we are now listening to Sutras. If you pay close attention, and listen singlemindedly, when the lecture is over you will feel as if a very short time had passed. If you don't pay attenion, what is it like? On the one hand you listen to the Sutras, and on the other you strike up false thinking, "Oh...it's still not over. How much time have we got left? Take a look, would you?"

This is like a student who said that when she sat in meditation she did not meditate but rather waited for the bell so she could get up and be "liberated." If you do that, how can you work at your meditation? If you do that, then when you sit, you feel the time drags on, and your legs start to hurt, and your back aches. But if you don't pay attenion to the time, then there's no leg or back pain; it's no problem. "Well, who hurts? Who aches?" Just ask, and it disappears. They sat for sixty small aeons and did not move in body or in mind. Their bodies didn't wiggle around or lean this way and that, and their minds also did not move.

LISTENING TO WHAT THE BUDDHA SAID...They listened to the Buddha Sun-Moon-Lamp Brightness speak the Dharma as if it were the time it takes to eat a bowl of rice, AS IF IT WERE BUT THE SPACE OF A MEAL.

AT THAT TIME IN THE ASSEMBLY THERE WAS NOT A SINGLE PERSON WHO GREW WEARY, EITHER PHYSICALLY OR MENTALLY. In the Dharma assembly, there wasn't a single person who got tired, and wanted to rest, to take a nap. Nobody wanted to rest or sleep.

If you were one who truly listened to Sutras, you wouldn't feel that it was tiresome to sit there. You should sit there and, the more you listened, the more delighted you would become. "Ah, the Dharma is really wonderful, inconceivably wonderful!" If you don't truly listen, you sit there and your legs wiggle and your hands jerk around and even though there's not wind, it looks like you're being blown back and forth, leaning all over the place. Or perhaps you get up and pace the floor, or you look to the east and look to the west. This is because your heart is not truly in it; you aren't truly listening to the Sutras, and you aren't tasting their true flavor. If you tasted the true flavor of the Sutras, I'll tell you, there would be nothing so important that it could interfere with your attendance at the lectures. You would certainly come to listen. "Everyday I miss a lecture, I will not eat," you'd say. "If I miss lectures for two days in a row, for two days I won't eat." If you pushed yourself like that, you wouldn't dare not come to listen. Say to yourself,"If you don't go listen, you won't get anything to eat!" That's a wonderful dharma. Try it out, if you dare. "So you don't want to listen to Sutras? All right, no food today. If you go hungry for a day then, next week, you will think, "I'm going to go listen to the Sutra lecture. Otherwise I'll go hungry!" Besides, not eating is really just not receiving the food of Dharma. In listening to the Sutras one receives the nourishment of Dharma.

Sutra:

AT THE END OF SIXTY SMALL AEONS, HAVING FINISHED SPEAKING THE SUTRA, THE BUDDHA SUN-MOON-LAMP BRIGHTNESS IMMEDIATELY ANNOUNCED TO THE ASSEMBLY OF BRAHMA, MARA, SHRAMANAS, BRAHMANS, GODS, HUMANS, AND ASURAS, "TODAY, AT MIDNIGHT, THE THUS COME ONE WILL ENTER NIRVANA WITHOUT RESIDUE."

Outline:

I3. similarity of announcing Nirvana

Commentary:

The Buddha Sun-Moon-Lamp Brightness spoke *The Dharma Flower Sutra* for a full sixty small aeons; in all that time not a single person in the assembly grew tired in body or in mind. AT THE END OF SIXTY SMALL AEONS, HAVING FINISHED SPEAKING THIS SUTRA, THE BUDDHA SUN-MOON-LAMP BRIGHTNESS IMMEDIATELY ANNOUNCED TO BRAHMA, the god, MARA, the demon king, SHRAMANAS, that is, the Bhikshus who have left home, THE BRAHMANS, one of the Indian outside ways who practice pure conduct. THE GODS, HUMANS, AND ASURAS...He made an announcement saying, "TONIGHT, AT MIDNIGHT, THE THUS COME ONE WILL ENTER NIRVANA WITHOUT RESIDUE. The Thus Come One Sun-Moon-Lamp Brightness today will enter Nirvana. The Buddha was born at noon and entered Nirvana at midnight. Noon is *yang* and night, *yin*. When the Buddha came into the world, it was as if the entire world was illuminated by the sun, moon, and lamplight. After the Buddha crossed into extinction, that is, entered Nirvana, it was like the darkness of the night. Not only was this the case with the Buddha Sun-Moon-Lamp Brightness, but all Buddhas are that way. They appear in the world at noon and enter Nirvana without residue at midnight.

NIRVANA is of four kinds, according to the explanation of the Consciousness Only School. Some texts give four kinds of Nirvana, but not the three kinds. What are the three?

1. The Nirvana of the purity of the nature. This type of Nirvana belongs to the virtue of the Dharmabody. The Buddha has three bodies: the Dharmabody, the Reward body, and the Transformation body. The Nirvana of the purity of the nature belongs to the virtue of the Dharma body, that virtue being that it is not produced or destroyed, not defiled and not pure, not increasing and not decreasing.

2. The Nirvana of perfect purity. This type of Nirvana belongs to the virtue of Prajna.

3. The Nirvana of the purity of expedient means. This belongs to the virtue of liberation.

The virtue of the Dharmabody, the virtue of Prajna, and the virtue of liberation are the Secret Storehouse of Great Nirvana, the three virtues of Nirvana.

The purity of expedient means refers to "from emptiness taking up a false (existence)" that is, what is not produced takes on production, and what is not extinguished takes on extinction. Although within the six paths of rebirth, there is no defilment and entry into nirvana entails permanent bliss, all actions and practices are conducted from within the Nirvana of expedient means purity. The three kinds of Nirvana are basically the same as the four kinds of Nirvana,

Here, the text says, NIRVANA WITHOUT RESIDUE. The first of the four kinds of Nirvana is the Nirvana of the purity of the self nature. This corresponds to the first of the three types of Nirvana, the Nirvana of the purity of the nature.

The second of the four types of Nirvana is the Nirvana with residue. What is meant by residue? It refers to those of the Two Vehicles. Although they have certified to the fruit, they still have bodies. Because their bodies remain, they still have suffering. As long as you have a body, you suffer. Without a body, there is no suffering. Why are you greedy, hateful, and stupid? It is because you take a thief for your son and search outside. Because you have a body, you have to take care of it; consequently, you are greedy, hateful, and stupid. If you have a body, you suffer. If you have a body, you undergo pain. This is called Nirvana with residue.

When you have emptied the body and dharmas, there is no attachment to self or to dharmas, and this is called the Nirvana without residue, the third of the four kinds; here, suffering has been ended, cultivation of Brahman conduct has been established, what was to be done has been done, and one undergoes no further becoming; one need not return to be reborn in the Three Realms.

The fourth is the Nirvana of no dwelling place which corresponds to the third of the three kinds of Nirvana discussed above, that of the purity of expedient means. The Nirvanas with and without residue correspond to the second of the three kinds, the Nirvana of perfect purity.

Sutra:

THERE WAS AT THAT TIME A BODHISATTVA BY THE NAME OF VIRTUE TREASURY TO WHOM THE BUDDHA SUN-MOON-LAMP BRIGHTNESS TRANSMITTED A PREDICTION, TELLING ALL THE BHIKSHUS, "THE BODHISATTVA VIRTUE TREASURY WILL NEXT BECOME A BUDDHA WITH THE NAME OF PURE-BODY-TATHAGATO 'RHAN, SAMYAKSAMBUDDHAH."

Outline:

I4. similarity of giving predictions

Commentary:

When the Buddha Sun-Moon-Lamp Brightness announced the news that he was going to enter Nirvana without residue, there was a Bodhisattva present by the name of

VIRTUE TREASURY. His virtuous practices were especially complete. THE BUDDHA SUN-MOON-LAMP BRIGHTNESS TRANSMITTED A PREDICTION to him. What is meant by "transmitting a prediction?" It is to announce a future event, one for which the time has not yet come. The event is still "hanging in the air." It hasn't yet "fallen to the ground." It is also said to be an advance prediction which refers to giving you a prediction in this life for your becoming a Buddha in a future life, saying, "You, in a future age, will be a Buddha with such and such a name..."

TELLING ALL THE BHIKSHUS, "THE BODHISATTVA VIRTUE TREASURY WILL NEXT BECOME A BUDDHA. After I have entered into Nirvana, he shall become a Buddha. His name will be PURE BODY Thus Come One. TATHAGATO'RHAN, that is Thus Come One, One Worthy of Offerings; SAMYAKSAMBUDDAH, one of Proper and Universal Knowledge." Originally the Buddha has ten titles, but here only three are used to represent all ten.

Sutra:

AFTER THAT BUDDHA HAD TRANSMITTED THE PREDICTION, AT MIDNIGHT HE ENTERED NIRVANA WITHOUT RESIDUE.

Outline:

I5. similarity of propagation of Sutra after Buddha's nirvana
J1. entering of nirvana

Commentary:

AFTER THAT BUDDHA HAD TRANSMITTED THE PREDICTION to the Bodhisattva Virtue Treasury, AT MIDNIGHT HE ENTERED NIRVANA WITHOUT RESIDUE. In the middle of the night, the Buddha went into Nirvana, he "completed the stillness."

Sutra:

FOLLOWING THE BUDDHA'S CROSSING OVER INTO EXTINCTION, THE BODHISATTVA WONDROUS LIGHT UPHELD THE <u>WONDERFUL DHARMA LOTUS FLOWER SUTRA</u> FOR A FULL EIGHTY SMALL AEONS, EXPOUNDING IT TO OTHERS. THE EIGHT SONS OF THE BUDDHA SUN-MOON-LAMP BRIGHTNESS ALL SERVED WONDROUS LIGHT AS THEIR MASTER.

WONDROUS LIGHT TAUGHT AND TRANSFORMED THEM, CAUSING THEM TO BECOME FIRMLY ESTABLISHED IN ANUTTARASAMYAKSAMBODHI.

THE PRINCES, HAVING MADE OFFERINGS TO LIMITLESS HUNDREDS OF THOUSANDS OF TENS OF THOUSANDS OF MILLIONS OF BUDDHAS, ALL REALIZED THE BUDDHA WAY. THE VERY LAST TO BECOME A BUDDHA WAS ONE NAMED BURNER OF THE LAMP.

AMONG THE EIGHT HUNDRED DISCIPLES WAS ONE NAMED SEEKER OF FAME, WHO WAS GREEDILY ATTACHED TO PROFIT AND OFFERINGS. ALTHOUGH HE READ AND RECITED MANY SCRIPTURES, HE DID NOT COMPREHEND THEM AND FORGOT MOST OF WHAT HE LEARNED. FOR THAT REASON HE WAS CALLED SEEKER OF FAME. BECAUSE HE HAD ALSO PLANTED GOOD ROOTS, HE WAS ABLE TO ENCOUNTER LIMITLESS HUNDREDS OF THOUSANDS OF TENS OF THOUSANDS OF MILLIONS OF BUDDHAS, MAKING OFFERINGS TO THEM AND HONORING THEM, VENERATING AND PRAISING THEM.

Outline:

J2. benefits derived from propagation of the Sutra after the Buddha's nirvana

Commentary:

FOLLOWING THE BUDDHA'S CROSSING OVER INTO EXTINCTION, THE BODHISATTVA WONDROUS LIGHT UPHELD THE WONDERFUL DHARMA LOTUS FLOWER SUTRA. He accepted, upheld, read and recited it FOR A FULL EIGHTY SMALL AEONS, EXPOUNDING IT TO OTHERS, explaining it to them.

THE EIGHT SONS OF THE BUDDHA SUN-MOON-LAMP BRIGHTNESS ALL SERVED WONDROUS LIGHT AS THEIR MASTER. They bowed to him as their teacher. WONDROUS LIGHT TAUGHT AND TRANSFORMED THEM, the eight sons, CAUSING THEM TO BECOME

FIRMLY ESTABLISHED IN ANUTTARASAMYAKSAMBODHI. He caused them to bring forth hearts which were solid and irreversible with respect to the Utmost Proper and Equal Right Enlightenment, that is, the Buddha-fruit. They only wished to go forward and had no thought of retreating. They were ever vigorous and never rested. The eight royal sons bowed to the Bodhisattva Wondrous Light as their teacher, and he carried out his responsibilities quite dutifully. He spoke to them all day saying things like, "Don't be lazy. Don't sneak off to rest or take naps, and don't go around stealing food!" That's how he kept track of them. Even though they were royal princes, they still have to cultivate truly. When Shakyamuni Buddha left the home-life to cultivate, he was by no means lazy. He meditated in the Himalayas everyday. Those who have left home must cultivate the Way if they are to receive the offerings from the ten directions. If you don't cultivate the Way, it can be very dangerous. Don't think that leaving home is all that easy.

THE PRINCES, the eight sons of the Buddha Sun-Moon-Lamp Brightness, after leaving home MADE OFFERINGS TO LIMITLESS HUNDREDS OF THOUSANDS OF TENS OF THOUSANDS OF BUDDHAS.Having cultivated both blessings and wisdom to perfection, they ALL REALIZED THE BUDDHA WAY.

What is meant by cultivating blessings and wisdom? MAKING OFFERINGS TO LIMITLESS HUNDREDS OF THOUSANDS OF TENS OF THOUSANDS OF BUDDHAS was the cultivation of blessings. Reciting and maintaining hundreds of thousands of tens of thousands of millions of Sutras which the Buddha had spoken was the cultivation of wisdom. Through accepting, maintaining, reading, and reciting, making offerings and paying honor, they perfected their blessings and wisdom and later became Buddhas.

THE VERY LAST TO BECOME A BUDDHA WAS ONE NAMED BURNER OF THE LAMP. AMONG THE EIGHT HUNDRED DISCIPLES WAS ONE NAMED SEEKER OF FAME. The Bodhisattva Wondrous Light had eight hundred disicples. One of them was called Seeker of Fame. Now, the Bodhisattva Wondrous Light was the Bodhisattva Manjushri. He was the master of the eight princes, and taught them all to become Buddhas. The last of the eight princes was called Burner of the Lamp. He was Shakyamuni Buddha's teacher and transmitted the prediction of Buddhahood to Shakyamuni Buddha. This means that the Bodhisattva Manjushri was Shakyamuni Buddha's grand-teacher, his teacher's teacher.

Manjushri now acts as Shakyamuni Buddha's disciple. The grand-teacher is now the disicple. What is the principle involved here? In the Buddhadharma, "The

Dharma is level and equal with nothing above or below." Everything in the world is, without exception, just like a play. People all watch the play and then, when it's over, they go home. Manjushri Bodhisattva acted in the Saha world as the disciple of Shakyamuni Buddha and Shakyamuni Buddha's teacher was Manjushri Bodhisattva's disciple. So, take a look: "The Dharma is level and equal, with nothing above or below," and so when Shakyamuni Buddha became a Buddha, Manjushri Bodhisattva had not yet done so, and so now he is Shakyamuni Buddha's disciple.

Among the eight hundred disciples was one named Seeker of Fame. He just loved to seek fame and profit. What was he like? He never cultivated; he just laughed and joked all day. He ran around outside, climbing on conditions at the homes of the wealthy people and influential officials. He schemed for his own advantage and he didn't cultivate. He didn't recited Sutras. Well, he recited them, but his heart wasn't in it. He recited them over and over, but couldn't remember them. Why not? Because his heart was heavy laden with schemes for climbing on conditions. If you can't remember your Sutra recitations, you should take a clue from Maitreya Bodhisattva for a warning. He couldn't remember the Sutras because he was too involved with climbing on conditions and seeking fame.

Why can't you remember your Sutra recitations? It's because, in your heart, you also seek fame and climb on conditions; you seek fame and profit. If you put down those two words "fame and profit,"then you'd be able to recite any book at all after reading it only once. You wouldn't have to put forth any special concentration to memorize it. Why? Because you'd have no other thoughts. Without thoughts of greed, hatred, or stupidity, or climbing on conditions, your intelligence and wisdom would come forth.

WHO WAS GREEDILY ATTACHED TO PROFIT AND OFFERINGS. See? Even Maitreya Bodhisattva had that flaw. He was greedy for profit, craved offerings, climbed on conditions, and got stuck on profit and offerings. Profit just means money. He was greedy for people to give him a little cash, like monks nowadays who receive offerings of money in little red envelopes. They open them up, and if there is a sizable amount of money in them, they are delightened. That is what is meant by being greedily attached to profit and offerings. If they get a little less, they grimace and groan. This is just a manifestation of greed for offerings. If you are truly a person of the Way, it won't matter how much they give. A little is a lot and a lot is a little. A little and a lot--it's all the same.

For example, last Saturday on the eighth day of the lunar month, one disciple saw that people were making offerings to the Dharma Master. Basically, I wouldn't even bring this matter up because it is likely to sound as if I'm asking for offerings, but unless I talk about it, no one will know. She saw that the Chinese people were all making offerings and so she also gave an offering. At the time I didn't know how much was in it. Later on, I opened it and saw that it was a penny. I was extremely happy.

You say, "How could a penny make you happy?"

Although it was only a penny, it showed that she had a sincere heart. I think on that day she didn't have any money and so she only gave a penny. That night, she made another offerings of four dollars and told me, "I didn't have any money today." I said, "I know. Your penny made merit and virtue for you perhaps as much as giving a hundred, a thousand, or ten thousand dollars would have, because you were sincere."In the Buddhadharma, as long as you are sincere, you obtain merit and virtue regardless of how much money you give as an offering. If you do not have a sincere heart, even if you give a lot, it's still a little. If you have a sincere heart, if you give a little, it's still a lot. You need only make offerings with a true heart.

ALTHOUGH HE READ AND RECITED MANY SUTRAS...At that time the Bodhisattva Seeker of Fame, Maitreya, one of the eight hundred disciples, read and recited Sutras. Like now, in the morning, the three who have left home along with several laypeople, recite the Shurangama Mantra, *The Vajra Sutra*, and *The Heart Sutra*. It would be good to recite the Great Compassion Mantra twenty-one times to seek a response and, whatever you seek, you may obtain. If you recite the Great Compassion Mantra, the lecture hall will be filled with a rare fragrance as that state arises when one recites it. If you recite Sutras sincerely a rare fragrance may also manifest. How does that happen? When you recite the Sutras, heavenly maidens will scatter flowers, and the fragrance will be manifest. But you must recite with a sincere heart, in the same way that you must make offerings to the Triple Jewel with a sincere heart. If you have a sincere heart, when you recite a single sentence of the Sutra, you can startle heaven and move the earth. The ghosts and spirits in heaven and earth will all know about it. If you don't have a sincere heart, you can recite the entire Sutra and all you do is strike up false thinking. What false thinking do you strike up? You think, "I'm reciting the Sutra today. I wonder if anyone will send me offerings? I'm reciting the Sutra so I can get offerings." If you have that kind of false thinking, then no one will make offerings to you. Why not? Because your heart is filled with the wish for offerings and so they will not appear. If you have thought, it is false thought. The thought arising is just false thought. Without thought, you may obtain a response. If you do not seek offerings, and they come, that is a response. Although he read and recited MANY SCRIPTURES, not one Sutra, but alot of them, HE DID NOT COMPREHEND THEM. He couldn't remember them. If you can't remember them, then you remember the first part and forget the last part, or remember the last part and forget the first part. If you remember the first and the last, you forget the middle part, and you can't recite it. You have to listen to the others and follow along with them. If you do that, the merit and virtue is theirs, not your own. Do you understand. You must be able to recite them on your own. You must comprehend them, recite them yourself, understand them, and be well-versed in them. Well-versed, you can recite them from the first part to the very end remembering them all.

Now, he read and recited them, but couldn't remember them. AND FORGOT MOST OF WHAT HE LEARNED. He didn't really recite. He recited the first part and forgot the last; forgetting a whole lot of it. FOR THIS REASON HE WAS CALLED SEEKER OF FAME. I believe that he probably did not give himself this name. Someone else probably gave it to him, saying, "All you do is seek fame and seek profit. We'll just call you Seeker of Fame Bodhisattva!"

BECAUSE HE HAD ALSO PLANTED GOOD ROOTS...Although he was called Seeker of Fame, he had also planted many good roots and cultivated many practices, cultivating blessings and cultivating wisdom. HE WAS ABLE TO ENCOUNTER LIMITLESS HUNDREDS OF THOUSANDS OF TENS OF THOUSANDS OF MILLIONS OF BUDDHAS, MAKING OFFERINGS TO THEM AND HONORING THEM, VENERATING AND PRAISING THEM. He made offerings to limitless Buddhas, honored them, venerated and praised them.

Sutra:

MAITREYA, IT SHOULD BE KNOWN, COULD THE BODHISATTVA WONDROUS LIGHT HAVE BEEN ANYONE ELSE? I, MYSELF,

WAS HE. AND THE BODHISATTVA SEEKER OF FAME WAS YOU, YOURSELF!

Outline:

J3. correspondence of the past and present

Commentary:

MAITREYA, IT SHOULD BE KNOWN, COULD THE BODHISATTVA WONDROUS LIGHT HAVE BEEN ANYONE ELSE? Do you know who he was? He wasn't anybody else but--who? I, MYSELF, WAS HE. He was just me--Manjushri Bodhisattva! Do you remember? AND THE BODHISATTVA SEEKER OF FAME, just who was he? YOU, YOURSELF! You, Maitreya Bodhisattva, you were the one who sought fame and profit. But now, you've improved yourself a lot, and made a lot of progress compared to the way you used to be.

Sutra:

THE PORTENTS NOW SEEN DO NOT DIFFER FROM THOSE, AND SO, IN MY ESTIMATION, TODAY THE THUS COME ONE IS ABOUT TO SPEAK A GREAT VEHICLE SUTRA CALLED THE WONDERFUL DHARMA LOTUS FLOWER, A DHARMA FOR INSTRUCTING BODHISATTVAS OF WHICH THE BUDDHA IS PROTECTIVE AND MINDFUL.

Outline:

F4. the conclusion

Commentary:

THE PORTENTS NOW SEEN...When Maitreya Bodhisattva heard Manjushri Bodhisattva give away his previous identity as the Bodhisattva who sought fame, he had already gotten rid of his mark of self; consequently, he wasn't embarrassed and he didn't feel, "All you do is talk about my bad points. You're really rude." He didn't think that way at all.

Manjushri Bodhisattva said to him, "I now see Shakyamuni Buddha emitting the white hair-mark light, along with the other portents, six in all, and they are just the same as those previously manifested by the

Buddha Brightness of Sun-Moon-Lamp. THEY DO NOT DIFFER FROM THOSE. "Those" refers to the portents manifested by the Buddha Sun-Moon-Lamp Brightness; "now" refers to those now manifest by Shakyamuni Buddha. The portents are the same. AND SO IN MY ESTIMATION, because of this, I now calculate, think about it...Actually, Manjushri Bodhisattva didn't need to think about it. He knew it all along. But he accords with worldly methods and says, "I have thought it over and it is my considered opinion that TODAY, THE THUS COME ONE IS ABOUT TO SPEAK A GREAT VEHICLE SUTRA CALLED THE WONDERFUL DHARMA LOTUS FLOWER, that was its title, A DHARMA FOR INSTRUCTING BODHISATTVAS OF WHICH THE BUDDHA IS PROTECTIVE AND MINDFUL.

Sutra:

AT THAT TIME MANJUSHRI, IN THE MIDST OF THE ASSEMBLY, WISHING TO RESTATE HIS MEANING, SPOKE VERSES, SAYING:

I RECALL THAT IN AGES PAST,
LIMITLESS, COUNTLESS AEONS AGO,
THERE APPEARED A BUDDHA, ONE HONORED
AMONG PEOPLE,
BY THE NAME OF BRIGHTNESS OF SUN-MOON-LAMP.
THAT WORLD HONORED ONE PROCLAIMED THE DHARMA,
TAKING LIMITLESS LIVING BEINGS ACROSS,
CAUSING COUNTLESS MILLIONS OF BODHISATTVAS
TO ENTER THE WISDOM OF THE BUDDHAS.

Outline:

E2. verse section
F1. extensive reference to what was seen in the past
G1. similarity with the first Buddha

Commentary:

AT THAT TIME, MANJUSHRI, IN THE MIDST OF THE ASSEMBLY, WISHING TO RESTATE THIS MEANING, thinking to repeat the principles once again SPOKE VERSES, SAYING,

I RECALL THAT IN AGES PAST/ Manjushri Bodhisattva says, "I,myself,remember that in the past, a long time ago LIMITLESS, COUNTLESS AEONS AGO/ THERE APPEARED A BUDDHA, ONE HONORED AMONG PEOPLE/ A Buddha who was venerated by both gods and humans BY THE NAME OF BRIGHTNESS OF SUN-MOON-LAMP/ THAT WORLD HONORED ONE PROCLAIMED THE DHARMA/ the wonderful Dharma of the Great Vehicle TAKING LIMITLESS LIVING BEINGS ACROSS/ He saved and liberated an unlimited number of them; it is not known how many beings he saved. AND CAUSING COUNTLESS MILLIONS OF BODHISATTVAS/ TO ENTER THE WISDOM OF THE BUDDHAS.

Sutra:

BEFORE THAT BUDDHA HAD LEFT HOME,

THE EIGHT ROYAL SONS BORN TO HIM,

SEEING THE GREAT SAGE LEAVE HIM HOME,

ALSO FOLLOWED HIM TO PRACTICE BRAHMAN CONDUCT.

Outline:

G2. similarity with the last Buddha
H1. similarity of what was seen in the past with what has already occurred in the present

Commentary:

BEFORE THAT BUDDHA HAD LEFT HOME/ Before the Buddha Brightness of Sun-Moon-Lamp had left the home-life, THE EIGHT ROYAL SONS BORN TO HIM/ SEEING THE GREAT SAGE LEAVE HIS HOME/ They knew that their father, the Great Sage, had left home ALSO FOLLOWED HIM TO CULTIVATE BRAHMAN CONDUCT/ They also renounced their kingdoms, cities, wives, and children; they gave them away, and followed their father to leave home and cultivate the clear, pure Brahman conduct.

Sutra:

THE BUDDHA THEN SPOKE A GREAT VEHICLE

SUTRA BY THE NAME OF LIMITLESS PRINCIPLES;
AMIDST THE ASSEMBLY, AND FOR THEIR SAKE,
HE SET IT FORTH IN EXTENSIVE DETAIL.
WHEN THE BUDDHA HAD FINISHED SPEAKING THE SUTRA,
SEATED IN THE DHARMA-SEAT,
HE SAT IN FULL LOTUS AND ENTERED THE SAMADHI
CALLED THE STATION OF LIMITLESS PRINCIPLES.
FROM THE HEAVENS FELL A RAIN OF MANDARAVA FLOWERS,
AND HEAVENLY DRUMS OF THEMSELVES DID SOUND,
WHILE ALL THE GODS, DRAGONS, GHOSTS, AND SPIRITS,
MADE OFFERINGS TO THE HONORED ONE;
AND, WITHIN ALL THE BUDDHA LANDS,
THERE OCCURRED A MIGHTY TREMBLING.
THE LIGHT EMITTED FROM BETWEEN THE BUDDHA'S BROWS
MANIFESTED ALL THESE RARE EVENTS.

Outline:

H2. similarity of what was seen in the past with what is occurring in the present, now.
- I1. similarity of the portents
  - J1. similarity of the six portents in this world

Commentary:

THE BUDDHA THEN SPOKE A GREAT VEHICLE/ The Buddha Brightness of Sun-Moon-Lamp spoke a Great Vehicle Sutra A SUTRA BY THE NAME OF LIMITLESS PRINCIPLES/ AMIDST THE ASSEMBLY, AND FOR THEIR SAKE/ in the Great Assembly HE SET IT FORTH IN EXTENSIVE DETAIL/ For the sake of the assembly, he spoke it in fine detail, explaining the wonderful principles of the Sutra.

WHEN THE BUDDHA HAD FINISHED SPEAKING THIS SUTRA/ *The Sutra of Limitless Principles*, WHILE SEATED ON THE DHARMA

SEAT/ He was then sitting on the Dharma seat where one sits while lecturing on the Sutras. HE SAT IN FULL LOTUS AND ENTERED SAMADHI/ He crossed his legs, sat in the lotus position and entered the concentration CALLED THE STATION OF LIMITLESS PRINCIPLES/ That was the name of the samadhi. FROM THE HEAVENS FELL A RAIN OF MANDARAVA FLOWERS/ At that time the gods sent down a rain of little white flowers and big white flowers, as well as little red flowers and big red flowers. AND HEAVENLY DRUMS OF THEMSELVES DID SOUND/ In the heavens, the celestial drums sounded without being struck. THE GODS, DRAGONS, GHOSTS, AND SPIRITS/ The gods and all the dragons and all the ghosts and spirits MADE OFFERINGS TO THE HONORED ONE/ They all made offerings to the Buddha, to the Dharma, and to the Sangha.

AND WITHIN ALL OF THE BUDDHA LANDS/ At that time, in all of the lands of the Buddha THERE OCCURRED A MIGHTY TREMBLING/ THE LIGHT EMITTED FROM BETWEEN THE BUDDHA'S BROWS/ The Buddha emitted white hair-mark light from between his eyebrows which MANIFESTED ALL THESE RARE EVENTS/ A great many rare and unprecedented things appeared.

Sutra:

THE LIGHT ILLUMINED TO THE EAST
EIGHTEEN THOUSAND BUDDHA LANDS,
REVEALING THE PLACES OF LIVING BEINGS'
KARMIC RETRIBUTIONS OF BIRTH AND DEATH.
SEEN, TOO, WERE BUDDHA LANDS ADORNED
WITH A MULTITUDE OF GEMS,
THE COLOR OF LAPIZ LAZULI AND CRYSTAL,
ILLUMINED BY THE BUDDHA'S LIGHT.
SEEN AS WELL WERE GODS AND PEOPLE,
DRAGONS, SPIRITS, AND YAKSHA HORDES,
GANDHARVAS AND KINNARAS,
EACH MAKING OFFERINGS TO THE BUDDHA.

Thus Come Ones, too, all were seen
As they naturally accomplished the BuddhaWay,
Their bodies' hue like mountains of gold,
Upright, serene, subtle, and fine,
As, within pure lapis lazuli
Would appear an image of real gold.
The World Honored Ones in those assemblies
Proclaimed the profound principle of the Law.
In all the Buddhas' lands,
Were Shravaka hosts, uncountable;
Through the illumination of the Buddha's light
Those assemblies all were fully seen.
There were also Bhikshus who,
Dwelt within the mountain groves,
Vigorously upholding the pure precepts
As if guarding brilliant pearls.
Also seen were Bodhisattvas
Practicing giving, patience, and so forth,
Their number like the Ganges' sands,
Illumined by the Buddha's light.
Seen too were Bodhisattvas who
Had deeply entered Dhyana samadhi,
With bodies and minds still and unmoving
They sought the Way unsurpassed.
Bodhisattvas, too, were seen who knew

THE MARK OF DHARMAS' STILL EXTINCTION;
EACH ONE WITHIN HIS BUDDHALAND
SPOKE DHARMA, SEEKING THE BUDDHA'S PATH.

Outline:

J2. similarity of the six portents in other worlds

Commentary:

THE LIGHT ILLUMINED TO THE EAST/ The light shone into the eastern direction. How far did it shine? EIGHTEEN THOUSAND BUDDHA WORLDS/ The eighteen thousand Buddha lands represent the eighteen realms of sense. REVEALING THE PLACE OF LIVING BEINGS/ The Buddha pointed out the places of all living beings KARMIC RETRIBUTIONS OF BIRTH AND DEATH/ where they were born and died, died and were reborn, the karmic retributions of their births and deaths.

Why is there karmic retribution?

It is because we people give rise to delusion. Giving rise to delusion is the production of ignorance. Once there is ignorance, then there is karmic activity, and karma is created. After karma has been created, one necessarily undergoes retribution. In the light of the Buddha these various circumstances appeared.

SEEN, TOO, WERE BUDDHALANDS ADORNED/ Some people saw other Buddha lands decorated WITH A MULTITUDE OF GEMS/ Various kind of treasures were used to ornament the Buddhalands THE COLOR OF LAPIS LAZULI AND CRYSTAL/ Some of the lands were adorned with lapis lazuli and others with crystal ILLUMINATED BY THE BUDDHA'S LIGHT/ It was through the illumination of the Buddha-light that these things were revealed.

SEEN AS WELL WERE GODS AND PEOPLE/ Not only were all the lands with their splendid and beautiful adornments seen, but also seen were all the gods in the heavens DRAGONS, SPIRITS, AND YAKSHA HORDES/ The dragons were there, and the spirits, and the ghosts, and so forth. GANDHARVAS AND KINNARAS/ The two classes of musical spirits, EACH MAKING OFFERINGS TO THE BUDDHA/ The gods, dragons, and the rest of the eight-fold division all brought forth their hearts to present offerings and make offerings to the Buddha.

THUS COME ONES, TOO, ALL WERE SEEN/ Also seen were all the Buddhas in other lands AS THEY NATURALLY ACCOMPLISHED THE BUDDHA WAY/ They brought forth the Bodhi-heart, good in the beginning, good in the middle and good at the end, right up until they became Buddhas, naturally realizing the Buddha path. THEIR BODIES' HUE LIKE MOUNTAINS OF GOLD/ Their bodies were the color of golden mountains, the color of burnished, purple-gold. UPRIGHT, SERENE, SUBTLE, AND FINE. The Buddha has thirty-two marks and eighty minor characteristics and is very majestic and fine. AS WITHIN PURE LAPIS LAZULI WOULD/ It is just like within a pure cylinder of lapis lazuli would APPEAR AN IMAGE OF REAL GOLD.

THE WORLD HONORED ONES IN THOSE ASSEMBLIES/ All the limitless Buddhas in the assemblies in the other Buddha-lands PROCLAIMED THE PROFOUND PRINCIPLE OF THE LAW/ They set forth and make known the extremely deep purport of the Dharma IN ALL THE BUDDHAS' LANDS/ In all the Buddha lands in other worlds WERE SHRAVAKA HOSTS, UNCOUNTABLE/ Because the Buddha Brightness of Sun-Moon-Lamp emitted the white hair-mark light illumining them, THOSE ASSEMBLIES ALL WERE FULLY SEEN.

THERE WERE ALSO BHIKSHUS WHO/ There were those who had left home, Bhikshus or Bhikshunis DWELT WITHIN THE MOUNTAINS GROVES/ They lived in the mountains, deep in the woods, in secluded valleys--places where no one ever goes--VIGOROUSLY UPHOLDING THE PURE PRECEPTS/ They were vigorous day and night. Day and night, they never rested. In what way were they vigorous? They forgot about eating; they forgot about sleeping; they forgot about wearing clothes.

Then what did they think of? They only thought to cultivate the Way with vigor. They were perpetually vigorous in the six periods of the day and night--always vigorous.

What are the six periods of the day and night? During the day there are three: the beginning of the day, the middle of the day, and the end of the day. During the night there are also three: the beginning of the night, the middle of the night, and the end of the night.

In the six periods of the day and night, they cultivated. They vigorously upheld the pure precepts, the clear, pure precious precepts. AS IF GUARDING BRILLIANT PEARLS/ They kept the clear, pure brilliant vajra precepts just like the dragon stands guard over his dragon pearl.

Those who have left home who uphold the precepts 1% have 1% of light; those who hold them 10% have 10% of light. If you hold them a full 100%, you will have 100% of light. The light is produced through the precepts, through samadhi, and through wisdom. If you don't hold the precepts, you will have no light. If you would like to have light, you must hold the precepts. Cultivating is not simply done to obtain light, but even up to the realization of Buddhahood, unless you keep the precepts, you won't be able to realize Buddhahood. Therefore, if you would like to become a Buddha, you must keep the precepts. The precepts are the most important thing.

There are Ten Shramanera Precepts and Two Hundred and Fifty Bhikshu Precepts. The study of the precepts is the most important. Those who have left home absolutely must follow the precepts. If they do not they are no different from lay people. Therefore, if you wish to realize the Buddha Way, you must start out by holding the precepts. That is why, in *The Dharma Flower Sutra* a great emphasis is placed upon the precepts. The precepts prohibit one from talking casually or in a confused manner, speaking in terms of right and wrong. You cannot, through your speech, cause living beings to become afflicted. It is said,

> Guard your mouth, collect your thoughts
> And with your body, don't transgress.
> Don't cause trouble for any living thing.
> Stay far away from useless bitter practices.
> A cultivator like this can save the world.

You should guard your mouth:

"How do I do that," you ask.

Just don't confusedly prattle. Keep your mouth shut like a bottle. Don't talk all day, talking about the useful and talking about the useless.If you do that, You are not guarding your mouth.

Collect your thoughts: If you collect your thoughts, then not only will you never say harmful things, but you will not even have evil thoughts within your mind. Your mind won't think about other people's rights and wrongs, and your mouth won't agitate about them. Your mind will not think about "right and wrong."

With your body, don't transgress: You cannot break the precepts with your body.

Don't cause trouble for any living thing: You should not hinder any living being in the world. To say nothing of people, you shouldn't even cause trouble for an animal or an insect.

Stay far away from useless bitter practices: Don't adopt bitter practices which are unbeneficial to you, to society, or to the world in general.

A cultivator like this can save the world: One who cultivates like this can teach and transform living beings.

Therefore, they keep and hold the precepts just as

they would guard a precious jewel. Perhaps you have a precious pearl, or perhaps a night-light pearl, or a wind-proofing pearl, or a water-proofing pearl, or a fire-proofing pearl.If you have a wind-proofing pearl you will not be bothered by windstorms. With the water-proofing pearl, the floods won't come, and with the fire-proofing pearl then everyone in your neighborhood will be able to borrow its light and their houses will not catch on fire.If you had such a precious gem, wouldn't you take special care of it? You would always protect that jewel.Holding the precepts is just like guarding such a precious gem, and so the text says, "As if guarding brilliant pearls."

ALSO SEEN WERE BODHISATTVAS/ Within the white hair-mark light emitted by the Buddha Brightness of Sun-Moon-Lamp, all the Bodhisattvas were seen, a great many of them, PRACTICING GIVING, PATIENCE, AND SO FORTH/ They cultivated the Six Perfections. The previous verse spoke of the Bhikshus practicing the Perfection of Morality. Now, the Perfections of Giving and Patience are mentioned. "And so forth," refers to the remaining Perfections, that is, Dhyana samadhi, Vigor, and Prajna--all six are included.

Giving is of three kinds: the giving of wealth, the giving of Dhamra, and the giving of fearlessness. If you have money, you may give money. If you understand the Buddhadharma, you can give Buddhahdarma. If you help others, causing them to get rid of the fear in their hearts, that is called the giving of fearlessness Patience is also of three kinds: Patience with production, patience with dharmas, and patience with the non-production of dharmas. And so forth...all the perfections were practiced. THEIR NUMBER LIKE THE GANGE'S SANDS/ How many Bodhisattvas were there practicing the Six Perfections and the Ten Thousand Conducts? There were as many as the grains of sand in the Ganges River. They gave away their kingdoms, cities, wives, and children.

Now, when I was lecturing this Sutra three weeks ago, I said that someone had given his wife away and there was a wife who asked me, "If someone was able to give his wife away, would it be possible to give one's husband away?" I told the questioner, "You should go at this gradually. Don't be so nervous." This problem is very difficult to solve, however, and so I told her, "If you want to give away your husband, you'll first have to find someone who wants to take him. If someone wants him, you can give him away; but if no one wants him, who are you going to give him to?" To date, she hasn't found anyone to take him. In the future, if she finds someone, she can give him away. For now, she'll just have to wait.

No doubt from ancient times until the present day, this is the first person who has ever wanted to give away her husband. And just who is this person? I don't know either! But I thought I'd tell you about it anyway.

So there were as many Bodhisattvas as the grains of sand in the Ganges River, and they were ILLUMINED BY THE BUDDHA'S LIGHT/ Because the light of the Buddha shone on them, all these states were visible.

SEEN, TOO, WERE BODHISATTVAS WHO/ Not just all the ones mentioned above, but again there were seen Bodhisattvas who HAD DEEPLY ENTERED DHYANA SAMADHI/ What is meant by "deeply entering?" It means that, with their full attention devoted to their work, they meditate throughout the six period of the day and night. If you don't meditate throughout the six periods of the day and night, then you haven't deeply entered. Those who cultivate the Way must do it with a true heart. Without a true heart, how can you expect to attain the Way? You must offer up your true heart and then not only can you attain the Way, but you can become a Buddha. So bring forth your heart and make it solid, sincere, and constant.

Your heart must be solid. You can't say, "Today, I have a solid heart, but tomorrow I'm likely to change." When tomorrow comes and you have changed, you are not longer solid. A sincere heart means that you actually and responsibly do the work. Constant means that you must persevere. It's not just a matter of day and night, but at all times, constantly, you must be the same.

Last summer, during the study and meditation session, many were very sincere in their study of the Buddhadharma. They were sincere to the point that they even studied when it was time to sleep. The summer session was a very short period of time. You brought forth the heart to cultivate the Way for that time, but you must cultivate and study the Buddhadharma like that forever. That counts as being true. Deeply entering Dhyana samadhi means to work hard at one's cultivation, constantly. WITH BODIES AND MINDS STILL AND UNMOVING/ Still and unmoving means that they had entered samadhi. They didn't fret, thinking, "My legs hurt!" and then rearrange them, or "My back aches," and then lean backwards against the wall. They didn't do anything like that because their bodies and minds were still and unmoving. THEY SOUGHT THE WAY UNSURPASSED/

They used determination and skill like this to seek the supreme path.

BODHISATTVAS, TOO, WERE SEEN WHO KNEW/ THE MARK OF DHARMAS' STILL EXTINCTION/ Also seen were very many Bodhisattvas who understood the mark of the still extinction of dharmas; the mark of still extinction is just the mark of Nirvana. Nirvana is just still extinction and still extinction is just Nirvana. They knew the wonderful aspect of Nirvana. EACH ONE WITHIN HIS BUDDHALAND/ Each one of the Bodhisattvas within his own land, SPOKE DHARMA, SEEKING THE BUDDHAS' PATH/ They taught and proclaimed the Buddhadharma. By speaking the Dharma, one increases one's blessings and wisdom, and they dedicated the merit and virtue thus accrued to the Buddha Way.

Sutra:

THEN THE FOUR-FOLD MULTITUDES

SEEING THE BUDDHA SUN-MOON-LAMP

MANIFEST GREAT AND POWERFUL SPIRITUAL PENETRATIONS,

IN THEIR HEARTS ALL REJOICED,

AND INQUIRED, EACH OF THE OTHER,

"WHAT IS THE REASON FOR THESE EVENTS?"

Outline:

I2. similarity of the doubtful thoughts

Commentary:

THEN THE FOUR-FOLD MULTITUDES/ At that time the Bhikshus, Bhikshunis, Upasakas, and Upasikas, SEEING THE BUDDHA SUN-MOON-LAMP/ When they saw the Buddha Brightness of Sun-Moon-Lamp MANIFEST GREAT AND POWERFUL SPIRITUAL PENETRATIONS/ Reveal the strength of his majestic spiritual penetrations and wonderful functions, IN THEIR HEARTS ALL REJOICED/ All their hearts were happy; this represents the portent of happiness. AND INQUIRED, EACH OF THE OTHER/ Each of of them had his own doubts, and so they asked each other, "WHAT IS THE REASON FOR THESE EVENTS? Just what is this all about? What's happening?"

Sutra:

THE HONORED ONE, REVERED BY GODS AND HUMANS,
JUST THEN FROM SAMADHI DID ARISE,
AND PRAISED THE BODHISATTVA WONDROUS LIGHT:
"YOU ACT AS EYES FOR THE WORLD,
ALL RETURN TO YOU IN FAITH; YOU ARE
ABLE REVERENTLY TO HOLD THE DHARMA-STORE.
DHARMA SUCH AS I DO SPEAK--
YOU ALONE CAN CERTIFY TO ITS UNDERSTANDING."
THE WORLD HONORED ONE HAVING PRAISED HIM,
AND CAUSED WONDROUS LIGHT TO REJOICE,
THEN SPOKE THE SUTRA OF THE DHARMA FLOWER.

Outline:

H3. similarity of what was seen in the past with what is about to happen in the present
I1. similarity of the persons for whom the Dharma was spoken

Commentary:

THE HONORED ONE REVERED BY GODS AND HUMANS/ That is, the Buddha, JUST THEN FROM SAMADHI DID ARISE/ He was very tranquil, very comfortable, and then he emerged from samadhi.What samadhi did he emerge from? The samadhi of the station of limitless principles. "Arise" means that he came out of samadhi. AND PRAISED THE BODHISATTVA WONDROUS LIGHT/ The Buddha Brightness of Sun-Moon-Lamp praised him saying, "YOU ACT AS EYES FOR ALL THE WORLD"/ You are the eyes of the people in the world. You are the world's bright-eyed learned advisor. You are the eyes for everyone and everyone relies upon you, Wondrous Light, to be their eyes. Why? ALL RETURN TO YOU IN FAITH; YOU ARE/ Everyone in the world finds refuge in you, pays respect to you, and has faith in you. They look up to you. And why? ABLE REVERENTLY TO HOLD THE DHARMA STORE/ It is because you can uphold the treasury of the Buddha's Dharma and cultivate according to the Dharma, propagate the Dharma, and teach and transform living beings according to the doctrines the Buddha taught in the Sutras.

DHARMA SUCH AS I DO SPEAK/ *The Wonderful Dharma Lotus Flower Sutra* which I speak, YOU ALONE CAN CERTIFY TO ITS UNDERSTANDING/ Only you, Bodhisattva Wondrous Light, can understand and certify to this kind of wisdom and know of the wonderful points found within the Sutra. THE WORLD HONORED ONE HAVING PRAISED HIM/ The World Honored One Brightness of Sun-Moon-Lamp, having thus praised the Bodhisattva Wondrous Light AND CAUSED WONDROUS LIGHT TO REJOICE/ He caused the Bodhisattva Wondrous Light to become very happy. So you see, Bodhisattvas also like to be praised. So, no matter who it is, take care not to speak ill of them. You should say things like, "You are truly fine. Your heart is good, and you are nice looking, too." No matter how ugly they are, don't just blurt out things like, "You're really ugly!" If you do that, they'll detest you. Even though they are ugly, if you bring it up, they aren't going to like it. If you don't mention it, there won't be anything they can do. After all, they were born looking like that and there's no place they can go to complain about it. But If you say, "You're grotesque!" they will most certainly get angry at you. "Oh yeah? Well, I've got something to say about that," they'll sputter. "I've got a belly full of temper and nowhere to put it. Since you say I'm ugly you can just take *that,* Buddy!!" And so the Buddha Brightness of Sun-Moon-Lamp praised the Bodhisattva Wondrous Light and THEN SPOKE THE SUTRA OF THE DHARMA FLOWER.

Sutra:

FOR A FULL SIXTY MINOR AEONS

HE DID NOT RISE FROM HIS SEAT.

THE SUPREME AND WONDROUS DHARMA THAT HE SPOKE,

THE DHARMA MASTER WONDROUS LIGHT

WAS FULLY ABLE TO RECEIVE AND HOLD.

Outline:

I2. similarity of the time

Commentary:

FOR A FULL SIXTY MINOR AEONS/ The Buddha Brightness of Sun-Moon-Lamp spoke *The Dharma Flower Sutra* for a full sixty small aeons, during which time HE DID NOT RISE FROM HIS SEAT/ He didn't get up from the Dharma seat for sixty small aeons while he spoke the Sutra. THE SUPREME AND WONDROUS DHARMA THAT HE SPOKE/ The most supreme, unsurpassed, deep, subtle and fine Dharma THE DHARMA MASTER WONDROUS LIGHT/ WAS FULLY ABLE TO RECEIVE AND HOLD/ He understood all of the doctrines in the Sutra. He relied upon that Dharma to cultivate, accepted it, maintain it, and accordingly taught it to others.

Sutra

THE BUDDHA, HAVING SPOKEN THE DHARMA FLOWER,
AND CAUSED THE ASSEMBLY TO REJOICE,
LATER, ON THAT VERY DAY,
ANNOUNCED TO THE HOST OF GODS AND HUMANS:
"THE MEANING OF THE REAL MARK OF ALL DHARMAS
HAS ALREADY BEEN SPOKEN FOR ALL OF YOU,
AND NOW AT MIDNIGHT, I
SHALL ENTER INTO NIRVANA.
YOU SHOULD SINGLE-HEARTEDLY ADVANCE WITH VIGOR,
AND AVOID LAXNESS, FOR
BUDDHAS ARE DIFFICULT INDEED TO MEET,
ENCOUNTERED BUT ONCE IN A MILLION AEONS."

Outline:

I3. similarity of announcement of Nirvana

Commentary:

The Bodhisattva Manjushri said, "THE BUDDHA, HAVING SPOKEN THE DHARMA FLOWER/ After the Buddha Brightness of Sun-Moon-Lamp had spoken the Sutra AND CAUSED THE ASSEMBLY

TO REJOICE/ and caused those assembled to be filled with the bliss of Dharma and gain unbounded happiness, LATER, ONE THAT VERY DAY/ "Later" means not long after that, very shortly after that, on that very same day. Which day? The day when he finished speaking *The Dharma Flower Sutra*. ANNOUNCED TO THE HOST OF GODS AND HUMANS/ He told those in the heavens and those among the humans as well as those of the entire eightfold division, "THE MEANING OF THE REAL MARK OF ALL DHARMAS"/ "All dharmas" means every dharma, all the eighty-four thousand Dharma-doors which the Buddha taught. All dharmas, as I often say, can be interpreted to mean "one single dharma," in this case "all dharma's," because if there are too many, one can't remember them clearly. It would be better for me to explain it as "one kind of dharma." Then if you remember one kind of dharma:

One is just the limitless.

If you understand the one kind of dharma, then you can hear one and understand ten, and you will be able to understand the other eighty-four thousand Dharma-doors as well:

Understanding one, all are understood--
Clear about one, clear about all.

If you can't understand that one dharma, how are you going to be able to understand a lot of them?

Someone once asked me, "Of the eighty-four thousand Dharma-doors taught by the Buddha, which is the most lofty? Which Dharma-door is number one? Which is most important?"

You could say this question is problematical; you could also say that it isn't. If you don't understand, it's problematical. If you understand the Dharma, then it's no problem! When he asked, I answered him in terms of his question and said, "Of the eighty-four thousand Dharma-doors, eighty-four thousand are the most lofty, eighty-four thousand are number one, and eighty-four thousand are the most important." Why did I say that?

Of the eighty-four thousand Dharma-doors, there is not one which is not for the purpose of curing the eighty-four thousand sicknesses of living beings. You need only apply that one Dharma-door which will effectively cure your sickness, and that Dharma-door becomes number one, the most lofty, and the most important. Why? Because it is useful to you. If it was of no use to you, suited for an illness other than the one you had, it would then become unimportant. It would not be number one, it would not be the most lofty Dharma-door. Now, speaking in terms of the real mark of all dharmas:

What is it? The real mark of all dharmas is the real mark of the number one dharma, the real mark of that most lofty, important dharma.

And what is the real mark?

The real mark is no mark. There is no mark. If you have a mark, then it is not the real mark. The real mark is not marked, and yet there is nothing unmarked. All marks are born from the real mark. Although they are born from the real mark, the real mark itself, in its basic substance, is without a mark. Because, in its basic substance, it is unmarked, it is therefore able to give birth to all marks. If it had a mark, then it could not be considered the real mark, for it would be empty and false. *The Vajra Sutra* says, "All with marks is empty and false. If you can see all marks as no marks, then you see the Thus Come One." That is why we say that the real mark is unmarked, and yet there is nothing which is not marked by it. This means that all dharmas are just that dharma. So the word "all" can be considered as an auxilliary particle, not as meaning "many." This way only one dharma is referred to. Which one? The meaning of the real mark, the doctrine of the real mark. *The Dharma Flower Sutra* speaks the Dharma-door of the doctrine of the real mark:

"THE MEANING OF THE REAL MARK OF ALL DHARMAS/ HAS ALREADY BEEN SPOKEN FOR ALL OF YOU/ The Buddha Brightness of Sun-Moon-Lamp said, "Now, I have already spoken to you the doctrine of the real mark of all dharmas. I'm done speaking. AND NOW, AT MIDNIGHT, I/ "I" says the Buddha Brightness of Sun-Moon-Lamp, referring to himself, "now, in the middle of the night, SHALL ENTER INTO NIRVANA/ I have done what I had to do, and so I should assume the position of permanence, happiness, true self, and purity. I should enter Nirvana."

Why did the Buddha enter Nirvana? There were many reasons. The most important reason was to prevent people from becoming dependent upon him. The Buddha could have postponed his entry into Nirvana indefinitely except for the fact that his disciples followed him, studying the Dharma under him everyday, and some of them might have become jaded. How? They might have gotten lazy, remiss, and thought, "It doesn't matter whether I cultivate or not because I can be with the Buddha everyday."

For example, I am now lecturing the Sutras to you everyday, and you can see your Master here everyday. You think, "When the Master lectures Sutras, I take notes, but I don't have to study them now. I'll wait until I have more time and then read them again." You take notes, but you don't study them. You put them high on the shelf for safe-keeping. However, after a time, you forget all about them, until the time comes when... you've completely forgotten!

However, in the human sphere there is "grief and joy, separation and reunion." If I, for special reasons, should have to leave all of you, at that time you may want to listen to the Sutras, but you won't be able to. You will wish to study the Buddhadharma and you will then realize how difficult it is, and you'll get out your old notes and review them, going over all the doctrines in the Sutras which the Dharma Master had taught you in the past. If I had never left, you would never have looked at your notes. Shakyamuni Buddha spoke the Dharma for forty-nine years and some of his disciples may have grown lax. This was not the case for Shakyamuni Buddha alone; every single Buddha, when he sees that some of his disciples have become dependent upon him will leave them and enter Nirvana. In this way, they don't become dependent upon him. It is a method for teaching living beings. Therefore, he charged them saying, "YOU SHOULD SINGLE-HEARTEDLY ADVANCE WITH VIGOR/ Just because he was afraid they would get lazy, he exhorted them, saying, "You who cultivate the Way, Bhikshus, Bhikshunis, Upasakas, and Upasikas, should concentrate singlemindedly and be vigorous. Don't be lax and don't be lazy. Cultivate the Way with a single thought. Don't strike up false thinking. Don't have a divided mind. That's what is meant by single-heartedly advancing with vigor.Be vigorous by day and vigorous by night; day and night, always, always be vigorous. Cultivate and work hard. Hard work is cultivation and cultivaiton is hard work. Be vigorous and single-hearted. AND AVOID LAXNESS, FOR/ You must not be lazy! Little Shramaneras, Big Shramaneras, Bhikshus of the Sangha, Bhikshunis of the Sangha: Do not be lax! Do not be lazy! Do not leave home and fail to cultivate. To leave home and not to cultivate is to neglect the Dharma; it is then just as if you had never left home. The ancients said,

> All day long, you can count up others wealth,
> When you haven't got half a cent yourself;
> If the Dharma you fail to cultivate,
> You're making the exact same mistake.

Bank-tellers, for example, handle other people's money all day, counting it up, "One thousand, two thousand, ten, twenty thousand, thirty thousand, fifty thousand, one hundred thousand, two hundred thousand, one million, ten million, one hundred million--too much money!" But none of it belongs to them. They just count it up for other people.

If you do not cultivate the Buddhadharma, it's just like counting other people's money.

Those who have left home must cultivate the Way. If you do not cultivate and insist upon being lazy, then do not leave home. Now, we are vigorous in the day and night. In the morning people recite Sutras and at night they recite Sutras, such as *The Vajra Sutra*. This is a very good idea because you should cultivate and you should not be lazy! You should think over the doctrine presented here in the Sutra: You should single-heartedly advance with vigor/ and avoid laxness, for/ Laxness just means being lazy and not cultivating.

BUDDHAS ARE DIFFICULT INDEED TO MEET/ The Buddhas, all of them, are extremely difficult to encounter. ENCOUNTERED BUT ONCE IN A MILLION AEONS/ It says a million aeons, but it may be several thousand, ten thousand millions of aeons before you meet with a Buddha appearing in the world.

Sutra:

ALL OF THE DISCIPLES OF THE WORLD HONORED ONE
HEARING OF THE BUDDHA'S ENTRY INTO NIRVANA,
EACH HARBORED GRIEF AND ANGUISH,
"WHY MUST THE BUDDHA TAKE EXTINCTION SO SOON?"
THE SAGELY LORD, THE DHARMA KING,
THEN COMFORTED THE LIMITLESS MULTITUDE:
"AFTER MY PASSAGE INTO EXTINCTION,
NONE OF YOU SHOULD WORRY OR FEAR,
FOR THE BODHISATTVA VIRTUE TREASURY,
WITH RESPECT TO THE NON-OUTFLOW MARK OF REALITY,
IN HEART HAS PENETRATED IT TOTALLY;
HE WILL NEXT BECOME A BUDDHA,
BY THE NAME OF PURE BODY, AND
WILL ALSO SAVE UNCOUNTED MULTITUDES.

Outline:

I4. similarity of giving predictions

Commentary:

ALL OF THE DISICPLES OF THE WORLD HONORED ONE/ The eight sons of the Buddha Brightness of Sun-Moon-Lamp, HEARING OF THE BUDDHA'S ENTRY INTO NIRVANA/ When they heard that the Buddha was about to enter Nirvana, EACH HARBORED GRIEF AND ANGUISH/ Basically, they all had a great deal of samadhi-power, but blood is thicker than water; because they had the relationship of father and son, master and disciple with the Buddha, they were struck with grief and anguish. Each one of them wept. They felt anguish and this means that they grew afflicted. The fact that they did so inwardly is indicated by the word "harbored." They did not let their grief show. They kept it within their hearts. The tears fell inside their hearts. They most certainly didn't let it show. Why not? Because the word "harbored" proves that they kept it inside. Although their hearts were filled with sorrow, it didn't show. It wasn't like people now who cry so that the tears fall and their noses run. Their tears fall and their noses run, but it's of no use whatsoever. That is why the eight royal sons harbored grief and anguish and thought, "WHY MUST THE BUDDHA TAKE EXTINCTION SO SOON?"/ Why must he enter Nirvana so quickly? Who are we going to cultivate under now? We assumed that our father, the Buddha, would stay in the world forever and at times we were lazy and snuck off to take it easy. We didn't cultivate vigorously and now, as they say, 'What a mess!' It may be a mess, but there's nothing we can do about it, now!"

They knew that their past actions were wrong. THE SAGELY LORD, THE DHARMA KING/ The Buddha is called the Sagely Lord and also called the Dharma King. THEN COMFORTED THE LIMITLESS MULTITUDE/ When the Buddha Brightness of Sun-Moon-Lamp saw his sons weeping within their hearts, and saw that some of the other people were crying outwardly, painfully weeping bitter tears, his compassionate heart couln't bear it, and so he comforted eveyone by saying, "Don't cry, everyone. Don't grieve and don't mourn. Don't be so upset. Although I'm going to enter Nirvana, AFTER MY PASSAGE INTO EXTINCTION/ in the future, NONE OF YOU SHOULD WORRY OR FEAR/ Don't worry, don't fret, or be afraid. Why? THE BODHISATTVA VIRTUE-TREASURY/ WITH RESPECT TO THE NON-OUTFLOW MARK OF REALITY/ With respect to the Dharma-door of the non-outflow real mark, IN HEART HAS PENETRATED IT TOTALLY/ His heart has penetrated to the absence of outflows and understood the Dharma-door of the real mark.

What is meant by no-outflows? It just means not flowing out! It means having no faults. Get rid of all your bad habits, your faults, your greed, hatred, and stupidity, pride and doubt, and break through ignorance. Once you have broken through ignorance, there are no outflows. If you haven't broken through ignorance, then you still have outflows.

How does one break through ignorance?

By studying the Buddhadharma. If you study the Buddhadharma until you understand it, then you will have no more ignorance. Why do you still have ignorance? It is just because you don't understand the Buddhadharma. When something happens, you lose your temper and you get afflicted. When the state arrives, you can't take it. Why can't you take it? Because you don't understand the Buddhadharma. If you understood the Buddhadharma, ignorance would be broken and the Dharma nature would manifest. You would be far removed from all affliction. There would be nothing good and nothing bad, no success and no failure. This is the wind and light of your native ground, your own familys' treasure. When you have obtained it, you will have no more ignorance. If you have no ignorance, you will have no outflows. If you have no outflows you obtain the real mark. You haven't obtained no-outflows? Then you haven't got the real mark. You don't understand the real mark. The Bodhisattva Virtue Treasury, however, has, in heart, penetrated the non-outlfow real mark. Don't think you are so outstanding. Take a look at the Bodhisattva Virtue Treasury. He has already completely understood the non-outflow reality mark.

HE WILL NEXT BECOME A BUDDHA/ After I have passed into extinction and entered Nirvana, he will become a Buddha BY THE NAME OF PURE BODY AND/ His name will be Pure Body Thus Come One WILL ALSO SAVE UNCOUNTED MULTITUDES/ He will also cross over and release an unlimited number of living beings.

Sutra:

THAT NIGHT THE BUDDHA PASSED INTO EXTINCTION,

AS A FLAME DIES ONCE ITS FUEL HAS BEEN CONSUMED.

THE SHARIRA WERE DIVIDED UP,

AND LIMITLESS STUPAS BUILT.
THE BHIKSHUS AND BHIKSHUNIS,
THEIR NUMBER LIKE THE GANGE'S SANDS,
REDOUBLED THEIR VIGOR IN ADVANCING
IN THEIR QUEST FOR THE UNSURPASSED PATH.

Outline:

I5. similarity of propagating the Sutra after the Buddha's extinction.
   J1. offerings and increasing vigor

Commentary:

THAT NIGHT THE BUDDHA PASSED INTO EXTINCTION/ The Buddha Brightness of Sun-Moon-Lamp on that day, at midnight entered Nirvana. AS A FLAME DIES ONCE ITS FUEL HAD BEEN CONSUMED/ What is the fuel? What is the flame? The fuel, in the Small Vehicle, is said to be the body. The dying of the flame is the attainment of Nirvana with residue. In the Great Vehicle it is said that living beings are the fuel, the firewood. The dying of the flame means that when the firewood is gone, there is no more fire.The living beings are the firewood and what is the flame?

The Buddha observes the potentials of beings in order to dispense the teaching according to their needs. He looks at the potentials of the beings in order to bestow the Buddhadharma and teach and transform them. This is called:

> Observing the potentials, dispensing the teaching;
> Speaking the Dharma according to the person.

The Buddha speaks that Dharma-door which is necessary to use to teach a particular individual. If someone should be taught by means of the Dharma-door of the Three Storehouses, the Buddha teaches that Dharma-door. If someone should be saved by means to the Vaipulya Dharma-door, he uses that one. If someone should be saved by means of the Dharma-door of Prajna, the Buddha speaks the Prajna Teaching. If someone should be saved by means of the Dharma Flower and Nirvana teachings, he gives them those teaching. This is to "observe the potentials and dispense the teaching." Taking a look at a person's potential affinities and speaking the Dharma according to the person.

Here, the potentials are no longer present. Those living beings which were to be crossed over have all been taken across. The flame has died out, and the method is no longer of use.

AS A FLAME DIES WHEN ITS FUEL HAS BEEN CONSUMED/ "As" means that this is an analogy. Don't think it is really talking about a fire going out when the fuel is all used up.

THE SHARIRA WERE DIVIDED UP/ After the Buddha had passed into extinction, all of that Buddha's relics were divided up AND LIMITLESS STUPAS BUILT/ Limitless high and manifest pagodas were raised.

THE BHIKSHUS AND BHIKSHUNIS/ The Bhikshu Sangha, and the Bhikshunis...Bhikshu has three meanings: a mendicant, frightener of mara, and destroyer of evil. Bhikshuni has the same three meanings.

What is meant by "mendicant." Bhikshus go out on begging round carrying their bowls.

What is meant by "frightener of mara?" When Bhikshus ascend the platform to receive the Bhikshu precepts they face the Three Masters and Seven Certifiers, ten Bhikshus in all who represent the Buddhas of the ten directions in transmitting the precepts. At the time they transmit the precepts, they ask, "Are you a great hero?"

The new preceptee says, "I am a great hero!"

Then they ask, "Have you brought forth the Bodhi heart?"

"I have brought forth the Bodhi heart!" The moment that they say they have brought forth the Bodhi heart, the heavenly demons in the Sixth Desire Heaven get the news flash, and they shudder with fright. Their hair stands on end, and they look at one another: "God! What are we going to do!!! This is terrible. We've lost a demon follower; the Buddha's gained a Buddha-follower. If this keep up, where's it all going to end?" They are afraid and so Bhikshus are called "frighteners of mara."

Bhikshu also means "destroyer of evil." How do they destroy evil? People are all unaware of the evil within themselves and they don't know that they should destroy it. To break through evil means to have no afflictions. When there are no afflictions, then genuine wisdom can come forth. So, here in America I have issued a very unfair law specifically to counteract afflictions and ignorance. Since this extremely unjust law has gone into effect, I have questioned my disciples a number of times, and they say that they have had no affliction and no temper. "Why not?" I ask, and they say, "I don't know." The law may be unfair, but it's extremely wonderful. It's wonderful because it's unfair. If it were fair, it wouldn't be wonderful.

The same three meanings also apply to the word Bhikshuni.

THEIR NUMBER LIKE THE GANGE'S SANDS/ There were as many of them as there are grains of sand in the Ganges River. REDOUBLED THEIR VIGOR IN ADVANCING/ Seeing the Buddha pass into extinction, the Bhikshus and Bhikshunis cultivated as if their lives depended on it. They cultivated for their very lives. If they starved to death, then they starved to death. So they didn't eat and they didn't sleep. They cultivated all day long. "Redoubled" means that they worked twice as hard. When the Buddha was in the world they sat for twelve hours a day, now they sat for twenty-four. They were extremely vigorous.

IN THEIR QUEST FOR THE UNSURPASSED PATH/ Why? They had no one to depend upon. "The Buddha has gone; how can we not cultivate now?" So they forgot about their slackness and got rid of their laziness. All they had left was vigor in their quest for the supreme Buddha Way.

Sutra:

THE DHARMA MASTER WONDROUS LIGHT
REVERENTLY KEPT THE STORE OF THE BUDDHA'S LAW;
FOR EIGHTY MINOR AEONS, HE
WIDELY SPREAD THE SUTRA OF THE DHARMA FLOWER.
ALL OF THE EIGHT ROYAL SONS
TAUGHT AND LED BY WONDROUS LIGHT,
BECAME SOLID IN THE UNSURPASSED PATH,
AND MET WITH BUDDHAS BEYOND ALL COUNT.
HAVING PRESENTED THEM OFFERINGS,

They accordingly practiced the Great Way,
And in succession, became Buddhas,
Transmitting prophecies in turn.
The last of these, a god among gods,
Was a Buddha by the name of Burner of the Lamp,
A guiding master of all the immortals,
Who brought release to countless multitudes.
The Dharma Master Wondrous Light
Had a disciple at that time
Whose heart harbored laxness, and who
Was greedily attached to fame and gain.
Seeking fame and gain untiringly,
He often visited the great clans;
He cast aside his recitations
Nelgelcted, forgot, and failed to comprehend them.
These, then, were the reasons why
He was given the name "Seeker of Fame."
Yet he also practiced many good deeds,
Enabling him to meet uncounted Buddhas,
And make offerings to all of them.
Accordingly he walked the great path,
And perfected the Six Paramitas.
Now he meets the Shakyan Lion;
Later, he will become a Buddha
By the name of Maitreya,

WHO WILL BROADLY TAKE ALL BEINGS OVER--
THEIR NUMBER FAR BEYOND ALL COUNT.

Outline:

J2. benefits derived from propagating the Sutra

Commentary:

THE DHARMA MASTER WONDROUS LIGHT/ REVERENTLY KEPT THE STORE OF THE BUDDHA'S LAW/ He reverently received the Buddha's Dharma-jewel, holding it, as it were, above his head FOR EIGHTY MINOR AEONS HE/ WIDELY SPREAD THE SUTRA OF THE DHARMA FLOWER/ ALL OF THE EIGHT ROYAL SONS/ The eight sons of the Buddha Brightness of Sun-Moon-Lamp, TAUGHT AND LED BY WONDROUS LIGHT/They bowed to the Dharma Master Wondrous Light as their Master, the Dharma Master Wondrous Light taught and transformed them so that they BECAME SOLID IN THE UNSURPASSED PATH/ They brought forth the solid resolve to seek the supreme way, the highest Buddha Way. AND MET WITH BUDDHAS BEYOND ALL COUNT/ They met a lot of Buddhas, an uncountable number of them. HAVING PRESENTED THEM WITH OFFERINGS/ They presented offerings to as many Buddhas as they met THEY ACCORDINGLY PRACTICED THE GREAT WAY/ They made offerings to the Buddhas and then followed them to cultivate and sought the Buddha Way. AND IN SUCCESSION, BECAME BUDDHAS/ The eight royal sons in successive order became Buddhas, TRANSMITTING PROPHECIES IN TURN/ Not only did they become Buddhas, but they bestowed predictions upon each other, right down the line. The first transmitted the prediction to the second, and the second to the third, and so forth to the eighth. THE LAST OF THESE, A GOD AMONG GODS/ The Buddha is called the God Among Gods. WAS A BUDDHA BY THE NAME OF BURNER OF THE LAMP/ A GUIDING MASTER OF IMMORTALS/ He was a mighty master and guide of all the gods and immortals WHO BROUGHT RELEASE TO COUNTLESS MULTITUDES/ It is not known how many living beings he saved.

THE DHARMA MASTER WONDROUS LIGHT/ HAD A DISCIPLE AT THAT TIME/ WHOSE HEART HARBORED LAXNESS AND WHO/ He didn't think to be vigorous. What he thought about all day was being lazy. If he wasn't thinking about sleeping, he was thinking about climbing on conditions, and when he returned from climbing on conditions, he went back to sleep. When he was done sleeping, he ran back out to climb on conditions. All day long he WAS GREEDILY

ATTACHED TO FAME AND GAIN/ SEEKING FAME AND GAIN UNTIRINGLY/ He had no other task all day but to seek for fame and profit. "What kind of scheme can I cook up to let everyone know my name," he thought. He advertised himself everywhere, saying, "I am so-and-so, do you know me? I've got the most cultivation! Among those who have left home, I work harder than anyone. I recite Sutras and I bow to the Buddha. I get up at three in the morning, and at midnight I haven't gone to sleep. What am I doing? Cultivating the Way. If I'm not investigating Dhyana, then I'm reciting the Buddha's name or bowing to the Buddha." He was always bragging about himself and buying himself billboards, advertising signs, and putting ads in the paper telling about how hard he cultivated and how devoted he was to his work. That's how he cultivated fame.

And what about seeking gain? Fame and gain together. If you have fame you'll have profit and if you have profit, you'll gain fame. He went around promoting himself, seeking for fame, afraid that people wouldn't know his name. Once they knew, some of the blind ones said, "That monk is a cultivator. Didn't he tell me so himself? We should all go make offerings to him!" and they all made offerings. Having sought fame, he got it and having sought gain, he got that, too. He sought them "untiringly." Why? Because he had an easy time getting what he wanted. He just asked, and it was given. He sought, and it was found. However, when he got them he wasn't satisfied. He received, but it was not enough. He was still unsatisfied. The more the better! He was insatiable when it came to profit and reputation. HE OFTEN VISITED THE GREAT CLANS/ "Often" means that he went there three, four, or five times a day. The first time he's come back with perhaps five hundred dollars. Then he'd think, "I didn't get very much. I'd better go out again."

"I have plans to do such-and-such acts of merit and virtue. Give me a little more," he'd say, and this time they would give him a thousand, twice as much. "Great clans" are wealthy, made up of many wealthy people. When they see a monk coming to beg, they will give him as much as he asks for. If he got five hundred, he'd ask for a thousand. When he returned with his thousand he'd think, "I didn't ask for enough. They'd have given me ten thousand if I'd asked for it," and that night he would return saying, "I have completed my acts of merit and virtue, and now I have yet another act of merit and virtue which must be done and it is extremely great.Give me but ten thousand dollars and I can complete the job." The wealthy person hears him say this and he takes out ten thousand dollars and gives it to him. He gets his way very easily. He goes out again and again to beg for money and ends up spending his whole life begging.

HE CAST ASIDE HIS RECITATIONS/ Because he was always out running around and climbing on conditions, if you asked him which Sutra he knew, he didn't know a single one. If you asked him, "Well, what about the Shastras,"Which one have you studied?"--he couldn't remember one of them. "Then what about the Vinaya?" He wasn't familiar with the Vinaya, either. He had cast it all aside; he didn't want to study. He didn't study anything at all. NEGLECTED, FORGOT, AND FAILED TO COMPREHEND THEM/ "Neglected" means that he put them away. There were Sutras around, but he didn't read them. He neglected them; because he didn't read them, he forgot and failed to comprehend them--that is, he couldn't remember them clearly.

THESE, THEN, WERE THE REASONS WHY/ HE WAS GIVEN THE NAME "SEEKER OF FAME."/ He was known as "Bodhisattva Seeker of Fame, Fame-seeking specialist."

YET HE ALSO PRACTICED MANY GOOD DEEDS/ Although he begged and was forever climbing on conditions, still, he did a lot of good things. Sometimes, when he begged, he didn't keep the money for himself, but used it to foster merit and virtue. He fostered merit and virtue, doing all manner of good deeds, thus ENABLING HIM TO MEET UNCOUNTED BUDDHAS/ Because of all the good he did, "borrowing flowers to give the Buddha"--he borrowed other people's flowers to present as an offering to the Buddha--he nonetheless had a bit of merit and virtue himself. AND MAKE OFFERINGS TO ALL OF THEM/ In the presence of the Buddhas he cultivated by making all manner of offerings.

ACCORDINGLY HE WALKED THE GREAT PATH/ He always accorded with living beings and sought the great, unsurpassed, great Way, AND PERFECTED THE SIX PARAMITAS/ Because he did many good deeds, he perfected the Six Paramitas: Giving: He went out to beg, and when he came back, he didn't keep what he got; he gave it away. Morality: He cultivated the precepts, the regulations. Patience: If someone scolded him, he pretended he hadn't heard it. How did he do that? His face was like rubber, as thick as an automobile tire. If someone scolded him, he paid no attention If someone hit him, he just pretended it didn't happen. He knew how to be patient.

With a face like rubber, no matter who treated him impolitely, it was as if nothing had happened. He looked like a beggar, and he begged for his food. Why do those who have left home take their bowls out to beg for food? They also want to adopt the style of a beggar and have no mark of self. No matter how impolite you are to them, they act as if nothing had happened.

Maitreya Bodhisattva's stomach was like the sea; you could float a boat in it. His heart was the heart of a Buddha, extremely compassionate. He has a short verse which I have explained to you before, but will repeat for you now:

The Old Fool wears a tattered robe,
And fills his belly with plain food.
He mends the rags to keep his body warm.
And lets the myriad affairs
just take their course.
Should someone scold the Old Fool,
The Old Fool just says, "Fine."
Should someone stike the Old Fool,
He just lies down to sleep.
"Spit right in my face," he says,
"And I'll just let it dry.
"That way I save my strength,
"And you have no affliction.
This kind of paramita,
Is the jewel in the wonderful.
Now that you know this news,
How can you worry about not attaining the Way?

The Old Fool is a very old man who wears ragged clothing. "When I eat," he says, "I don't use oil or salt. I eat until I'm full and then forget it." That's how he cultivates the practice of patience. He can endure hunger and thirst, heat and cold. So it says, "He fills his belly with plain food." It may be tasteless, but when he eats it, it tastes just fine.

When his clothes rip, he patches them, to keep out the cold, and whatever happens just happens. It's all taken care of according to conditions. They come, they go; they come, they go, according to the way things are, they take their course.

If someone starts scolding the Old Fool he just says, "I must really thank you! You're a very good scolder; you've scolded me wonderfully well. I simply love to hear the sound of your voice scolding me." That's how he handles it. If someone stikes him, he just lies down. If you hit him again, he just goes to sleep. "Go ahead and beat me as you please," he says. "Spit right in my face and I'll just let it dry by itself. That way I don't have to put out the energy to wipe it off, and naturally you're not going to have any way to fight me because I'm just like a wooden statue, without feeling and without awareness."

He says, "This kind of Paramita, this perfection to patience, is the jewel in the wonderful. If you know this news, how can you worry about not completing the Way?"

So although on the one hand it looks as if Maitreya Bodhisattva seeks name and profit, he also truly does the work and is not afraid of bitterness, of bitter practices, in his cultivation. What are bitter practices? The more difficult something is, the more you should want to do it. You should do the things others cannot do. "The things than other people don't want to do, I do."

For example, wherever Maitreya Bodhisattva goes, he specializes in cleaning the toilets. That's the dirtiest work there is, but he does it exclusively. He gets up early, sneaks into the bathroom and cleans the toilets until they sparkle. He does the most difficult work, the things no one else wants to do. And in doing it, he's not afraid of suffering. The more he does it, the more he likes to do it. So there he is, Maitreya Bodhisattva, with his big belly, always opening his mouth to laugh. He doesn't fear suffering while he works. He's not like us who type for a while and then feel that our hands ache, or print a few sheets and find it too much trouble. In the beginning, it was very interesting work, but after two and a half, not even three, days: "Ugh! Too much trouble. Too much work!"

Who told you to do it in the first place? Huh? When you started out, you didn't find it troublesome, but after a while it gets tiring. That's simply too stupid! Wouldn't you say it was stupid? When you do merit and virtue, you undergo some bitterness. You can't just do it for one or two days. No matter what people do--haven't I told you this before?--they should be solid, sincere, and persevering? You should have these three qualities. Your resolve must be solid. No matter what kind of work you are doing, you must be firm. Sincerity doesn't mean that you do it today and detest it tomorrow. You should think, "In the beginning, I liked it, and I will continue to like it." That's sincerity. Then, you must persevere. Anyone can work for two and a half, not yet three, days. What's hard about that? It's no problem at all. The several decades we live as human beings is not a long time. Think about all the great aeons Maitreya Bodhisattva cultivated the practice of patience, cultivated giving, cultivated morality, cultivated vigor, cultivated Dhyana samadhi, and Prajna. All those great aeons were to him just like a single day. And we work for two and a half days and are fed up. Didn't you know when you began, if you work, of course it's going to be trouble. It you don't want to be troubled, the best thing to do would be to go to sleep. That's no trouble at all. Or go out and beg, climb on conditions. That's no trouble either. When you get there say, "I am a monk. You should make offerings to me. I now need five thousand. Hand it over," and they'll give it to you. It will take no effort on your part at all. However, things that take no effort have no real worth or value, and they create no merit or virtue to speak of because it is merit and virtue which you told other people to do. You didn't do it yourself.

Therefore, you should be like Maitreya Bodhisattva. You should have his patience and vigor. It shouldn't be the case that someone makes a remark, and you can't let go of it and start to cry, or that someone treats you unkindly and you lose your temper. When you listen to the Sutras, you must actually put into practice what you hear. If you don't actually practice, what's the use of listening to them? Every night you listen to the Sutras for two hours, and when you're done listening it's just like the wind had been blowing past your ears; it goes in one ear and out the other. What's the use of that? It's utterly useless. You must truly, actually cultivate, do the work. If you have genuine wisdom, *genuine* wisdom, you should not just do such stupid things. And genuine wisdom is only gained in exchange for suffering. It is not obtained without the least bit of effort. It is not obtained without the slightest bit of cultivation, nor it it obtained by being afraid of bitterness, hardship, or poverty. How can you get any wisdom that way? Then, if you are not afraid of these things and you cultivate for a long period of time, you can have some accomplishment.

Maitreya Bodhisattva cultivated the Six Paramitas perfectly. "Perfectly" means that he possessed all six of them.

NOW HE MEETS THE SHAKYAN LION/ The Shakyan Lion is Shakyamuni Buddha. LATER, HE WILL BECOME A BUDDHA/ After Shakyamuni Buddha, Maitreya Buddha will succeed the Buddha-position. He is waiting to become a Buddha in the future. BY THE NAME OF MAITREYA/ He is known as the Venerable Maitreya Buddha who will descend in the future. WHO WILL BROADLY TAKE ALL BEINGS OVER/ He will save all living beings, a great, great many of them. THEIR NUMBER FAR BEYOND ALL COUNT/ An uncountable number of them.

Sutra:

AFTER THAT BUDDHA HAD PASSED INTO EXTINCTION,
THE INDOLENT ONE WAS YOU,
AND THE DHARMA MASTER WONDROUS LIGHT,
WAS I, MYSELF, NOW PRESENT HERE.

Outline:

J3. past corresponding with the present

Commentary:

AFTER THAT BUDDHA HAD PASSED INTO EXTINCTION/ Who would you say "that Buddha" was? It was the Buddha Brightness of Sun-Moon-Lamp. THE INDOLENT ONE WAS YOU/ The lazy Bodhisattva was you, you Maitrya Bodhisattva! AND THE DHARMA MASTER WONDROUS LIGHT/ Who was he? WAS I, MYSELF, NOW PRESENT HERE/ Now, presently, I myself, Manjushri Bodhisattva, was the Dharma Master Wondrous Light.

Sutra:

I SAW THE BUDDHA BRIGHTNESS OF LAMP;
HIS LIGHT AND PORTENTS WERE LIKE THESE.
THUS I KNOW THE PRESENT BUDDHA,
WISHES TO SPEAK THE DHARMA FLOWER SUTRA.

Outline:

F2. conclusion
G1. about to speak The Dharma Flower Sutra

Commentary:

I SAW THE BUDDHA BRIGHTNESS OF LAMP/ In the past I saw the Buddha Brightness of Sun-Moon-Lamp. HIS LIGHT

AND PORTENTS WERE LIKE THESE/ His bright portents were like the ones now manifest by Shakyamuni Buddha. THUS, I KNOW THE PRESENT BUDDHA/ Because I saw it in the past, I know that now Shakyamuni Buddha WISHES TO SPEAK THE DHARMA FLOWER SUTRA/ He wants to speak *The Wonderful Dharma Lotus Flower Sutra*.

Sutra:

THE PRESENT MARKS ARE LIKE THE PORTENTS PAST,
EXPEDIENT DEVICES OF THE BUDDHAS.
THE BUDDHA NOW PUTS FORTH BRIGHT LIGHT,
TO HELP REVEAL THE REAL MARK'S MEANING.
ALL OF YOU NOW SHOULD UNDERSTAND, AND
WITH ONE HEART, JOIN YOUR PALMS, AND WAIT;
THE BUDDHA WILL LET FALL THE DHARMA RAIN,
TO SATISFY ALL THOSE WHO SEEK THE WAY.

Outline:

G2. a dharma for teaching Bodhisattvas

Commentary:

THE PRESENT MARKS ARE LIKE THE PORTENTS PAST/ Right now, the portents revealed by Shakyamuni Buddha's white hair-mark light are like the ones previously seen at the time of Sun-Moon-Lamp Brightness Buddha. EXPEDIENT DEVICES OF THE BUDDHAS/ They are dharmas of expediency employed by all the Buddhas. THE BUDDHA NOW PUTS FORTH BRIGHT LIGHT/ The Buddha Shakyamuni emits the white hair-mark light from between his brows TO HELP REVEAL THE REAL MARK'S MEANING/ He wants to speak the real mark doctrine of the Great Vehicle's *Wonderful Dharma Lotus Flower Sutra*.

ALL OF YOU NOW SHOULD UNDERSTAND, AND/ You should know, be aware, WITH ONE HEART, JOIN YOUR PALMS, AND WAIT/ Put your palms together, focus your attention, concentrate, and wait for the Buddha to speak the supreme wonderful Dharma.

THE BUDDHA WILL LET FALL THE DHARMA RAIN/ The Buddha Shakyamuni is about to let fall the great Dharma rain, TO SATISY ALL THOSE WHO SEEK THE WAY/ The rain reaches those of all three dispositions: those of superior, average, and inferior dispositions, that is, the intelligent, the ordinary, and the dull. It moistens both the bright and the dull. The Dharma rain is like the rain from the sky which is received in due measure by the flowers, grasses, and trees, each according to the amount it requires. The Buddha now speaks the Dharma, and those of the Great Vehicle disposition receive the Great Vehicle Dharma. Those disposed to the Small Vehicle understand the Small Vehicle Dharma. Common folk understand the doctrines of common people. The rain of Dharma satisfies all those who seek the Way.

Sutra:

THOSE WHO SEEK THREE VEHICLES,

SHOULD THEY HAVE DOUBTS OR REGRETS,

THE BUDDHA WILL REMOVE THEM NOW,

SO THAT THEY VANISH AND NONE REMAIN.

Outline:

G3. of which the Buddhas are protective and mindful

Commentary:

THOSE WHO SEEK THREE VEHICLES/ Now, all of the Bodhisattvas, Sound-Hearers, and Condition-Enlightened Ones, the people of the Three Vehicles, SHOULD THEY HAVE DOUBTS OR REGRETS/ If you have any doubts or questions, THE BUDDHA WILL REMOVE THEM NOW/ He will now answer your questions, SO THAT THEY VANISH AND NONE REMAIN/ He will cause you not to have the slightest bit of doubt. He will resolve all of your doubts--they will vanish without a trace.

When people cultivate the Way, they must *cultivate* it. If they don't cultivate it, there is no Way. Only if you cultivate, can there be a Way. Therefore, speaking in terms of cultivation, if you don't cultivate, there are no problems at all. As soon as you begin to cultivate, however, the problems come. Why do they come? It's because in former lives your actions resulted from a conflux of causes and conditions. Amidst these various different causes and conditions, there were a lot of "books"which you did not keep accurately. And because these books weren't clear, in your present life, as soon as you begin to cultivate the Way, the demon king wants to do battle with you, to liquidate you. He causes you to feel that if the afflictions aren't coming from one direction, they are coming from another. Afflictions come at your from the north, east, south, west, the fourpoints in between and from above and below--all ten directions. If you aren't afflicted over people, you get afflicted over things. Hah! If you aren't afflicted over things, then you get afflicted over animals. If you are not afflicted over animals, you are afflicted because of ghosts. If you aren't afflicted because of ghosts, then you are afflicted towards the spirits. Ahh...even to the point that you get afflicted at the Bodhisattvas and angry at the Buddha! You even get angry at yourself!

Why does this happen?

It's because in the past you were too muddled. You did things too unclearly and so now you run into all kinds of afflictions. Some people cultivate and make a vow not be become afflicted. Before they made the vow, there really wasn't any affliction, but as soon as they make the vow, the affliction arrives quite promptly. Before they made a vow to eat only one meal a day, they didn't feel particularly hungry, but as soon as the vow was made and they finish eating, they're hungry, so hungry they can't stand it. "I'm starved! I'm exhausted. I can't even stand up and I can't sit comfortablly either." It's strange, *very strange.*

What is the principle involved? Well, when you go to school, after you have studied for a while, you take a test. If you pass the test, you can ascend a grade. If you don't pass, you have to repeat the course. Cultivation is the same. If you cultivate the Way, the demons will test you to see, ultimately, if you can endure it or not, if you can bear it or not. I often tell you that you must:

endure what others can't endure,
take what others cannot take,
eat what others cannot eat, &
do what others cannot do.

That's how you should be. That's the basic job of cultivating the Way and one who can do this can be considered a cultivator.

END OF CHAPTER ONE--*THE DHARMA FLOWER SUTRA*

INDEX*

*Index includes entries from Volume One, pp. 1-66.

A BRIGHT STAR IN A TROUBLED WORLD:

THE CITY OF TEN THOUSAND BUDDHAS

Located at Talmage, California, just south of Ukiah and about two hours north of San Francisco, is Wonderful Enlightenment Mountain, and located at its base is the 237 acre area holding 60 buildings which is called the City of Ten Thousand Buddhas which is fast becoming a center for religious, educational, and social programs for world Buddhism.

At present, the complex houses Tathagata Monastery and the Great Compassion House for men, Great Joyous Giving House for women, the campus of Dharma Realm Buddhist University, and a large auditorium. Plans are underway to present many kinds of programs to benefit people in spirit, mind, and body--a home for the aged, a hospital emphasizing the utilization of both eastern and western healing techniques, and alternaltive mental health facility, and educational programs ranging from pre-school through Ph.D. Cottage industries, organic farming, and living in harmony with our environment will be stressed. The City is an ideal spot for conventions where people of all races and religions can exchange their ideas and unite their energies to

Image of Kuan Yin Bodhisattva in the Hall of Ten Thousand Buddhas

promote human welfare and world peace.

Religious cultivation will be foremost and the City will be instrumental in the transmission of the Orthodox Precepts of the Buddhas, thus developing bhikshus and bhikshunis to teach and maintain the Buddhadharma. Rigorous cultivation and meditation sessions will be held regularly and the grounds of the monastery and convent will provide and pure and quiet setting in which to pursue study and meditation. A number of facilities are available for those found qualified to retreat for long periods of time into total contemplative seclusion as well.

The spacious grounds have more than a hundred acres of pine groves, meadows, and a running stream, and will soon be organically cultivated with a wide variety of fruits and vegetables.

At a time when the world is torn with strife and spiritual awareness steadily declining, the City of Ten Thousand Buddhas appears as a guiding star, a place where people can work together, each in their own way, to develop and express the wonderful spiritual nature inherent in all living beings, to discover life's true meaning and pass it on to future generations.

***

A SPECIAL APPROACH

Focus on values: examining the moral foundations of ancient spiritual traditions, relating those traditions to space-age living, and finding what it takes to live in harmony with our social and natural environments.

Focus on change: a key to understanding ourselves, our relationships, and the crises of the modern world. What we seek is to be open to new ways of seeing ourselves, to new modes of relating to friend and stranger, and to new methods and technological aids that supplement and open up for us the limitless store of human wisdom, past and present.

Total environment education where teacher and student are partners in the educational process and share responsibility for it. Learning takes place both in and out of the classroom in a community which is involved in the complex problems of society.

Personally tailored programs in which education need not be constricted by traditional department boundaries. The emphasis will be on meaningful learning, not just the accumulation of facts and test-taking skills.

Education for young and old where the different generations come together to share in the experience of learning and thereby enrich that experience. The University also especially encourages those with valuable life experience to apply for special experimental learning credits.

GUIDING IDEALS

These are the ideals which will guide education at Dharma Realm University:

To explain and share the Buddha's teaching;
To develop straightforward minds and hearts;
To benefit society;
To encourage all beings to seek enlightenment.

XIV.

CAMPUS

The main campus of Dharma Realm University is located at the foot of Cow Mountain National Recreation Area in the beautiful Ukiah valley. It is surrounded by the woods, meadows, and farmland of the City of Ten Thousand Buddhas.

The University will be housed in several large buildings set among trees and broad lawns. One classroom building has been newly refurbished for educational use. Residential and recreational facilities, including auditorium-gymnasium, and swimming pool, will be provided students by the City of Ten Thousand Buddhas.

The air is clean and fresh, and the climate is pleasant and temperate (av. min. temp. 43.2 deg; av. max. temp. 76 deg.) Rarely falling below freezing in the winter and usually dry in the summer, the area is very fertile with much grape and fruit tree cultivation. Close by are the Russian River, Lake Mendocino and Clear Lake, several hot springs, redwood and other national forest lands, and the scenic Pacific Coast.

PROGRAMS-Undergraduate and graduate, full-time and part-time

The University intends to provide quality education in a number of fields, with an emphasis (wherever possible) on matching classroom theory with practical experience. The curriculum is divided into three main program areas:

The Letters and Science Program: In addition to a regular curriculum of Humanities, Social, and Natural Sciences, special emphasis will be laid on East-West studies, with strong offerings in Asian languages, literature, philosophy, and religion. We expect pioneering interdisciplinary approaches in many of these areas, combining the best of Asian and Western approaches to education. Education for personal growth and the development of special competencies will be the twin aims of the program.

The Buddhist Studies Program will emphasize a combination of traditional and modern methods including actual practice of the Buddhadharma as well as scholarly investigation. Offerings will range from introductory fundamentals to advanced meditation and will include advanced seminars in both English and canonical languages.

The Arts Program: Practical Arts will concentrate on putting knowledge to work right away in workshops for building a living community: ecology, energy, gardening and nutrition, community planning, management, etc. Creative Arts offerings will include the meeting of East and West in a whole panorama of studio arts. There will be special courses in Chinese calligraphy, in the creation of Buddha images, and in music and dance. Individual Arts workshops will include t'ai-chi ch'üan, yoga, meditational techniques, wilderness survival, etc.

THE INTERNATIONAL TRANSLATION CENTER

The Translation Center will sponsor courses, workshops, and special programs concerned with translation techniques for a wide range of languages and will coordinate a unique degree program in translation.

THE WORLD RELIGIONS CENTER

The World Religions Center will sponsor workshops, conferences, and other special programs to aid in mutual understanding and good will among those of different faiths.

SPECIAL INTERNATIONAL STUDENT PROGRAM

In the future, there will be special emphasis on welcoming students from Asian countries to complement the University's strong offerings in East-West studies. Areas of special interest to Asian students will be added to the curriculum as well as a strong English as a Second Language (ESL) Program.

DONATIONS

Dharma Realm University welcomes your help with donations. In addition to financial assistance, the University needs home and office furniture, books and scholarly journals, supplies and equipment, and the services of volunteers. *All donations are tax deductible.*

XVIII.

THE BUDDHIST TEXT TRANSLATION SOCIETY

Chairperson: The Venerable Master Hua
Abbot of Gold Mountain Dhyana Monastery
Professor of the Tripitaka and the Dhyanas

PRIMARY TRANSLATION COMMITTEE:

Chairpersons: Bhikshuni Heng Yin, Lecturer in Buddhism
Bhikshuni Heng Ch'ih, Lecturer in Buddhism

Members: Bhikshu Wei Sung, Lecturer in Buddhism
Bhikshu Heng Kuan, Lecturer in Buddhism
Bhikshu Heng Pai, Lecturer in Buddhism
Bhikshu Heng Yo, Lecturer in Buddhism
Bhikshu Heng Sure, Lecturer in Buddhism
Bhikshuni Heng Hsien, Lecturer in Buddhism
Bhikshuni Heng Chen, Lecturer in Buddhism
Bhikshuni Heng Ch'ing, Lecturer in Buddhism

Upasaka Huang Kuo-jen, Kung Fu Master, B.A.
Upasaka I Kuo-jung, Ph.D., UC Berkeley
Upasaka Kuo Yu Linebarger, M.A., San Francisco State University

REVISION COMMITTEE:

Chairpersons: Bhikshu Heng Yo
Upasaka I Kuo-jung

Members: Bhikshu Heng Kuan
Bhikshu Heng Sure
Bhikshuni Heng Yin
Bhikshuni Heng Hsien
Bhikshuni Heng Chen

Professor L. Lancaster, UC Berkeley
Professor M. Tsent, San Francisco State University
Upasaka Hsieh Ping-ying, author, professor, editor
Upasika Phoung Kuo-wu
Upasaka Lee Kuo-ch'ien, B.A.
Upasaka Li Kuo-wei, M.A.
Upasaka Kuo Yu Linebarger
Upasika I Kuo-han, B A.
Upasika Kuo Ts'an Epstein
Upasika Kuo-chin Vickers

THE BUDDHIST TEXT TRANSLATION SOCIETY

The Buddhist Text Translation Society is dedicated to making the genuine principles of the Buddhadharma available to the Western reader in a form that can be put directly into practice. Since 1972, the Society has been publishing English translations of Sutras (the sayings of the Buddha), instructional handbooks in meditation and moral conduct, biographies, poetry, and fiction. Each of the Society's Sutra translations is accompanied by a contemporary commentary spoken by the Venerable Master Hsüan Hua. The Venerable Master Hsüan Hua is the founder of Gold Mountain Monastery and the Institute for the Translation of Buddhist Texts, both located in San Francisco, as well as Gold Wheel Temple in Los Angeles and the new center of world Buddhism, City of Ten Thousand Buddhas near Ukiah, California.

The accurate and faithful translation of the Buddhist Canon into English and other Western languages is one of the most important objectives of the Sino-American Buddhist Association, the parent organization of the Buddhist Text Translation Society. Since 1959 it has been establishing monasteries, temples, meditation centers, schools, and translation institutes so that people can cultivate the teachings of Shakyamuni Buddha and so that Buddhism can flourish throughout the world.

EIGHT REGULATIONS FOR TRANSLATION SOCIETY TRANSLATORS:

The translation of the Buddhist Tripitaka is work of such magnitude that it could never be entrusted to a single person working on his own. Above all, translations of Sutras must be certified as the authentic transmission of the Buddha's proper Dharma. Translations done under the auspices of the Buddhist Text Translation Society, a body of more than thirty Sangha members and scholars, bear such authority. The following eight regulations govern the conduct of Buddhist Text Translation Society translators:

1. A translator must free himself from motives of personal gain and reputation.
2. A translator must cultivate an attitude free from arrogance and conceit.
3. A translator must refrain from advertising himself and denigrating others.
4. A translator must not establish himself as the standard of correctness and supress the work of others with his fault-finding.
5. A translator must take the Buddha-mind as his own mind.
6. A translator must use the wisdom of the selective Dharma-eye to determine true principles.
7. A translator must request the Virtuous Elders from the ten directions to certify his translations.
8. A translator must endeavor to propagate the teachings by printing Sutras, Shastras, and Vinaya texts when his translations have been certified.

The Buddhist Text Translation Society

The Buddhist Text Translation Society is dedicated to making the genuine principles of the Buddhadharma available to the Western reader in a form that can be put directly into practice. Since 1972, the Society has been publishing English translations of Sutras (the sayings of the Buddha), instructional handbooks in meditation and moral conduct, biographies, poetry, and fiction. Each of the Society's Sutra translations is accompanied by a contemporary commentary spoken by the Venerable Master Hsuan Hua. The Venerable Master Hsuan Hua is the founder of Gold Mountain Monastery and the Institute for the Translation of Buddhist Texts, both located in San Francisco, as well as Gold Wheel Temple in Los Angeles and the new center of world Buddhism, City of Ten Thousand Buddhas near Ukiah, California.

The accurate and faithful translation of the Buddhist Canon into English and other Western languages is one of the most important objectives of the Sino-American Buddhist Association, the parent organization of the Buddhist Text Translation Society. Since 1959 it has been establishing monasteries, temples, meditation centers, schools, and translation institutes so that people can cultivate the teachings of Shakyamuni Buddha and so that Buddhism can flourish throughout the world.

Buddhist Sutras:

The Amitabha Sutra, with commentary by the Venerable Master Hsuan Hua. Shakyamuni Buddha spoke the Amitabha Sutra to let all living beings know of the power of Amitabha Buddha's great vows to lead all who recite his name with faith to rebirth in his Buddhaland, the Land of Ultimate Bliss, where they may cultivate and quickly realize Buddhahood. 204 pages, $5.95

The Vajra Sutra, with commentary by the Venerable Master Hsuan Hua. Prajna or transcendental wisdom, the subject of this Sutra, is of central importance in the Buddha's teaching. The Buddha spent 20 years speaking the Prajna sutras and declared that they would be disseminated to every land. The Sutra says, "One should produce a thought without dwelling anywhere." The Sixth Patriarch, the Great Master Hui Neng, heard this sentence and awakened to the Way. 192 pages, $5.95

The Shurangama Sutra, Vol. I, with commentary by the Venerable Master Hsuan Hua. "There is a samadhi called the Foremost Shurangama King of the Great Buddha Summit, which is the fullfillment of the 10,00 practices. It is the one door to the transcendent and wonderfully adorned road of the Thus Come Ones of the ten directions." The Sutra explains the samadhi (state of still concentration) of the Buddha and the 50 kinds of demonic samadhi which can delude us in our search for enlightenment.

The Lotus Sutra, Vol. I, with commentary by the Venerable Master Hsuan Hua. The Buddha appeared in the world in order to lead all living beings to understand the teaching of the Lotus Sutra. 'For the sake of all living beings, I preach the One Buddha-Vehicle. If you are able to receive these words with faith, you shall all be able to become Buddhas. This vehicle is wondrously pure and supreme. In all the worlds throughout the universe there is nothing more exalted.'

Sutra of the Past Vows of Earth Store Bodhisattva, with commentary by the Venerable Master Hsuan Hua. The power of Earth Store Bodhisattva's compassion is unusually great, a strength which most other Bodhisattvas cannot match: he alone has made the vow to go to the hells and rescue living beings there. "If I do not go to the hells to aid them, who else will go?" Before he entered Nirvana, Shakyamuni Buddha went to the Heaven of the Thirty-three to speak this Sutra on behalf of his mother. It is one of the most popular Buddhist scriptures in China, describing the heavens and hells, the workings of karma, and the virtue of filial piety. The first translation into English. 235 pages, $6.75 paper, $12.75 cloth.

The Sixth Patriarch's Dharma Jewel Platform Sutra, with commentary by the Venerable Master Hsuan Hua. The Sixth Patriarch said, "Unenlightened, the Buddha is a living being. At the time of an enlightened thought, the living being is a Buddha. Therefore, know that the ten thousand dharmas exist within your own mind. Why do you not see the true suchness of your original nature from within your own mind?" The sutra is the founding text of Ch'an (Zen) Buddhism, consisting of the teachings of the Venerable Master Hui Neng, the illiterate Patriarch. Second edition. 380 pages, $10.00

The Dharani Sutra, with commentary by the Venerable Master Hsuan Hua. The Sutra speaks of compassion, which relieves us of suffering and gives us joy. The Bodhisattva Who Regards the World's Sounds (Avalokiteshvara) embodies this infinite compassion. The Dharani Sutra shows how by the practice of compassion and the recitation of the Great Compassion Mantra we can gain the thousand hands and thousand eyes of Avalokiteshvara and rescue living beings in distress by means of wholesome magic and healing. The first translation in any Western language. Illustrated with woodcuts from the Secret School. 352 pages, $10.00

The Sutra in Forty-two Sections, with commentary by the Venerable Master Hsuan Hua, "When the Shramana who has left the home-life puts an end to his desires and drives away his longings, he knows the source of his own mind and penetrates to the profound principles of Buddhahood. He awakens to the Unconditioned, clinging to nothing within and seeking nothing without." The Sutra in which the Buddha gives the essentials of the Path.

Buddhist Practice:

The Shramanera Vinaya and Rules of Deportment, with commentary by the Venerable Master Hsuan Hua. The Buddha instructed his disciples to take the Vinaya (the moral code) for their Master once he himself had entered Nirvana. Those who seek to end birth and death and to save all living beings from suffering must base their practice on proper morality. 112 pages, $3.95

Pure Land and Ch'an Dharma Talks, "From limitless aeons past until the present we have accumulated uncountable states of mind in the field of our eighth consciousness. Sitting quietly allows these states to come forth in a way that they can be recognized, just like the moon's reflection in still water." Instructions by the Venerable Master Hsuan Hua in the practice of reciting the name of Amitabha Buddha and in the self-investigating meditation called Ch'an. 72 pages, $3.00

Buddha Root Farm, Further instructions by the Venerable Master Hsuan Hua in meditation on the name of Amitabha Buddha of the Western Land of Ultimate Bliss. "The water flows, the wind blows, whispering his name. And when he takes you by the hand to the Happy Land, you'll be so glad you came." 72 pages, $3.00

Biographical:

Records of the Life of the Venerable Master Hsuan Hua, Part I. "The Master was 19 years old when his mother passed away. At this time, he left the home life, taking the ten precepts of a Shramanera. He then went to his mother's grave site,and built a 5' X 8' hut out of five-inch sorghum stalks. The hut kept out the wind and rain, but there was little difference between the inside and the outside. Here the Master observed the custom of filial piety by watching over his mother's grave for a period of three years. Clothed only in a rag robe, he endured the bitter Manchurian snow and the blazing summer sun. He ate only one meal a day and never slept lying down." an account of the Master's early years in China. 96 pages, $3.95

Records of the Life of Ch'an Master Hsuan Hua, Part II. "In the late afternoon, after a day of work at the construction site of Tz'u-hsing Monastery, the Master would go back down the mountain to catch the ferry to Hong Kong. Even then he did not rest, but delighted his fellow passengers by giving informal Dharma talks during the 45-minute crossing. With no effort on his part, he attracted an ever-increasing gathering on those ferry boat rides, who listened as the Master made good use of the time by expounding the Dharma for them." The events of the Master's life as he taught and transformed his followers in Hong Kong, containing many photographs, poems and stories. 229 pages, $6.95

World Peace Gathering, A moving document of American Buddhism in action, commemorating the successful completion of an extraordinary 1,100 mile journey made by two American Buddhist monks in 1974. With Heng Yo at his side, Heng Ju walked from San Francisco to Marblemount, Washington, bowing to the ground every third step, praying for peace for all humankind. With numerous photographs. 128 pages, $3.95

Buddhist Poetry and Fiction:

The Ten Dharma Realms Are Not Beyond A Single Thought. Verses and explanation of the ten realms of existence by the Venerable Master Hsuan Hua. 72 pages, $3.00

"The way of men is harmony,
With merit and error interspersed.
On virtuous deeds you rise, offenses make you fall.
It has nothing to do with anyone else at all."

Celebrisi's Journey. A novel by David (Kuo Chou) Rounds. Where is the realm beyond the senses? What happens when a modern man sets out ot find it? This is the story of a search pursued across the landscape of America from New Jersey to Maine to the Dakotas to California, through despair to understanding, through the cloud of thoughts to the bright stillness, into the mind, beyond the self. 178 pages, $3.25

Three Steps, One Bow, "Even before we left San Francisco to begin the pilgrimage, people were doubtful about how we would obtain the basic requirements for survival. But the Master had said that if one is completely sincere and genuine, survival would not be a problem. The Master has completely proved this is in his own life, and after a while on our trip we too found it to be true without fail. We discovered very quickly, though, that what is tacitly assumed by this principle is equally true: if your heart is not sincere, survival *will* be a problem." *Three Steps, One Bow* is Heng Ju's and Heng Yo's own story of devotion, humor, and hardships overcome on their extraordinary pilgrimage for world peace.

Vajra Bodhi Sea

The monthly journal of the Sino-American Buddhist Association since 1970, Vajra Bodhi Sea makes Buddhist writings and Buddhist news available to readers everywhere. Each issue contains Sutra translations, biographical sketches of high masters of antiquity, and biographies of contemporary Buddhists of the Sangha and lay communities. Also included are feature articles, world Buddhist news, poetry, book reviews, a series of Sanskrit lessons and vegetarian recipes. $15 for a one-year subscription, $42 for a three-year subscription. Subscription free with membership in the Sino-American Buddhist Association.

____Please enroll me in a subscription to Vajra Bodhi Sea for:

____one year, $15

____three years, $42

____Please send me a copy of "A General Introduction to the Sino-American Buddhist Association" (22 pages, $1.25)

ORDER FORM

To order books of the Buddhist Text Translation Society, fill out the form below and send it with your check to:

The Buddhist Text Translation Society
1731 Fifteenth Street
San Francisco, California 94103

Qty.	Title	Unit Price	Total
	Amitabha Sutra	5.95	
	Vajra Sutra	5.95	
	Dharani Sutra	10.00	
	Earth Store Sutra (cloth)	12.75	
	Earth Store Sutra (soft)	6.75	
	Sixth Patriarch Sutra	10.00	
	Shurangama Sutra Vol. I		
	Lotus Sutra Vol. I		
	Song of Enlightenment		
	Sutra in 42 Sections		
	Shramanera Vinaya	3.95	
	Pure Land & Ch'an Talks	3.00	
	Buddha Root Farm	3.00	
	Records of the Life, I	3.95	
	Records of the Life, II	6.95	
	World Peace Gathering	3.95	
	Three Steps, One Bow		
	Ten Dharma Realms	3.00	
	Celebrisi's Journey	3.25	
		Sub-Total	
		6% Sales Tax California Residents Only (BART Counties 6.5%)	
		Shipping & handling (add 10%)	
		Amount Enclosed